'SLEEPWALKING TO SEGREGATION'?

Challenging myths about race and migration

Nissa Finney and Ludi Simpson

First published in Great Britain in 2009 by

The Policy Press
University of Bristol
Fourth Floor, Beacon House
Queen's Road
Bristol BS8 1QU

Tel +44 (0)117 331 4054
Fax +44 (0)117 331 4093
e-mail tpp-info@bristol.ac.uk
www.policypress.co.uk

North American office:
The Policy Press
c/o International Specialized Books Services
920 NE 58th Avenue, Suite 300
Portland,
OR 97213-3786, USA
Tel +1 503 287 3093   Fax +1 503 280 8832
e-mail info@isbs.com

British Library Cataloguing in Publication Data
A catalogue record for this book is available from the British Library

Library of Congress Cataloging-in-Publication Data
A catalog record for this book has been requested

ISBN 978 1 84742 007 7 paperback
ISBN 978 1 84742 008 4 hardback

Cover design Qube Design Associates, Bristol
Illustrations kindly supplied by Tim Hunkin, www.timhunkin.com
Front cover: photograph kindly supplied by Getty Images
Printed and bound in Great Britain by Hobbs, Southampton
The Policy Press uses environmentally responsible print partners

Contents

—

List of tables, figures and boxes

Tables

Figures

Boxes

Acknowledgements

Much of this book crystallises research developed over several years, to which countless people have contributed through their comment and their own work. Where possible we have cited the work of those who have influenced us. Here we would like to thank those who helped shape the book by reading and commenting on draft chapters, including Sue Argent, Rob Berkeley, Gemma Catney, Tony Champion, Danny Dorling, Katie Finney, Vivien Finney, John Gillott, Virinder Kalra, Alan Marshall, Dave Marshall, Jacky Marshall, Ceri Peach, Debbie Phillips, Ian Plewis, Steve Schofield and Ann Simpson. An early version of Chapter Two was published in *Radical Statistics* in 2002; our analysis of friendship groups data in Chapter Five relies on unpublished work by Nisha Kapoor. We are grateful to The Policy Press for being so accommodating and professional throughout.

Output from the censuses of Britain and the census questionnaire partly reproduced in Figure 2.1 are Crown copyright and are reproduced with the permission of the Controller of HMSO and the Queen's Printer for Scotland.

1

Introduction

Race and migration have never been far from the top of Britain's political and media agendas in the first decade of the 21st century. As in the 20th century, the question is how a successful diverse society can be created. This question is a difficult one, and an important one, because it determines people's opportunities and experiences, it affects the order of society and the identity of society. In recent years, the question has become shrouded in pessimism; and the pessimists see a future of division and conflict, with British society sleepwalking to segregation, amid a culture clash brought on by unsustainable immigration.

We see this pessimism as unnecessary and unwarranted. We find that many of the claims surrounding segregation, immigration and dangerous cultures turn out to be myths, unsustainable in the face of evidence. Our focus in this book is on how numbers have misleadingly become central to fears and forecasts of the state of ethnic relations. Race and statistics are a potent mix and evidence expressed as numbers is central to claims about immigration, race relations and integration. This is not a new phenomenon: numbers have been part of race debates since those debates began. In the 19th and 20th centuries the arguments were whether intelligence tests proved that races have different abilities and whether eugenic policies were needed for the progressive development of Western society. At the beginning of the 21st century the arguments take new twists: Britain is dangerously segregated – or is it? Diverse cities consist of communities living parallel lives – or do they? Immigration is bad for Britain's existing residents – or is it?

In examining claims of race and migration we are not arguing that statistics have no place in policy debate. On the contrary, it is our contention that democracy functions better if everyone has access to the best possible information. Thus, it cannot be in the interest of our society for debate about such important issues to be based on myths.

We believe that much of the evidence is ignored in exaggerated beliefs and claims about race and migration. For example, segregation is said by politicians to be increasing and reaching the levels of American ghettos. It is neither. Terrorists are said by security forces to be aided by residential concentrations of Muslims. But the proportion of Muslims charged with terrorist offences in Britain is no greater in Muslim concentrations than in other areas. Opinion surveys regularly expose that in the public imagination numbers of immigrants are exaggerated. Academic research is not immune to exaggeration and untested assumptions, often referring to areas of immigrant settlement as 'problem areas' where crime, low political involvement, and unemployment are supposed to be a result of the inadequacy of immigrants themselves. The evidence base for many claims about race and migration crumbles when subjected to investigation. The problem is not that the evidence is poor, but that much of it is ignored by those pursuing the pessimistic perspective. The evidence for our counterclaims in this paragraph is to be found in this book.

This book therefore aims to set the record straight on current claims about Britain's 'immigration burden', about the level of racial or ethnic segregation and about minority ethnic groups' willingness to integrate. As authors we hope to have some influence on the powerful stories that have currency on the street, in the media, in political debate and in academia. Far from belittling the role of statistical evidence, we hope that we employ it in this book fairly and openly, with our sources open to inspection and further investigation. Racial statistics may have developed historically in response to assumptions about the superiority of a white European elite, but we do not believe that interpretations of race statistics have to be based in elitism. In the tradition of both liberal and radical writing we see a role for rigorous science, in this case numerical description of the world, to defend and to extend human rights.

It is fair to ask why myths of race and migration persist if persuasive evidence exists to lay them to rest. How do such powerful stories circulate and continue in spite of their status as myths? We tackle this question first by discussing how ethnicity has come to be defined and measured; how race has become quantifiable, and the implications of that. Second, we discuss the roles of the media and institutional spokespeople in repeating claims without concern for their truth. We do not attempt to pin down the motivations of the actors in this numbers game, but we do point to a number of reasons for their prominence. All-powerful myths are sustained by the value of sensationalism to the media, and a lack of questioning of statistical evidence, but politics also create a momentum for believed myths. These particular myths of migration are sustained by politics of xenophobia and racism, which play on naïve conservatism or fear of change. These particular myths and myth-makers allow the scapegoating of minorities, at a time of economic downturn and war in Islamic countries, making them complicit in the unsavoury pastime of 'playing the race card'. The result is that evidence is selectively presented, at times ignored and at times creatively invented, supporting a misleading interpretation of the world.

Our own motivation is to challenge a set of claims that we think are not only untrue but are having the effect of setting people in Britain against each other. We believe that equality of treatment is the basis of respect and of self-respect. A successful complex society demands respect for others but not that everyone makes the same life choices or holds the same beliefs, only that those choices do not infringe other people's choices. What constitutes respect and infringements are matters for Britain's democratic and legal framework, which is quite experienced and capable when it comes to dealing with differences of opinion and behaviour. Democratic forums and the courts do have to discuss how groups' rights affect individuals and vice versa, as they always have done (think of the rights of political parties, trades unions or community organisations). These are also the ways of solving housing, employment, public disorder and economic problems rather than through blaming or making demands of groups of people defined by their immigrant, religious or minority status. Our own promotion of refugee rights and action against racism involves a broad concern for equality of treatment, which we hope to support using our more academic and technical research skills.

This book is intended for a broad audience: anyone interested in understanding more fully the debates and evidence about race and migration as well as the academics, students and those involved in making public policy whose job it is to grapple with these ideas. As such we have tried to write in a direct and accessible way. We hope that those involved in social scientific study will benefit from the pulling together of debates on integration from a number of disciplines, from the new evidence presented and from discussion of how research can challenge myths. We hope that those involved in implementing policies of integration and diversity will benefit from clarification of evidence on these issues. We hope that all readers will enjoy the challenges to common ways of thinking about race and segregation.

Contemporary debates of migration and race

The problem of the (mis)use of statistics in contemporary migration and race debates is well illustrated with the example of how the issue of segregation has gained social and political prominence in Britain. Segregation, an issue largely confined to the pages of academic journals between the 1970s and the early 21st century, was thrown into the limelight by the strong language used in official reports after disturbances in northern towns in 2001:

–

We have focused on the very worrying drift towards self-
segregation, the necessity of arresting and reversing this
process.... The Bradford District has witnessed growing
division among its population along race, ethnic, religious
and social class lines – and now finds itself in the grip of
fear.[1]

The team was particularly struck by the depth of
polarisation of our towns and cities. The extent to which
physical divisions were compounded by so many other
aspects of our daily lives, was very evident. Separate
educational arrangements, community and voluntary
bodies, employment, places of worship, language, social
and cultural networks means that many communities
operate on the basis of parallel lives. These lives often
do not seem to touch at any point, let alone overlap and
promote meaningful exchanges.[2]

These two authoritative inquiries reported communities physically
divided, 'self-segregated' on religious and ethnic lines. Later we will
show that the communities referred to could equally be described as
highly mixed, but here we are simply concerned with examples of the
claims of segregation. The religious and ethnic divisions of concern
to the inquiries were mainly those between families living in Britain
for many generations and those who have immigrated in recent
decades. The Bishop of Rochester highlighted multiculturalism as
the conduit from immigration to segregation, and 'Islamic extremism'
as its legacy:

[The] novel philosophy of 'multiculturalism' ... required
that people should be facilitated in living as separate
communities, continuing to communicate in their
own languages and having minimum need for building
healthy relationships with the majority. Alongside these
developments, there has been a worldwide resurgence of
the ideology of Islamic extremism. One of the results of
this has been to further alienate the young from the nation
in which they were growing up and also to turn already
separate communities into 'no-go' areas where adherence
to this ideology has become a mark of acceptability.[3]

MigrationWatchUK adds its focus on immigration when praising the Commission for Racial Equality's warning of growing segregation (these two organisations will feature frequently in this book):

> The very high rates of immigration in recent years are creating areas in which children with two UK born parents are in a minority. This poses serious difficulties for effective integration as there will increasingly be no core culture with which to integrate.... The Chairman of the Commission for Racial Equality (CRE) has warned that 'we are sleepwalking our way towards segregation'. He also said that 'The fact is that we are a society which, almost without noticing it, is becoming more divided by race and religion. Residentially, some districts are on their way to becoming fully fledged ghettos'.[4]

Trevor Phillips, the Chair of the former Commission for Racial Equality and now Chair of the Equality and Human Rights Commission,[5] links increased segregation more to cultural diversity than to immigration. His warnings of racial and religious divisions have been repeated by David Cameron as leader of the Conservative Party as well as by Tony Blair when Prime Minister:

> We like our diversity. But how do we react when that 'difference' leads to separation and alienation from the values that define what we hold in common? ... [T]he reason we are having this debate is not generalised extremism. It is a new and virulent form of ideology associated with a minority of our Muslim community.[6]

The argument is generally that 'the pace of change' in local neighbourhoods arising from ideas and behaviour new to Britain has led to retreat by religious and ethnic groups into 'their own communities' such that people of different communities are living separate and parallel lives. The emphasis on immigration, cultural distrust or politics depends on the author but, so the argument goes, the separate behaviour is both resulting in and reinforced by residential clustering. In short, 'segregation – residentially, socially and in the workplace – is growing'[7] and is a problem requiring urgent action. The Commission for Racial Equality has rightly argued that segregation must not be understood solely in residential terms; but it places residential patterns central to understanding the problems:

'None of the factors leading to [residential] segregation … should necessarily lead to the formation of communities that are shut off from the outside world. But that is what we are seeing emerging'.[8] The Commission has used copious statistics to lend authority to these claims:

> In England, the number of people of Pakistani heritage in what are technically called 'ghetto' communities trebled during 1991-2001; 13% in Leicester live in such communities (the figure was 10.8% in 1991); 13.3% in Bradford (it was 4.3% in 1991).[9]

> It should not surprise us that in Birmingham the concentration has reached extreme proportions. Overall 29.6% of Birmingham's population comes from ethnic minority groups. But this figure masks a vast variation among the city's wards. At one end sit what can only be described as largely white areas to the south and north of the city, with ethnic minority proportions of under 5%; Northfields and Sutton Four Oaks for example. On the other hand, Lozells itself boasts an almost totally non-white population at 82.6%. It is hard to imagine how, even with the best will in the world, white, black and brown families can hope to share their hopes, dreams and ambitions.[10]

The language here is racially selective. A minority population under 5% is said to make an area 'largely white', while the presence of a relatively large white population of over 15% makes an area 'almost totally non-white'. As so often, the lack of a white population is seen as 'extreme' in a way that the lack of minority ethnic groups is not. This description of ethnic composition is coloured by an assumption that large minority populations are a concern. But more important in the logic of these extracts is the leap of causal explanation between minority ethnic concentrations and divisive segregation. It is simply assumed that people who do not live in the same area cannot share the same values, and that racial, ethnic and religious divisions are greater than other divisions, for example by wealth. We shall see later that this passage contains falsehoods as well as these linguistic and logical assumptions. The allusion to a technical definition of ghettos is a pure invention, for example, and while Leicester and Bradford's minority ethnic populations are growing, in recent years more white residents have moved *into* these two cities' most concentrated minority areas than have moved out.

The Commission for Racial Equality and its successor the Equality and Human Rights Commission draw on a variety of statistical evidence to paint an equally bleak picture of segregation in schools and in friendship groups. But where does this evidence come from? Can we rely on it? What evidence is ignored? In this book we critique this evidence and the use of it. Our aims in this should not be misinterpreted: we do not intend to negate the very good work of the government equality bodies. Our own aims are not at odds with theirs. However, our concern is that by promoting messages based on misinterpretations and invention of evidence, the Equality and Human Rights Commission and other powerful institutions are sustaining myths that will be damaging to their own agendas of integration.

What is segregation?

There is easily cause for alarm that the goal of integration is not being achieved when that goal is ill-defined and the goal posts are continually moving. While politicians and their advisors battle with constructing the best systems to create an integrated society, researchers develop theories and evidence to understand and explain the state of society and how it is changing.

Theories of segregation and integration have a history over many decades. Different aspects of the theories are elaborated in the chapters of this book. What the continued theorising tells us, however, is that there is no straightforward answer to 'what is segregation?' and 'what is integration?'. The concepts are complex and dynamic and continue to be contested.

Segregation and integration theory has predominantly been developed by scholars in the US and this thinking has influenced scholarship elsewhere, including in Britain.[11] Thinking on segregation and integration has changed as paradigms in social science have shifted. Over the last few decades, theories of segregation and integration have been framed within paradigms concerned with identity and social change. Changes in race relations thinking, and the associated policy initiatives, are outlined in Chapter Two and also discussed in Chapters Four and Five.

From early studies, distinctions have been made between different types of integration. In particular, concepts of spatial, structural and cultural integration remain important.[12] Spatial integration is about where people live; structural integration is about engagement with structures of society such as employment and education; cultural integration is about engagement in values, traditions and customs. The variety of dimensions of integration – from housing choice, to political engagement, to economic achievement – means that the phenomenon is studied within a number of disciplines, although traditionally it has been the remit of sociologists and geographers. It is these scholars who have theorised the relationship between types of segregation and integration, in particular the implications of spatial segregation for other forms of segregation.[13] Theories of spatial integration are discussed in Chapter Six.

Early theories of integration suggested that the newcomers or minority ethnic groups would adapt to the 'majority culture' in a straightforward one-way process. Structural and cultural integration – or assimilation – was thought to occur over time as migrants dispersed residentially from immigrant settlement areas.[14] By the 1960s this 'straight line' view of integration was being challenged.[15] Theories began to incorporate ideas that change occurred dynamically throughout society rather than entirely on the part of immigrants; and that integration happened in different ways in different places and for different populations.[16] It was recognised that retention of ethnic or migrant affiliations and networks was a part of, rather than contrary to, integration.[17]

In recent years, theories have returned to the significance of the spatial dimensions of integration. This reflects broader social scientific concerns with space and scale; and with the contemporary social and political processes of globalisation and localisation. What is happening locally, and how this differs, is seen as important. The defining aspect of integration in political terms has become whether neighbourhoods are 'cohesive'; whether contact between ethnic groups results in conflict or cooperation. Theories diverge about whether local diversity is beneficial or detrimental for social cohesion.[18] Recent debate is also engaged around the extent to which immigration and diversity has led, and is leading, to social change in Western societies. Some have argued that societies are being remade as a result of international migration while others argue that the changes do not extend to the deepest roots of society's values and culture.[19]

So, when MigrationWatchUK talks about the 'core culture with which to integrate' being under threat, many questions are raised. Is it possible to define this 'core culture'? Has it ever existed? Who defines it? Who has a right to define it? How is integration to this 'core culture' assessed? It is partly because integration and segregation are chaotic concepts that myths around them can grow. In the chapters that follow we attempt to highlight the assumptions and concepts used in the myths as well as to question their accuracy and appropriateness in relation to what scholarship tells us about segregation and integration.

The role of statistics

In evaluating claims of race and migration we also examine the statistical evidence behind them. It sometimes seems that statistics are used to support both sides of a political argument, and the audience is left wondering which are the most believable or accurate. How do you know that we have used evidence more robustly than the myth-makers we seek to challenge? We are fortunate in this book to have space for sufficient evidence to enable the reader to consider both sides. We hope to be responsible critics of the claims we investigate. We try to avoid 'hit and run criticism', which might point out some small flaw and pretend it invalidates the whole claim. We also attempt to put forward alternative views and to provide evidence that enables the reader to judge between the claim and the alternative.[20]

At times the public discussion of race and migration involves evidence that we find is simply incorrectly stated. These 'errors of commission' are the easiest to describe and to match to reliable sources of bona fide statistics. This is the case, for example, with the claim that government statistics show an increase in segregation, discussed in Chapter Six. At other times claims are made without evidence. These are 'errors of omission', which we tackle by providing evidence with which to judge the claims, as in the expectation of 'Minority White Cities' by 2011 discussed in Chapter Seven. We are frankly appalled by the way in which evidence is ignored and invented in order to support major social policies, and wish to provide an antidote that treats evidence with more respect. In all cases we provide detailed references to publications or to websites that the reader can investigate themselves if they are so inclined. We have acknowledged the varied origins and meanings of race statistics (in Chapter Two) and have taken care not to combine data from different sources inappropriately, or to make a case based on data that we believe to be unreliable. We are happy to discuss further any of the evidence should readers wish to get in touch.

In challenging the myths we also take issue with interpretation of evidence, usually when it is used out of its context, without acknowledgement of alternative explanations or without due respect for the quality of the evidence. The increase in immigration to Britain in recent years is portrayed by some as shockingly high, but is shown in Chapter Three to be very close to the world average. Rather than stimulating a panic about Britain's predicament and policies, the same data taken in context stimulate an understanding of the global rise of mobility and structural changes that are most likely here to stay. In another example, data supposed to reveal alarming ethnically exclusive friendship groups can be alternatively interpreted as revealing surprisingly broad friendships; these same data are contradicted in both detail and interpretation by reports from much larger and better organised surveys, as discussed in Chapter Five.

At times, interpretation of data does depend on what perspective one brings to it. We have already described our own perspectives in favour of human rights and against discrimination and prejudice. These are very broad points of departure that we imagine most readers will agree with, but nonetheless our aim is not simply to tell our story. Our aim is to allow readers to assess the claims made in common debate, drawing on our experience as researchers to give evidence that is open and rigorous, emphasising what we understand to be clear results rather than nit-picking minor criticisms of others, or claiming a unique interpretation where we know others exist.

Within the book we have made a strong case that some widely publicised views have no basis in evidence, including views promoted by government spokespeople and government organisations. We do not expect to be free of criticism ourselves but look forward to a debate based on examination of evidence. We hope to induce a little more respect for the widely abused term 'evidence-based policy'.

Abuse of statistics in times of uncertainty

There is no doubt that statistics have authority. It is no surprise that governmental and non-governmental organisations employ them in their arguments. The development of science and scientific method has lent authority to quantitative evidence. The focus of social sciences in the 1950s and 1960s on evidence from surveys and censuses has instilled a sense of their importance for issues of public policy. Politicians pepper their speeches with statistics to avoid accusations of being merely popularist. We agree on the importance of clear descriptions of reality. But we think that as a society we do not treat this statistical evidence with the critical scrutiny that it deserves.[21]

Such scrutiny is particularly important in times of uncertainty, when myths and moral panics thrive.[22] The late 20th and early 21st centuries have been a period of uncertainty in many ways. Britain, like many other societies, is in a period of rethinking issues of immigration and diversity. The issues are not new; they have been a constant in social and political debates since the beginning of the 20th century and particularly since the 1950s, when Britain first experienced large-scale labour recruitment from the Caribbean and the Indian subcontinent. However, we are now in a new phase, a phase that has been identified as having begun in the 1990s and that is referred to as a period of new migration and super-diversity.[23]

A number of characteristics define the current era. First, there are changes in international migration. There has been a rise in international migration globally and Britain has experienced increased numbers of people emigrating and immigrating. On balance, Britain's population has grown through immigration since the early 1980s.[24] This phase of immigration, however, differs from previous ones in its diversity: diverse reasons for migration, diverse legal (and illegal) channels through which it is achieved and diverse places of origin of immigrants.

Many migrants come to Britain for work. This may be short or long term and may or may not be through specific company or employment-sector schemes. Migrant workers engage in a range of employment, from low-skilled to high-skilled work, spanning the wage scale. Migrants also come to study, to join their family, and as asylum seekers or refugees – forced migrants in search of refuge. Migrants now come from every continent, from places that are far more varied in location, culture, history and politics than the Commonwealth countries that were the predominant source of immigrants in the second half of the 20th century. These changes in international migration have led to increased diversity in Britain along many lines: country of origin, legal status, employment and housing experience, ethnicity, religion, language, education, gender and age.

Uncertainty in this period of new migration and super-diversity has been dramatically increased by international events in the early years of the 21st century. The attacks on New York and other US cities in September 2001 led to the 'war on terror' between 'the West' and 'the Muslim terrorists'. The resultant wars in Afghanistan and Iraq and attacks in Spain and Britain have shifted the official context for thinking about race, migration and diversity. The anti-racist and multicultural optimism of the late 20th century has been replaced by fear and suspicion, particularly with regard to Muslims.

Consequently, there is ongoing debate about the best policy responses to issues of diversity and integration within this changing context. The questions are challenging: in a time of greater international tension and migration, how can commitment to globalisation, individual human rights and equality be protected, diversity respected and welcomed, while unity in the national polity is nurtured? One response, powerful because it has been adopted by government, has linked immigration, religion and violence. The adoption of multiculturalism has been blamed for strengthening divisions between ethnic and religious groups. In its place are ideas of integration, community cohesion, national identity and citizenship.[25] This line of thinking became evident in the White Paper *Secure Borders, Safe Haven* published in 2002 and was reinforced in *Our Shared Future*, the 2007 report of the government Commission on Integration and Cohesion.[26]

The Foreword to the Commission's report signifies the challenges and changes for policy thinking, making explicit the vision of a society 'where people are committed to what we have in common rather than obsessing with those things that make us different'.[27] Its focus on citizenship had been proposed by the government's earlier Community Cohesion Panel, which hoped that policies would 'be applied with greater vigour to break down segregated areas and be monitored on a regular basis'.[28]

In *Our Shared Future*, there is also acknowledgement of the problematic line of recent debates: 'It is clear that whilst there are significant challenges, the mood of pessimism that some hold is not justified. Excessive coverage about residential segregation for example serves to spread a view that the whole of England is spatially segregated. It overstates and oversimplifies the problem and leaves us "sleepwalking into simplicity"'.[29] It is our contention that overstatement and oversimplification are just two ways in which evidence has been abused in this debate.

The role of legends and myths

Given this context of quite intense political and social change, it is not surprising that debates on race and migration are awash with myths. But what is a myth and what roles do myths play?

Myths, as understood in this book, are legends or powerful stories that have influence but are not true. Legends — one can think of them as stories with a message — are abundant in society. Legends claim truths about the corruption of power, or the benefits of eating an apple a day, or what makes a celebrity successful, or the incompatibility of religion and politics. One key purpose of legends is to help society understand where it is at; to help people share and discuss understandings about how things happen. Legends are an important and normal way of maintaining a viewpoint. For any group of people, be that, for example, residents of a nation, people of a shared generation or those who happen to attend the same school, legends provide a means for defining and expressing beliefs and attitudes. They also sustain political viewpoints. In the context of this book, legends often become pervasive – common-sense – ways of expressing, thinking about and understanding issues such as immigration and integration.

All legends contain some warning or advice, some kind of 'moral message'. It is this warning that makes them memorable, gives them social currency and encourages them to be repeated, whether or not they are believed. It is this warning that makes the legends culturally ingrained and therefore difficult to challenge; if the warning, or the 'moral message', resonates with the audience, the legend will be passed on. An apple a day is worth the effort if it avoids illness. Immigration should be stopped if that would reduce unemployment.

Myths are legends that are untrue, as in 'that's just a myth'. Nevertheless, they can be widely believed and have considerable impact on behaviour if they provide an explanation for the way society works. The warnings are taken on board and the symbolism remembered even if there is scepticism about the evidence delivered in the myth.[30] Legends may have varying degrees of truth and often rely on an acceptance of their assumptions, which are rarely made explicit. Most legends are expressed in ambiguous terms and so are not easy to dismiss.

Legends are not problematic per se. But they become problematic when they are inaccurate but nonetheless constitute the framework for policy debate, and the context for interpretation of evidence. Legends get in the way if they misinform and limit our views of society.[31] Contemporary myths of race and migration are particularly problematic because they encourage division and tension, prejudice, fear, hostility and discrimination between groups and also within groups.

The mythical properties of 'the segregation problem' can be identified. The warning in this legend is quite clear: if we allow ethnic groups to grow apart there will be deviance, caused by those 'outside the mainstream' 'playing by their own rules'. The end result is also explicit: 'crime, no-go areas and chronic cultural conflict'.[32] The legends and their warning have become influential, through repetition by prominent social commentators.[33] That the Chair of the Equality and Human Rights Commission expressed such concern is significant. It has legitimised other vocal proponents of race and migration myths such as MigrationWatchUK and the British National Party.[34] It has contributed to the claims being used to frame political thinking, media reporting and public opinion. Counterarguments, or legends with a different message, are heard, although not so frequently as the myths. These counterarguments often refer to a common humanity, or to neighbours' common conditions and interests. They have rarely held the weight, pervasiveness and strength of contemporary myths in early 21st-century thinking but this is not, as we will demonstrate, because of lack or inadequacy of evidence to support them.

Contemporary myths of race and migration, therefore, have a number of defining characteristics: they express values and warning, they use symbolism, they use evidence selectively and, we argue, incorrectly, and they have social currency and impact. In the chapters that challenge myths we unpick the evidence that underpins them and in doing so we aim to change the status of the widely accepted truth that Britain is 'sleepwalking to segregation' into a rejected falsehood. We hope to open up more space for discussion of alternative arguments and to demonstrate that the picture is far less bleak than the myth-makers lead us to believe.

Clarifying important terms

There are a number of important concepts and terms that are central to this book that need definition: 'race', ethnicity, segregation, integration, multiculturalism and migration. These are sometimes contentious and ambiguous terms, and it is important to clarify how we understand and use them.

'Race' has its origins in distinctions of biology or colour but is now usually used (often in inverted commas, although not subsequently in this book) to distinguish between people on the basis of a number of characteristics through which racism could be expressed. We use race in this book to refer to socially significant difference associated with migration, origin and colour, as in Black or Asian. *Ethnicity* is a newer concept and term than race, and one that embraces a broader idea of difference. Ethnicity usually refers to self-adopted identity based on a mixture of physical attributes, birthplace, legal status (nationality), but also and in particular on family origins, beliefs (including religion) and practices (language and culture).

However, the distinction between race and ethnicity is often blurred both in common usage and in serious analytical writing. Racism can be directed against Travellers or Polish people or Muslims without reference to migration, origin or colour. At the same time, the official measurement in Britain of 'ethnic group' in censuses and surveys, which provides much of the evidence in this book and elsewhere, mixes labels of appearance (White, Black, Asian, ...) with an instruction to indicate one's 'cultural background' from choices including African, Chinese, Irish and Pakistani (and does not include an explicit dimension of religion). Thus, we cannot attempt to divide the evidence on race and ethnicity and do not attempt to make that distinction except where we can explain our meaning clearly and helpfully. We do not use race in any biological sense. We will usually refer to ethnicity and signal where we refer to specific aspects of ethnicity. When referring to ethnic group we will usually have in mind the official categories used in British statistics, and capitalise White as well as other groups.[35] When thinking of all groups other than White we will often refer to minorities or ethnic minorities, although at times we may specifically include White minorities too.

Segregation is used in this book to refer to separation between people of different ethnicities. It is such a slippery term because different authors may refer to the separation of individuals or whole communities, where the separation may be voluntary or involuntary, and may be complete or slight. If lack of segregation means a mixed area, is a mixed area one where two groups co-exist in equal numbers or where each group is represented in its national proportions? What degree of separation counts as segregation? In Chapter Six we will define and explore four different meanings of segregation that are each in common usage. Separation can be residential, in social networks or in housing, employment and education. Although we are concerned with all of these aspects of segregation, much of the discussion in this book is about residential segregation or where people live. This is because much of the evidence quoted in support of claims about segregation in Britain only describes physical or geographical separation, and also because it is often claimed that residential segregation is the root of other divisions. This is made explicit by conflict theorists who claim that those of different ethnicity can only co-exist without conflict by merging into a common ethnicity (this is further discussed in Chapter Six). More often, however, the claim that geographical segregation of any degree is a negative and undesirable feature of our society is made implicitly, often by allusion to violence and deprivation in alleged or imminent 'ghettos', rather than explored explicitly as we try to do in this book. For those who think that over time integration must eliminate differences between groups, all degrees of geographical separation are signs of backwardness, and this justifies our close look at the evidence for residential segregation. For us, residential clustering has historical and social roots, and is not of itself negative, just as group differences, if they are not expressions of discrimination, are not of themselves negative.

Integration is not the opposite of segregation. We think that a degree of separateness is compatible with participation in work, education, housing and political processes, which we believe are the key elements of integration. We use the term integration in this general sense in the book, to mean a desirable outcome of harmonious diversity without discrimination. However, it is worth signalling that this is quite different from assimilation – the elimination of all differences – and different too from a general reduction of differences in all behaviour and life choices. That seems to us a crude and indeed repressive view of integration, demanding that our family origins and religious choices have no impact on our behaviour.

Multiculturalism in social policy respects distinct group identities based on shared histories or cultures or languages or practices. A multicultural perspective does not see group identities as being at odds with integration and does not view affiliation with one group as meaning detachment from or opposition to other groups. While a multicultural social policy was never defined explicitly with that label, in Britain from the 1980s to 1990s government funding and policy recognised group differences as a legitimate guide to the spectrum of needs in an integrated society. For example, school dietary and dress guidelines were extended to allow for some non-Christian religious preferences, and local community centres aiming to involve specific cultural heritages were supported to increase civic involvement and to demonstrate the state's acceptance of Britain's growing diversity. The term multicultural is often used in a more general way to mean cultural or ethnic diversity but we use it in this book to refer specifically to this recognition of diversity in social policy. It is not the role of this book to evaluate multicultural policy, but in various places we note that along with immigration, multiculturalism has been attacked at the start of the 21st century as an important stimulant of segregation in Britain. Our evidence that the growth of segregation is in fact a myth may in that sense make multiculturalism a legitimate option in social policy.

Migration is perhaps the most straightforward concept to introduce. It is about the residential movement of people. There are two forms of migration that have significance for this book: international migration and internal migration. International migration involves movement across international boundaries: emigration is movement out of a country and immigration is movement into a country. Internal migration refers to a change of address within a country: out-migration is movement out of a defined area such as a city or local authority district to other areas of the country, and in-migration is movement into a defined area. International migration is important because it changes the ethnic composition of the nationally resident population and internal migration is important because it changes the distribution – and therefore the segregation – of that ethnically differentiated population.

Finding your way around the book

Seven chapters follow this introduction, laying out and critiquing evidence and arguments on key aspects of current race and migration debates. To make this book as direct and accessible as possible we have used specialist language minimally and references have been placed in endnotes to chapters and in the bibliography, rather than throughout the text. To enable the book to be 'dipped into' as well as read sequentially, each chapter is self-contained, although ordered such that the discussion in one feeds into the next.

Chapter Two begins that discussion by questioning the meaning and value of race data, presenting perspectives from North America and France in addition to Britain. The chapter aims to assess the historical and current uses of ethnic group data in order to better understand how they might be of positive purpose.

Chapters Three to Seven are the myth-breaking chapters and combine reviews of existing work with new evidence. In each chapter we begin with a claim and its origins and move on to assess it and the evidence that has been used to underpin it. Five specific myths are addressed. They are included because they are prominent myths and ones that represent concerns about both immigration and the integration of immigrants and their families. Immigration is the first myth addressed in the book (Chapter Three) because of its importance in bringing ethnic diversity to Britain. The concerns about post-Second World War mass labour immigration are echoed today in reactions to the immigration of asylum seekers and workers from Eastern Europe. This chapter argues that current levels of immigration are not problematic; that immigration is economically beneficial; and that Britain's immigration experience is quite unexceptional when viewed in an international context.

The other four myths that the book addresses relate to integration. Chapter Four deals with concerns about structural and cultural integration. It argues that growing minority populations are not creating a crisis of space, housing availability or service provision.

Chapter Five discusses the myth that divisions are created by a lack of effort to integrate by minority populations. Evidence is reviewed on where young people aspire to live, their attitudes to mixing, and the association of terrorism with areas of high proportions of Muslims.

Chapter Six then turns directly to the myth of spatial segregation. It clarifies recent debate by demonstrating that there are no ghettos in Britain. Evidence shows an increase in the number of mixed areas at the same time as the size of minority populations is growing. The chapter challenges the idea of 'white flight'; and the fundamental assumption that residential separation is a problem.

The final myth (Chapter Seven) addresses fears that cities are becoming minority white. The chapter questions why there is such fascination with this demographic 'landmark' and presents the best available evidence about the future pluralisation of Britain's cities.

Chapter Eight draws together the book's arguments, discusses why the myths are so persistent, questions what may motivate those who maintain and promote the myths and suggests alternative ways of thinking about race and migration.

At the end of the book, we have compiled a summary of the arguments and evidence, which provides a concise myth-breaking reference source.

Notes
[1] Ouseley (2001, Foreword).
[2] Cantle (2001, p 9).
[3] Michael Nazir-Ali, Bishop of Rochester, 7 January 2008, www. telegraph.co.uk/news/main.jhtml?xml=/news/2008/01/06/nislam106. xml (all web links cited in this book were accurate and accessible in September 2008).
[4] MigrationWatchUK (2006).
[5] The Commission for Racial Equality merged with the equivalent government bodies for gender and disability equality, to create the Equality and Human Rights Commission in 2007.
[6] Blair (2006).
[7] CRE (2007, p 1).

[8] Trevor Phillips, speech at the Royal Geographical Society Annual Conference, London, 30 August 2006.

[9] Trevor Phillips, speech at the 1st Yousaf Inait Lecture, 3 March 2006.

[10] Trevor Phillips, speech at Keele University, 30 November 2005, http://83.137.212.42/sitearchive/cre/Default.aspx.LocID-0hgnew09i. RefLocID-0hg00900c002.Lang-EN.htm

[11] Alba and Nee (2005) provide an in-depth discussion of theories of integration since the 1920s.

[12] These distinctions were made in the work of the Chicago School in the 1920s (see Park, 1950 and Park, 1952). Gordon's (1964) influential model of assimilation made an explicit distinction between structural and cultural assimilation, breaking each down into constituent dimensions.

[13] Massey and Denton's (1993) book *American Apartheid* is a seminal work that illustrates the detrimental effects of residential segregation for minorities in the US. In the UK context, Ceri Peach has considered the implications of ethnic enclaves (for example, Peach, 1996a). Roger Andersson, Sako Musterd and colleagues discuss this issue from a perspective of Continental Europe (for example, Andersson et al, 2007).

[14] Massey and Mullan (1984) provide an exemplification of the theory of spatial assimilation and Alba et al (1999) reassess it in a US context. Alternatives to this theory have been proposed, including Zelinsky and Lee's (1998) idea of heterolocalism.

[15] Glazer and Moynihan's (1963) book *Beyond the Melting Pot* was particularly influential in changing the direction of thinking on integration.

[16] The concept of 'segmented assimilation' was introduced by Portes and Zhou (1993).

[17] Alba and Nee (1997) and Gans (1997) provide reviews and a critique of assimilation theory.

[18] Putnam (2007) argues that diversity reduces social solidarity while Stein et al (2000) and Marschall and Stolle (2004) argue to the contrary.

[19] Alba and Nee (2005) argue that immigrant assimilation has fundamentally changed US society. Portes (2008) has argued that the changes are to the visible, surface levels of institutions and organisations.

[20] Bross (1960) and the Radical Statistics Education Group (1982) discuss the nature of responsible criticism in research, the latter in the context of educational research into the impact on pupil progress of teaching styles, selective schools and school effectiveness.

[21] We are in agreement here with the Royal Statistical Society, which has attempted to address this problem including by launching the Statistical Excellence in Journalism award in 2007.

[22] For discussion of moral panic, including moral panic on immigration, see Cohen (2002).

[23] For discussion, see Koser and Lutz (1998) and Vertovec (2007).

[24] See Salt (2006) for an overview of patterns in international migration, to which we will return in Chapter Three.

[25] See Kundnani (2007a) for an overview of political thinking on these issues.

[26] Home Office (2002); Commission on Integration and Cohesion (2007).

[27] Commission on Integration and Cohesion (2007, pp 2-4).

[28] Community Cohesion Panel (2004).

[29] Commission on Integration and Cohesion (2007, p 3).

[30] See Whatley and Henken (2000) for an introduction to and definition of contemporary legends and folklore.

[31] Lomborg (2001) makes the same argument in defending his book, *The Skeptical Environmentalist*, which challenges environmental myths.

[32] These phrases were used by Trevor Phillips (2005) in a speech blaming terrorist atrocities on the impact of physical and cultural segregation.

[33] Repetition of messages by key actors is an important part of the process by which they gain social currency; see Kitzinger (1999).

[34] MigrationWatchUK is a thinktank, established in October 2001, that promotes anti-immigration arguments. The British National Party (BNP) is an extreme right-wing party with representation at local government level.

[35] Ethnic group categories from the 2001 Census are given in Figure 2.1. For brevity, and to avoid associations between nationality and ethnicity, we sometimes use 'White Briton', 'Caribbean', 'African' and 'Irish' instead of 'White British', 'Black Caribbean', 'Black African' and 'White Irish'. See Chapter Two for discussion of the development of ethnic group categories.

2

Making sense of race statistics

It is extremely difficult to define 'coloured' precisely at all; and it is impossible to define it precisely in a way that will work in a census. We did not (and will not) attempt it, but used the unequivocal and objective concept of birthplace instead. This leaves you with the awkward 'white Indians' and 'black Englishman' but there is no practicable way of identifying them in a census. *John Boreham, Chief Government Statistician*[1]

Introduction

In Britain and the US, the terms 'race', 'ethnicity', 'ethnic group' and 'ethnic minorities' are now ubiquitous in politics and social science alike, with abundant statistics to match. But less than 50 years ago, Britain's chief government statistician ruled that it was impossible to measure in a census what was then termed 'coloured'. Britain is still the only country in Europe to regularly make such measurements in national inquiries. The measurement of ethnicity remains a contentious issue because the question of what is being measured is inseparable from the (political) purposes for which the statistics are intended. The historical development of race statistics informs how we think about and understand race today.

It is the role of this chapter to take a historical, political and statistical view of the official collection of data that are currently labelled 'ethnic group', in order to better understand how they are used in the making of myths and, indeed, in the counterarguments to those myths. The first section of this chapter presents a roughly chronological review of the development of race statistics in Britain in relation to specific policy arenas. It considers the influence of pre-20th-century eugenics, immigration control, anti-discrimination legislation, multicultural policy and community cohesion agendas. The second section gives examples from three countries – Britain, France and the US – of solutions to the dilemmas of how to measure race. The chapter thereby aims to demonstrate that the categorisation and measurement of race is highly contentious, with data serving several specific policy agendas. Nevertheless, the chapter concludes, ethnic group statistics in Britain have meaningful potential for assessing social conditions and social change.

Politics, policy and race statistics

Eugenics

The development of statistics as a scientific discipline more than 100 years ago has a direct link with racist ideology. Francis Galton, one of the founding fathers of both statistics and demography and a cousin of Charles Darwin, built the theory of variation between populations on the belief that '[i]t would be quite practicable to produce a highly gifted race of men by judicious marriages during several consecutive generations' ... 'as much superior mentally and morally to the modern European, as the modern European is to the

—

24

lowest of the Negro races'.[2] Such eugenic views were a common motivation for statistical developments up to the 20th century. The measurement of correlation between personal characteristics was developed in response to eugenic concerns in Britain that the genetic stock of prosperous families was weakened by classes and races whose genetic composition was considered to be inferior.[3]

Other statisticians also supported eugenicist theories. Ronald Fisher, who laid the foundation of modern statistical theory, argued that '[t]o increase the birth rate in the professional classes and among the highly skilled artisans would be to solve the great eugenic problem of the present generation and to lay a broad foundation for every kind of social advance'.[4] The leading official demographer in the US, P.K. Whelpton, was able to comment approvingly on Nazi laws to sterilise the disabled population: 'By means of eugenic sterilization, it is planned to lower the incidence of certain undesirable qualities in the next generation ... this plan should be watched carefully by populationists in all parts of the world and such tests of its effectiveness made as are possible'.[5] There are plenty of other great names of statistics and demography – Dublin, Edgeworth, Spearman and Thompson – who made similarly enthusiastic statements about the need to breed out disadvantage.[6] The historical association of statistics and racist eugenics is one reason why statistics of race are viewed with suspicion.

The eugenic perspective was weakened with the defeat of Nazi fascism, its most successful proponent, and is no longer a pervasive view in Britain or among statisticians. Modern studies of genetics and behaviour do search for group differences, for example between males and females, but most are cautious about exploring racial explanations. A minority, however, continue to pursue ideas that race can be an indicator of inferiority or superiority.[7]

Immigration control

From the early 20th century a new context emerged for race statistics: controlling immigration. Controlling immigration was seen as 'necessary to improve race relations. The fewer the blacks, the easier their integration. No blacks, no problem: it was all a matter of numbers'.[8] Immigration control and race relations debates were intertwined from the beginning. Frequently, minority or non-British residents are used to represent the immigration of the past and it is often overlooked whether the move was by the person concerned or by their parents or by earlier ancestors. Some academics whose work stems from immigration policy talk of 'immigrant populations' and 'foreign–origin populations', notably David Coleman whose association with the MigrationWatchUK campaign became a public issue in 2007.[9] 'Foreign' is a pernicious term to use for the five million citizens of the UK, half of these born in the UK, who happen not to have a long British heritage, as it implies a status below those who are not of immigrant origin.

Immigrant origin is identifiable in government surveys and the 10-yearly census. Up to 1971, an individual's own place of birth was the only means of understanding the mix of origins in Britain. Birthplace is categorised finely to reveal those born in each country of the world, and published tables from British censuses divide the world into more than 20 countries and regions. The censuses up to 1971 report the sex and age composition of those born outside Britain but not their social conditions. Interest in the population size and characteristics of immigrants and their descendants born in Britain gained strength in the 1960s and 1970s as immigration became a strong political issue.

At the same time, minority populations made their organised contribution in many areas, and racism was resisted strongly by Black organisations stimulated by political traditions new to Britain including the Black Power movements of the Caribbean and the US. Immigration was high on the government statistical agenda. Immigration policy and anti–racists alike focused on the minority population as a whole without focusing on groups of different origin, and this was not to change until multicultural policies came to the fore in the 1980s.

The census of 1971 extended the question on country of birth to each person's parents following a firm rejection of a question on race by the government Chief Statistician. The extended birthplace question was the basis of government estimates of the 'New Commonwealth and Pakistan' population: those born in, or with parents born in, the New Commonwealth or Pakistan.[10] The census reports for each part of the country gave numbers and age structures for the group as a whole, which corresponded well with Britain's 'coloured' minority population. The government's aim was a demographic profile of the minority population but political debate about the statistics continued to focus on whether the immigrant population had been exaggerated or undercounted. These debates informed the politics of immigration.[11]

The immigration debate is ongoing and continues to be racialised as indicated by *The Observer* headline declaring 'The last days of a white world'.[12] The immigration debate – and population projections – are dealt with in Chapters Three, Four and Seven of this book.

Anti-discrimination

The introduction of legislation in the 1970s outlawing racial discrimination gave a new imperative to the collection of race statistics. Implementation of anti-discrimination laws, including the prosecution of employers for recruitment malpractice, has depended on the comparison of employment and population statistics with an ethnicity dimension. This is a very different motivation from the eugenics of earlier racial categorisation. Race and ethnic group statistics provide official measures of the results of discrimination and therefore of rights denied. Statistics are required and encouraged by government anti-discrimination legislation, which charges the Equality and Human Rights Commission to ensure that progress towards (or away from) equality is statistically monitored and gives it powers to investigate suspected discrimination.[13]

The 1976 Race Relations Act was much stronger than those of the 1960s, and came after awareness of discrimination in housing and employment markets, and street skirmishes involving young Black and Asian people in the early 1970s, in particular in response to disproportionate attention from the police. The Race Relations Act did not stave off the first significant 'race riots', in Bristol in 1980[14] and Liverpool and London in 1981, but by focusing on the rights and conditions of people in Britain it gave a purpose other than immigration policy for statistically monitoring the conditions of Britain's Black populations or what were by then called ethnic minorities.

Race statistics are useful for anti-discrimination in a number of ways: they can reveal differences between ethnic groups, inform targets for reducing inequalities and be used to explain ethnic differences. Race statistics are powerful for demonstrating inequalities; they can tell stories of human tragedy that should inform public policy. The 91 deaths in the period February 2000 to April 2001 either from racist attacks, or while in police custody, or of asylum seekers each signal the end of a human life, the brutal cutting short of potential. There were successful prosecutions in only about half of these cases.[15] Powerful descriptive statistics in government reports show that:

> Overall, people from minority ethnic communities are
> more likely than others to live in deprived areas and in

27

unpopular and overcrowded housing. They are more likely to be poor and to be unemployed, regardless of their age, sex, qualifications and place of residence. As a group they are as well qualified as White people but some Black and Asian groups do not do as well at school as others, and African-Caribbean pupils are disproportionately excluded from school.[16]

Such statistics undermine any claim that there is no problem for government to address.

Targets for equality, for example equal employment, are set based on demographic analysis of ethnic group data. Home Office statistics for 2008 show West Yorkshire police with 4% minority officers compared to its 14% adult minority population,[17] highlighting that police recruitment does not reflect the policed population; the pattern is repeated in each of the major conurbations of Britain. In this case, the targets demanded by anti-discriminatory policy involve short-term projections of the number of Black and Asian adults of working age. They also imply monitoring not just of whether the targets are met, but how. Greater recruitment, perhaps from overseas as suggested by the London Metropolitan Police, will not itself change the discriminatory police behaviour observed by potential recruits and deterring their applications.[18]

Statistical modelling takes further the descriptive differences between groups in the population. It attempts to measure the 'causal path' of inequality by associating some of the group differences with other variables. For example, the high unemployment rate of minorities in Britain has remained throughout the last 40 years, and has been approximately double the white unemployment rate. About half of this excess unemployment is associated with characteristics such as minorities' place of residence within Britain in unemployment hotspots, and poorer qualifications, but the remainder is an excess unemployment for minorities in the same locations and of the same individual characteristics as white peers, and therefore is likely to be mainly due to discriminatory practices.[19] Differences in residence and qualifications are also achieved after discriminatory processes in education, immigration, housing and employment, entrenched within Britain's institutions, and therefore the excess unemployment associated with them also partly reflects discrimination, albeit from a more indirect causal path.[20]

Discrimination in the job market has also been measured experimentally (sometimes referred to simply as 'testing'). For example, in one study, when pairs of identical job applications were sent to a range of employers, English-named candidates were twice as likely as Asian-named candidates to get an interview.[21] The results of experiments are powerful, but they are not so easy to achieve.

Thus, it seems that race and ethnicity categories are useful to monitor and to expose oppression and its resulting disadvantage. In the US, where there is also a history of anti-discrimination legislation and associated statistics, community campaigners have defended those statistics when they have come under threat, because they are viewed as a means to improve services to those who have been excluded.[22]

But collection of statistics does not automatically lead to a reduction in the discrimination that they may reveal. Shortly before the British census first asked a direct question on 'ethnic group', a critical review of social research on ethnic inequalities considered that data collection was already outstripping its value: 'The crux of the matter lies not with data production however. It is the absence of political will on the part of the government to act upon data that is the major stumbling block to the fight against racial disadvantage and discrimination'.[23]

Twenty years later, disadvantage and discrimination continue on a similar scale and the political will to act to reduce it remains limited. The disadvantage varies between minority groups, and is perhaps worst in the economic arena. Minority group unemployment for men born in the UK is higher than white male unemployment by 7%. Only a quarter of this difference can be associated with poorer qualifications or less helpful social networks (human and social capital, according to the experts in this field).[24] The remainder may be due to a variety of factors that put minority groups in a disadvantaged position within the labour market, including direct and indirect discrimination. This disadvantage is no less than it has been in the past 40 years.[25]

Legislation has stipulated that public service employers must conform to race equality in employment and delivery of services. It is no longer acceptable for mainstream politicians or public servants to openly condone discrimination and racist behaviour. Voluntary and funded programmes encourage diversity and cooperation and aim to stamp out racism whether on estates or in sport. But serious incidences of racism within the police and other public bodies continue, and the private sector is not included in the main race discrimination legislation. Campaigns and legislation have not been sufficient or sufficiently used to prevent regular xenophobic tirades in the national press and far-right political parties, and racist behaviour in some of Britain's neighbourhoods severely restricts the ability of minority groups, including those of White Eastern European origin, to exercise their rights. Having race statistics has, if anything, illuminated the failure of anti-discrimination legislation.

Multiculturalism

The fourth way in which government policies demand racial statistics is to promote diversity and support the needs of different minority ethnic groups. Multicultural policies make demands of statistics in several ways. Categories of separate ethnic identities are required in order to understand and accommodate differences rather than to reduce them. Roy Jenkins' formulation of racial integration in 1966 as 'equal opportunity accompanied by cultural diversity in an atmosphere of mutual tolerance'[26] was acted on in the 1980s through a barrage of race awareness training and the development of diversity policies in education, social services and other public arenas.

For policies of promotion of diversity, unlike anti-discrimination legislation, statistics are *permanently* needed: there will never be a time when there is no diversity to promote. Government resources are specified to ensure that each minority (or majority) group can express itself and be appreciated within regulatory limits. Ethnic and religious organisations have supported and indeed led new arguments for measurement of both ethnic group and religion as official categories, because such recognition allows resources to be claimed.[27]

Multicultural policy expects that we all have an ethnic background, a different priority from the focus on discriminated social groups, or on immigrants. In this assertion of ethnicity it is acceptable to have more than one identity, although in statistical practice it is rare to measure the richness of multiple affiliations. Promotion of diversity readily includes Welsh and Scottish, Jewish and Latvian as well as Caribbean and African. Organisations that obtain resources on the basis of measured community size would be only too pleased to welcome you into their category. Opposition in Britain to the collection of ethnicity in census data has been minimal since the government adoption of anti-discrimination and multicultural policies.

However, there have been some critics. Kenan Malik has argued that if labelled ethnic categories lead to resources then the danger of competition and animosity inevitably follows. In the context of schooling he illustrates how statistically salient labels give a misleading racial focus to investigations:

Class and poverty seem more important determinants of poor educational performance than race. Yet so obsessed are we by racial categories that the question remains 'Why do black boys do so badly?' rather than 'Why do boys from poor background of whatever race, ethnicity or faith do so badly?'. Racism clearly shapes the lives of many Bangladeshis and African Caribbeans but race (or culture or faith) cannot be a one-stop explanation for all problems.[28]

Community cohesion

The final policy arena that demands statistics of race or ethnicity is labelled community cohesion. It results from a series of Home Office reports that have been critical of multicultural policy.[29] They complain that rather than celebrating and protecting ethnic diversity, multicultural policies have led to self-segregation of communities. Thus there is a need for those communities to become more integrated in society. In the same way, the government has demanded an oath of allegiance to Britain and a sufficiency of English from new immigrants since 2004.

The government accepted the Home Office recommendation that all local authorities should monitor community cohesion, without prescribing how it might be measured. The reports' depiction of communities experiencing parallel lives indicated remedies of interaction and of sharing the same workplaces, play places and neighbourhoods. The goal of integration places emphasis on comparison with the indigenous majority, rather than the diversity emphasised by multiculturalism, which affects how statistics are presented more than their collection. Importance is laid more on indices of segregation and friendship networks than on individual characteristics and inequality. The emphasis on segregation and ethnic separateness had been absent from policy for several decades, and represents a shift from material to cultural explanations of different experiences.[30]

Evidence of disadvantage in employment for a minority ethnic group, for example, is now as likely to be associated with ethnic difference and disengagement with British society, as it used to be associated with disadvantage associated with individual and institutional racism. Government policy encourages community cohesion and discourages public spending on group-specific resources. This shift in explanations of inequality does not deny the existence of racism but adds pressure on minority ethnic groups to feel responsible for the predicaments that they may face, including disadvantage. It is a shift that is noticeable in other areas of government policy. For example, in making local areas responsible for their sustained regeneration, regional policy has shifted away from structural economic understanding of spatial inequalities resulting from government and company decisions.[31] Ironically, monitoring the success of policies of community cohesion demands similar descriptive and local statistics to those required by multiculturalism.

The measurement and interpretation of 'ethnic group': policy concepts in statistical practice

The political and policy demands on race statistics have shifted over the decades of the 20th and early 21st centuries. This has raised many challenges for the measurement of ethnicity, some of which have already been alluded to. In this section, recent solutions to the dilemmas of measuring (or not) ethnicity are presented for Britain, France and the United States.

Britain's early experience

Despite the usefulness of ethnic group statistics for monitoring inequalities, setting policy targets and explaining ethnic differences, the introduction of an ethnic group question in the census in Britain was not straightforward. The strength of the anti-discrimination movement led the government to propose a direct question on ethnic origin in the White Paper preparing for the 1981 Census, not much more than a decade after the chief statistician had said it was impossible, in the quote that starts this chapter. 'Authoritative and reliable information about the main ethnic minorities' was now needed:

> In order to help in carrying out their responsibilities under the Race Relations Act, and in developing effective social policies, the Government and local authorities need to know how the family structure, housing, education, employment and unemployment of the ethnic minorities compare with the conditions in the population as a whole.[32]

So it was acknowledged that minority workers and their families were, as campaigning Black organisations sometimes put it, 'here to stay, here to fight'. And government, while turning the screws to restrict immigration, also wanted to prepare the mechanisms of social control that would monitor and reduce the impact of the racist institutional practices of the British state and commerce, although the term institutional racism was yet to be coined. At this distance and accustomed to ethnic group data from the censuses of 1991 and 2001, researchers and statisticians might well assume that an ethnic group question was a welcome advance. In fact the tests for an 'ethnic origin question' in the census were not successful. In particular the 1979 test in Haringey was held at a time when police were allowed to pick up and pick on anyone in the street on suspicion that they might commit a crime.[33] They picked up predominantly Black youth. The media at the time gave credence to the repatriation politics of the far right. Many of the Black respondents in tests of the census objected to the question asking their origins, although it gained support from the newly established Commission for Racial Equality.

The British Society for Social Responsibility in Science, a radical science movement with some influence among researchers who debated the content of the census, had published a broadsheet arguing very strongly against the asking of the question. It said that in the atmosphere of fear about repatriation and racist policing, with little evidence of a commitment to prosecute racists, there was little purpose for the question. To help its readers empathise with the situation that Black people in Britain faced with a census question on race, it hypothesised a public debate on euthanasia at 65 and asked whether elderly people would be right to worry if there was a new census question on age.[34]

Others have argued that the collection of race data for whatever purposes reinforces the racial thinking that constitutes racial prejudice, or at the very least encourages explanations of disadvantage based on racial difference, and when resources follow ethnic patterns the competition encourages tensions between areas and social groups rather than unites them against causes of inequality. There were also concerns about the way in which race statistics were used in research. In 1972 the staff of the Institute of Race Relations had felt the urgent need to resolve 'the conflicting aims of objective, unbiased research on the one hand and policy-oriented research on the other: shifting the focus of race research from black people to white institutions, from the done-to to the do-er, from the victim to the perpetrator'.[35]

In the face of significant public and professional opposition the 1981 Census did not include a question on ethnic origin, for fear of jeopardising cooperation with the rest of the census questions.[36]

—

Nonetheless, in 1981 the social conditions of the Black and Asian population were for the first time measured in the census and presented in published tables, using information on place of birth. For the first time, census data were also readily available on computers for each small area in Britain, so the establishment of ethnicity as a regular dimension of British social demography can be dated to 1981. The question on parents' country of birth had been dropped, but a tabulation of overcrowding, housing quality and car ownership was given for residents whose head of household had been born in the New Commonwealth with Pakistan (NCWP). Very few children of immigrants were yet old enough to have left home to head their own household, so the category 'Head of household born in NCWP' fitted the minority population very well in the same way as parental country of birth had done in 1971, as discussed earlier in this chapter.

The 1981 Census showed clearly that the minority groups on average had considerably worse social and housing conditions than the population as a whole. At that time 'NCWP' was still presented as one group, and separately from statistics of the whole population. Statistics of specific origins were not presented in published tables. Since the 1980s, however, with the dawning of multicultural policies, there has been interest in the separate experiences of different ethnic groups. In 1991 and 2001 the censuses collected ethnic group information directly, allowing the study of many immigrant–origin groups.

Britain's ethnic group census question

Even after three decades of research and experience of wording a question, and after sociological and governmental studies into ethnicity and race over 40 years, debate persists in Britain about how best to measure ethnicity. The 1991 and 2001 Censuses both used a direct question on ethnic group, and the 2011 Census plans to continue this tradition, unique within Europe. The question has developed through the three censuses but has not fundamentally changed. This section focuses on the 2001 Census whose ethnic group question is reproduced in Figure 2.1.[37]

This is by far the longest of the 35 questions in the 2001 Census for each individual. It asks 'What is your ethnic group?' and requests that respondents select the category that best indicates their 'cultural background'. The available categories are hierarchically structured, with a first level marked by five bold headings that equate to colour or race: 'White', 'Mixed', 'Asian or Asian British', 'Black or Black British', and 'Chinese or other ethnic group'. Under each of these five

34

Figure 2.1: 2001 Census question used in England and Wales

8   What is your ethnic group?

♦   Choose ONE section from A to E, then
    ✔ the appropriate box to indicate
    your cultural background.

A   White

☐ British   ☐ Irish

☐ Any other White background,
  please write in

B   Mixed

☐ White and Black Caribbean

☐ White and Black African

☐ White and Asian

☐ Any other Mixed background,
  please write in

C   Asian or Asian British

☐ Indian   ☐ Pakistani

☐ Bangladeshi

☐ Any other Asian background,
  please write in

D   Black or Black British

☐ Caribbean   ☐ African

☐ Any other Black background,
  please write in

E   Chinese or other ethnic group

☐ Chinese

☐ Any other, *please write in*

headings are subcategories, which indicate a country or region of origin – British, Irish, Indian, Pakistani, Bangladeshi, Caribbean, African and Chinese – and opportunity to write in an answer should these labelled categories not be appropriate. Although ethnic group is self-identified in that the form is self-completed, choices are restricted by the categories presented.

The question 'worked' in the sense of achieving response rates of over 97%, higher than questions on health, qualifications and employment.[38] There was no public campaign against the question prior to its use in 2001, except in Wales where 'Welsh' became a popular write-in answer. This technical success can be seen as the main result of consultation prior to the census. However, the mixed purposes and policies that motivate the question are evident in several ambiguities within it.

The focus on detailed differences among categories other than White emphasises a distinction between indigenous and foreign populations from the politics of immigration and social cohesion. 'Cultural background' is indicated by the question wording, but the categories offered are countries or regions of family origin. Peter Aspinall points out that '[t]he option for the Irish-descended population in which "Irish" is set against "British" will not enable the full size of the "Irish" cultural background group to be captured'. He expects that those with Northern Ireland Protestant backgrounds may especially choose British over Irish. This is an example of a mixture of geographical, national and cultural origins within a single 'ethnic group' category, which social research cannot currently disentangle.[39] For other writers, family origin would capture a more constant, less socially constructed demographic variable than cultural background.[40] But 'origin' is also a difficult concept to measure for anyone whose known origins cannot be traced to a single country, and that includes most people who care to think about it. The use of colour within the question leads to ambiguous interpretation by researchers. For example, the British Household Panel Survey uses 'RACE' as its name for ethnic group categories from the census.[41]

The way that nationality is used in the question has also come under scrutiny.[42] 'British' is used as part of the Asian and Black main headings, but a final category of 'British' is only allowed under the main heading 'White'. On purely technical grounds, this is a mistake, confirmed by enumerators reporting that some Asian respondents had ticked 'British', having seen it as the first box and wishing to confirm their British identity and nationality.[43] In response to the demand in Wales for a 'Welsh' category, government and the Equality and Human Rights Commission now recommend use of the 2001 Census question expanded to include 'Welsh', 'Scottish' and 'English' in addition to 'British' and 'Irish', but again only under the 'White' heading. The 2011 Census is likely to include these options in a separate question about 'national identity'.

The use of 'mixed' categories, new for the 2001 Census, was justified from the multicultural camp as reflecting new cultural identities. It has a seriously negative impact on the effectiveness of employment discrimination statistics, by reducing the number in the discriminated population (for example 'Black') without demanding that the employing organisations re-survey their workforce to exclude 'Mixed' from the 'Black' employees and applicants.[44] Mixed unions have importance as a positive sign of the most intimate form of integration, but are also a threat to the standard categories of identity used to address discrimination.[45] It can also be argued that the four choices offered for 'Mixed' do not reflect the multiple sources that define people's mixed identity.

The upcoming census in 2011 will be the third to include ethnicity. New questions on year of arrival in Britain for those born overseas, languages spoken, passports held, and national identity have also been tested, reflecting the current political focus on immigration. The set of categories for ethnic group in 2011 will be different from 1991 and 2001, driven by politics, pragmatism and coherence. Once included, any category is hard to remove if it has been embraced by a significantly large population, and so the number of categories has increased from 10 in 1991, to 16 in 2001, and three more have been tested for 2011: Arab and Gypsy/Romany/Irish Traveller are additions throughout the UK, while English, Welsh, Irish and Scottish are added respectively in those four countries. Chinese has been shifted to join Indian, Pakistani and Bangladeshi under the heading Asian for the first time, and Black or Black British has been pushed further towards the end of the question at each asking.

These changes are partly an attempt to better represent the diversity of the UK, but change makes it more difficult for statisticians to compare data from different censuses. The question of reliability is important when comparing data from different censuses, and when interpreting data from any one census. Comparison of census answers for those present in both 1991 and 2001 shows that inconsistent answers were not unusual, especially for minority group residents born in the UK who are increasing in number. Among those born in the UK and recorded as Pakistani or Bangladeshi in 1991, more than 5% were recorded as something different in 2001. More than 10% of UK-born Indians in 1991, and more than 20% of UK-born Africans and Caribbeans in 1991, were recorded as something different in 2001.[46]

The census leads official statistical categorisation by providing baseline population figures for other studies. One can sympathise with the impossibility of its satisfying the conceptual approach of such a variety of motivations that demand the statistics. But in other studies there is an opportunity to plan the instruments of data collection to suit particular purposes. Professional advice suggests that ethnicity as such is not measurable as a single variable. Most writers recommend that the means of measurement should be related to the purpose of the research. The *British Medical Journal* adds:

> If it is unknown which of ethnicity, race or culture is the most important influence then an attempt should be made to measure all of them. A range of information is best collected: genetic differences, self assigned ethnicity, observer assigned ethnicity, country or area of birth, years in country of residence, religion.[47]

Without doubt, ethnicity is difficult to conceptualise and to measure. Adding a religion question to the census since 2001 has compounded the conceptual and motivational confusion. Things were certainly easier before ethnicity came along. Sivanandan, writing in 1983, suggested that ethnicity was a backward move both conceptually and in the struggle for equality: 'Ethnicity was a tool to blunt the edge of black struggle, return "black" to its constituent parts and at the same time, allow the nascent black bourgeoisie, petit-bourgeoisie really, to move up in the system'.[48]

—

To add to the conceptual difficulties, planning must involve prediction (as plans are about the future), and therefore some constancy of categories over time. But this is not possible with measurement of ethnic affiliation. We each have many cultural affiliations, which we express differently in different contexts. We change our affiliation over time too, in response to the changing environment in which our declarations of difference take place, and in response to our own development and understanding. What we are willing to declare as our identity within official enquiries depends not only on what is acceptable to ourselves but what we understand is socially acceptable and to our advantage. That will differ according to what we feel the enquiry will be used for. Changes in affiliation are also observed according to the political context and who fills in the form.[49]

Although definition and measurement of ethnicity in Britain is contested, ethnic group data from the census and other sources provide a rich resource for understanding the nature of social differences between ethnic groups. Exploring the meaning of ethnic group in terms of how it is measured can be as revealing as results about different ethnic groups. Most social data are politically sensitive in some way and data about ethnicity are a prime example. This should not prevent their use, but users should be aware that what they have is a contested representation of society.

France's experience

The politics of race statistics in France are in stark contrast to those in Britain. Whereas in Britain the collection of data on ethnicity is now commonplace and disputes are mostly about the specific categories that should be used, in France there are few such data and their collection is felt by many to be a betrayal of the secular values of French republicanism. The view is that to make a person's ethnic affiliation a matter of government enquiry is to interfere in private concerns, and is itself suggestive of discrimination on grounds of race or religion. Thus, the anti-racist activists in *SOS Racisme*, whose slogan 'Don't touch my pal' (*Touche pas à mon pote*) has been so effective in uniting sentiment against extreme racism in France, published a petition headed 'Don't label my pal' (*Fiche pas mon pote*) signed by over 100,000 people in November 2007. The petition said:

> I refuse to answer anyone who asks my colour of skin, my origin or my religion. I refuse to answer the same questions about my spouse, my children, or my parents. I

refuse to accept that my identity is reduced to the criteria of another time, that of colonial France, or Vichy. I refuse to accept the idea that the fight against discrimination and the effort for integration require the creation of ethno-racial categories. To claim this is intellectual and political manipulation. I refuse to accept that the focus and investigation be on the victims rather than on the authors of discrimination. Knowledge of the reality of discrimination is necessary and must be gained by other means, such as testing. I want discriminatory practice to be properly identified and diagnosed to sanction it more severely. I refuse to accept an alleged scientific guarantee that consolidates racist stereotypes which unfortunately continue to be used within French society. I refuse to accept the State's rehabilitation of an ethnic, racial or religious framework to draw up 'ethnic statistics'. I refuse to modify the fundamentals of our Republic, and demand that the Constitutional Council do not pass article 63 of the law on immigration.[50]

The main target was not immigration law but a 'survey of trajectories and origins' planned by France's statistical agency INSEE and national demographic research institute INED. INED staff were divided in their approach to collection of ethnicity data, with several of its researchers signing the *SOS Racisme* petition and writing in *Le Monde* to protest the 'return to racial eugenics', which they associated with asking questions related to colour and family origins.[51]

The organisers of the survey aimed to analyse the impact of ethnic and racial origins on access to resources including public services, education, employment and housing. The survey would ask cultural, social and geographical origins in an attempt to assess their impact on helping or limiting access to resources. Colour of skin, religion and country of origin would be asked in order to understand the place of ethnicity in personal identity and in social and work trajectories. The survey organisers continued:

Testing has its use to reveal open discriminatory practices. It does not allow construction and comparison of social and work trajectories, to get to the root of inequalities and to measure their possibly unintended consequences. In fact in choosing to present candidates as 'blacks' or 'arabs' or 'maghrébins' or 'French whites', testing uses categories that are themselves a construction of discrimination. One does not escape categorisation so easily![52]

The collection of ethnic statistics became a political issue in the 2006 French presidential campaign when the conservative winner Sarkozy favoured ethnic statistics while the socialist Royal did not. But both camps in the struggle over a French extension of statistics into an ethnicity dimension include serious anti-racists. One can perhaps identify those against ethnicity statistics as those who see no role for the state in race relations beyond penalising discrimination. They also feel that the use of ethnic labels reinforces racialist choices more than it could undermine them through a better intellectual understanding of society's inequalities. In 2008, the French survey of trajectories and origins went ahead, without the direct question involving labels of colour.

The US's experience

About half of all countries ask a question or questions related to ethnicity.[53] The US's census question on race has its origins in slavery, asking White, Black or Mulatto in 1850, but now with 15 categories including American Indian or Alaska Native, Black or African American, Native Hawaiian, Filipino, Japanese and White. Respondents can choose more than one category to indicate mixed racial affiliation. An additional question distinguishes Hispanic and Latino ethnic origins from others. The particular details of debate over the categories is specific to the US but its motivation is a familiar mix of political desire to be counted (on the part of minorities whose status and access to resources are enhanced by government recognition), practical limitations on data collection (too many questions, too complicated questions or widely unacceptable questions are rejected) and academic concern, for example about the incoherence of categories that mix concepts of physical appearance and country of family origin.[54] Population projections with a racial dimension are made by the US government, but their value is unclear since racial categories will change over the period projected. Plans made to respond to projected population diversity cannot have much rationale if even the categories that will be salient in the future cannot be predicted.[55]

Conclusion

Statistics of ethnicity are not as straightforward as they appear. In Britain and elsewhere, race statistics have developed (or not) in response to changing political and policy arenas. In Britain, their development has been particularly influenced by eugenicist thinking, immigration control, anti-discrimination legislation, multicultural policies and community cohesion agendas. As a result of these multiple and shifting demands there are many ambiguities in the leading instruments of government measurement of ethnicity, particularly the meaning of each ethnic group category. One can question whether the monitoring of ethnic differences and inequalities that has been facilitated by race statistics, has had any impact on reducing inequalities or improving integration.

Despite the criticisms of measurement of ethnic groups in Britain, the data provide a rich resource for studying social conditions and social change. The caveats placed on these data are not unique; all social data come with contentions and questions. With appropriate and careful use, ethnic group statistics can reveal a great deal about the state of society. It is our aim to use ethnic group data transparently and carefully so as to recognise their limitations. For example, nowhere do we combine data from sources where ethnic group measurement has different meanings; and we focus on strong patterns and trends – such as the growth of minority populations and counterurbanisation – that can be identified whichever combination of ethnic group categories is analysed.

This chapter has aimed to place the figures used in this book – by the myth-makers and in the counterarguments – in context, to raise questions about the purpose of the statistics and their meaning. In this book we take the statistics as we must with their inherent strengths and weaknesses. We use them as robustly as we can and focus on pulling from them pictures of Britain in the 21st century.

Notes

[1] In Institute of Race Relations, Newsletter, March 1966, p 11, quoted in Leech (1989).

[2] From the prefaces of Galton's (1869, 1892) *Hereditary Genius*.

[3] The link between statistical development and eugenics is explored, for example, by MacKenzie (1999) and Zuberi (2001). Eugenic concerns focused on the supposed genetic impact of mixing between classes and races, and of the lower birth rates of the favoured classes.

[4] Fisher (1917, p 206).

[5] Whelpton (1938, p 183).

[6] See MacKenzie (1999) and Zuberi (2001) from whom the quotes have been taken.

[7] Gould (1996) provides a clear and detailed account of the attempts to measure intelligence as innate and genetic qualities. Herrnstein and Murray (1994) are among the new eugenicists, reviewed, for example, by Zuberi (2001).

[8] Sivanandan (1990, p 11).

[9] For example, *Times Higher Education*, 2 March 2007, or Teresa Hayter in *The Guardian*, 16 March 2007.

[10] Pakistan was not a member of the Commonwealth between 1972 and 1989.

[11] Peach and Winchester (1974).

[12] Browne (2000).

[13] The Equality and Human Rights Commission has been the single government agency supporting its anti-discrimination legislation since 2007, when it replaced separate agencies on race, gender and disability, including the Commission for Racial Equality.

[14] Joshua et al (1983).

[15] Athwal (2001).

[16] Cabinet Office (2000, p 7).

[17] *Bradford Telegraph & Argus*, 22 April 2008; ethnic composition of population from the Office for National Statistics, for 2005, www.statistics.gov.uk/StatBase/Product.asp?vlnk=14238

[18] Black and Asian members of the public put discriminatory behaviour by the police ahead of any other service, according to the opinion survey reported by the Home Office (2001).

[19] Leslie et al (2001); Twomey (2001); Blackaby et al (2002); Heath and Li (2007).

[20] In other contexts, the standardisation or explanation of differences between groups is justified and necessary when it involves variables that

are not social or cannot be the result of discrimination, as age is in some cases. Thus, people in Black and Asian categories have low crude illness rates when expressed as the number of people ill as a proportion of the group's population; but this is mainly due to their young age structures, where few people have reached the ages where illness is much more common. Age-standardised ratios show relatively high illness among Black and Asian groups, and low take-up of caring services among Asian groups who are much more likely to care for their elderly and sick within the community and without state support.

[21] Jobseekers for hospital jobs were twice as likely to get an interview without an Asian-sounding name as with one, when using the same CV (Esmail and Everington, 1993). Hubbuck and Carter (1980), Brown and Gay (1985) and the Commission for Racial Equality (CRE, 1996) found similar results from testing. Early British tests influenced the content of the 1976 Race Relations Act (Daniel, 1968), and have been repeated in Continental European countries with similar results.

[22] Wyly and Holloway (2002).

[23] Booth (1988, p 262).

[24] Heath and Li (2007).

[25] Leslie et al (2001).

[26] In a speech to the National Committee for Commonwealth Immigrants in June 1966, included in Jenkins (1967, p 267).

[27] For example, Boag (2001) and Southworth (2001).

[28] Malik (2007).

[29] The major reports were those of Cantle (2001) and Denham (2001). Kundnani (2002) gave an immediate critical analysis, while various authors discuss the practical implementation of local community cohesion policies in Flint and Robinson (2008).

[30] Phillips, D. (2006) traces the growth of social cohesion's focus on segregation. Kalra and Kapoor (2008) review the adoption of cultural indicators of integration to replace material disadvantage, and associate this shift with the academic adoption of social capital theories.

[31] Amin (2005) shows the emphasis on community responsibility.

[32] HM Government (1978, para 24).

[33] Then known as the 'sus laws' and restricted from the 1980s. Similar police powers of 'stop and search' have been reintroduced in the 2000s.

[34] BSSRS (1981).

[35] Bourne (2001, p 9).

[36] Leech (1989) provides a full account of the course of proposals in the 1970s and 1980s for a question on ethnic group in the national census of Britain.

[37] For analysis of ethnicity in the 1991 Census, four volumes published by the UK statistics agencies are invaluable, including Coleman and Salt (1996).

[38] www.statistics.gov.uk/census2001/pdfs/editimputevr.pdf

[39] Aspinall (2000, p 114).

[40] For example, Berthoud (1998).

[41] The British Household Panel Survey (BHPS) began in 1991 and every year surveys the same representative sample of individuals in households across Britain, allowing analysis of change over time on a range of social issues. From 2009 the BSPS will be incorporated into the UK Household Longitudinal Study with a substantial sample of minority ethnic groups.

[42] CRE (2002). The Office for National Statistics now recommends that surveys include a further question of 'National group' to elicit one response from 'English/Scottish/Welsh/Irish/British/Other/Not stated' and that further work on ethnic group 'calls for an approach that transcends statistics and embraces sociological and political considerations as well' (www.statistics.gov.uk/nsbase/themes/compendia_reference/ articles/ns_ethnic_classification.asp, 2002). The Department for Children, Schools and Families' annual schools census has already taken a different line, including 'Cornish, English, Scottish and Welsh' as subcategories of White British (www.teachernet.gov.uk/management/ ims/datacollections/sc2008/).

[43] Experiences of taking the census in 2001 are surveyed in Simpson and Brown (2008).

[44] In the US, those who tick 'Multi-racial' on the census to declare their identity know which box to tick for affirmative action employers, but may not realise that the first decision may restrict the effectiveness of the latter (Wright, 1994).

[45] Rocheron (1997) takes apart a preoccupation with mixed unions within French demography. In the British government-sponsored feasibility study for population projections with an ethnic group dimension, three chapters focus on the mixed group as requiring major technical innovation (Haskey, 2002).

[46] Simpson and Akinwale (2007, p 203).

[47] BMJ (1996). Very similar advice is given by Modood (1992), Berthoud (1998) and Aspinall (2001).

[48] Sivanandan (1983, p 4).

[49] Wallman (1986); Simpson (1997).

[50] www.fichepasmonpote.com/index.php [authors' translation].

[51] Blum et al (2007).

[52] Manifesto against the petition, personal communication from Patrick Simon [authors' translation].

[53] Morning (2008).

[54] Prewitt (2005).

[55] Ellis (2001).

3

Challenging the myth that 'Britain takes too many immigrants'

Immigration is now on an unprecedented scale ... immigration will result in an increase in the population of the UK of 6 million in the 27 years from 2004 ... the pressure on our borders continues. *MigrationWatch UK*[1]

Introduction

For MigrationWatchUK, immigration is the source of Britain's major problems. Their views are shared by others and their spokesperson consulted whenever immigration is in the news. The solution they campaign for is an annual limit so that immigration is no more than emigration. But is it really that straightforward? In a globalised world where travel is commonplace, shouldn't we expect more migration and less rigid borders? Does Britain really take more immigrants than other countries? Is population growth because of immigration actually a problem? Is immigration in fact economically costly?

The sense that immigration and immigrants are a major problem permeates British culture and government thinking. The increase in immigration and the projected population increase reported in the quote above are not in dispute. Although we do take issue below with the accuracy of figures used in the debate, we also wish to investigate the claims that immigration poses a burden. The claims are that immigration must be limited because it is causing population growth and because it is changing the composition of the population to be more ethnically diverse. Both these impacts are seen by the pessimists to have detrimental impacts on the existing population (it is not usual to hear arguments, for example, that immigration is a bad thing because it is making our population more educated, which is indeed the case[2]). The next chapter deals with the claims that increased cultural diversity is problematic. Here we address concerns about immigration causing population growth by asking whether Britain takes more than its fair share of immigrants and whether these immigrants are economically costly. The chapter ends with a study of claims made specifically by MigrationWatchUK.

The origins of the myth

Concern about overpopulation is longstanding and has not always been linked to immigration. It seems logical enough to be concerned that an increased population puts demands on a nation's resources. This contention has been central to population debates for a long time. Underpopulation has also been a constant concern – from the threat that declining fertility posed for recruitment into 20th century armies, to the current alarm that a declining workforce will be insufficient to support the elderly population.

The English political economist Thomas Malthus proposed the Principle of Population in 1798.[3] In his theory, population growth was set against the resources of the earth and Malthus predicted that the exponential growth in population would soon outstrip the arithmetic growth of resources (food). The result would be population decline through excess deaths over births until the population was within the carrying capacity of the resources. Although it is generally regarded that production of resources has kept pace with population growth and averted catastrophe – that necessity and demand have fuelled production and inventiveness – Malthus's ideas have been extremely influential for thinking about societal evolution.

Today, debates about sustainability include concern that the population is already too large. These debates began in the mid-20th century when a humanist shift in thinking on economic organisation, and the energy crisis of the early 1970s, ushered in the beginnings of the modern environmental movement.[4] Now, the question is not only about whether production can meet the needs of the population, but also whether the means of production are themselves reducing the carrying capacity of the earth.

Both the modern debates and the historical ones rely on quantification of production and consumption, costs and benefits, people and resources. Throughout the decades the problem of immigration, and of sustainability more generally, has been understood through numbers. For migration arguments, quantitative evidence has been particularly important because, until recent years, studies have predominantly been economic-oriented, measuring people and their impacts in terms of costs and benefits.

However, the numbers-based arguments are usually infused with moral and political assumptions. In particular, the 'problem' of population has historically been used to suggest that there are too many people of particular races and classes. Class politics was inherent to Malthus's theories in the 18th century: his proposals for restrictions to population growth were only to be applied to the working and poor classes; it was they who were responsible for social ills. Arguments against immigration today usually choose to highlight flows from poor countries or of poor people as a greater burden than immigration of Western professionals.

Since they were first introduced, British immigration laws applied only to particular, undesirable migrants. The first immigration Act, the 1905 Aliens Order, restricted entry of Jewish migrants from Eastern Europe and 'coloured' seamen from all around the world. Subsequent legislation was similarly racialised, responding to fears of racial violence, as experienced in Cardiff, Glasgow, Liverpool, London and South Shields in 1919. The migrants themselves were assumed to be to blame for the disturbances.

After the Second World War non-White immigration and settlement reached unprecedented levels in response to Britain's need for labour during an economic boom. Colonial administrations that had facilitated the recruitment of colonised citizens into the fight against fascism now recruited labour. It was at this time that the immigration numbers game and political manoeuvring to increase restrictions on immigration really began. Concerns about the impact of immigration were evident at the highest levels of government: immigrants represented a threat to 'the racial character of the English people'.[5] Only four years after the *Empire Windrush* transported the first recruits from the Caribbean to the UK, by 1952 Labour and Conservative governments had

> instituted a number of covert, and sometimes illegal, administrative measures designed to discourage Black immigration ... [these actions] amounted to the construction of an ideological framework in which Black people were seen to be threatening, alien and unassimilable and to the development of policies to discourage and control Black immigration.[6]

Through the middle decades of the 20th century, race and immigration policies continued to be entwined, and the argument that there were 'too many' immigrants was repeated time and again. It was clear that the key issue was 'not numbers of immigrants, but numbers of "coloured" immigrants'.[7] Restrictions were placed on movement from the Commonwealth and elsewhere via legislation in 1962, 1965, 1967, 1968, 1971, 1981, 1987 and 1988. Successive governments resolved to limit the number of 'coloured' people to a level that was assimilable, although the precise level was never specified. The abstract notion of assimilability was understood as a level of immigration that would not result in changes to Britishness; that would not lead to clusters of Black people which would enable them to make demands; that prevented racial conflict; and, in Cold War years, that restricted communist influence.[8]

The scene is thus set for anti-immigration movements of the 21st century and the cementing of assumptions that there is too much (of certain types of) immigration and that a fair share or ideal level of immigration can be specified. The claims are evident in political arguments, in the media and in public opinion. Extreme positions are taken by the right-wing political party the British National Party (BNP) and the campaigning organisation MigrationWatchUK. The BNP stance on immigration is quite clear: there is too much and all further immigration must be halted. For the BNP, immigration is a problem because 'we, the native British people, will be an ethnic minority in our own country within sixty years' (see Chapter Seven for an examination of this forecast). The BNP claims that immigration has resulted in 'reverse discrimination' towards 'indigenous people'.[9]

Anti-immigration sentiment has been pervasive in the British media. A large body of research has considered media coverage, particularly press coverage, of immigration with the overwhelmingly consistent finding (not only in Britain but also in Europe and North America) that immigration and race are given negative coverage with immigrants and ethnic minorities presented in stereotyped ways as a problem or threat.[10] An analysis of the content of the British press in the mid-1990s found that immigration and asylum politics were a strong thematic focus for all newspapers, making up 37% of news coverage in *The Guardian*, 46% in *The Times* and 55% in the *Daily Mail*.[11] A review of media coverage at the start of the 21st century concluded that immigrants and asylum seekers received the same type of stigmatising coverage which Black and Asian minorities received 15 years earlier.[12] The types of headlines characterising this coverage are illustrated in Box 3.1.

The press coverage in some newspapers was considered so biased by The Federation of Poles in Great Britain that it made a formal submission to the Press Complaints Commission in 2008 about persistent emotive anti-Polish language in the *Daily Mail*. The Federation demonstrated that newspapers choose how to report migrants, noting that 'when on July 17th 2007 the *Daily Mail* headline screams "Influx of Immigrants costs Every UK Household £350 a Year", the equivalent article in *The Independent*, based on the same government report, is headed "Home Office: Migrants Work Harder, Earn More and Pay More Taxes than Britons"'. The *Daily Mail* defended itself by claiming balanced coverage and that 'The Mail is entitled to run stories about immigration, the more so as the last 10 years have witnessed immigration on a [greater] scale [and] at a vastly increased rate than at any time in this country's history since and including the Norman invasion of the 11th century'.[13] This 2008 complaint followed similar concerns expressed in 2003 about inaccurate and unbalanced press coverage of refugee and asylum issues.[14] The complaint, put forward by a number of organisations

Box 3.1: Front-page headlines claiming too much immigration

'Lunatic Asylum, 3,200 new illegal immigrants set up home in Great Britain every month' (*The Sun*, 14 February 2001)

'Stop the Asylum Invasion' (*Daily Express*, 22 August 2001)

'2m migrants for Britain in next decade' (*Daily Telegraph*, 5 August 2002)

'Immigration chaos engulfs Labour' (*The Times*, 2 April 2004)

'500,000 illegal immigrants says Home Office' (*The Sunday Times*, 17 April 2005)

'Asylum chaos and 250,000 people avoid deportation' (*The Times*, 19 July 2005)

'Crackdown sought on hiring illegal immigrants' (*Financial Times*, 14 June 2006)

'Permit scheme to cut flow of East Europeans' (*The Guardian*, 25 August 2006)

'Reed faces crisis over new immigrant flood from Sangatte' (*The Sunday Times*, 8 April 2007)

'Polish immigrants take £1bn out of the UK economy' (*Daily Mail*, 27 June 2007)

'Migration "far higher than stated"' (*The Sunday Times*, 2 September 2007)

'Europe to open borders to 20m Asian and African workers' (*Financial Times*, 13 September 2007)

'Fears for NHS and schools as 1000 children are born a month: the Polish baby boom' (*Daily Mail*, 25 November 2007)

including the Information Centre on Asylum and Refugees and MediaWise, was upheld by the Press Complaints Commission, which issued guidelines to the newspaper industry that included the instruction not to use 'misleading or distorted terminology' in coverage of asylum issues.

Thus, it is the scale of immigration and claimed problematic consequences that have characterised media discourses. This is evident in the language used: metaphors of swamping, flooding and waves, and terminologies of natural disasters or military invasions characterise news coverage. The media frequently use binary categories such as bogus/genuine and legal/illegal to identify immigrants as negative and opposite to 'native' British residents. Such criminalising descriptions reinforce the claim that immigration is a problem, and legitimise repressive state responses.[15]

Indeed, the policies of British governments since the beginning of the 1990s are framed by the belief that there is too much immigration, of the wrong types. They are restrictive, particularly to asylum seekers, and favour trained workers for specific industries. Seven Acts relating to immigration have been passed since 1990 (in 1993, 1996, 1999, 2002, 2004, 2006 and 2008). Several of these Acts are titled 'Immigration and Asylum', indicating the rise in political significance of immigration for refuge – and the desire to place restrictions on this movement.[16] The Criminal Justice and Immigration Act 2008 provides special immigration status for terrorists and serious criminals who cannot be removed from the UK.

From early 2008 a points-based 'managed migration' scheme has been in place in the UK. Points are partly allocated according to the demands of the UK economy, and community relations are monitored to inform levels and types of immigration that are acceptable. Refugees are now accepted primarily through United Nations (UN) quota systems according to what the UK feels it can accommodate, and within the country the dispersal policy aims to 'spread the burden' of asylum seekers.[17] Despite these moves towards more transparent, demand-led systems, the Joint Council for the Welfare of Immigrants argues that 'it would be precipitate to argue that race is out of the picture on immigration, either at the level of policy formation or public debate'.[18] Despite the clear rules, a 'culture of disbelief' leads to 'perverse and unjust decisions' in an under-resourced system according to the Independent Asylum Commission reporting in 2008.[19]

Given this historical, political and media context, it is not surprising that the claims of too much immigration, that certain types of immigration are the problem, and that there is some identifiable ideal level of immigration, pervade public opinion. Since 1989, MORI polls have found that over 60% of respondents agreed that there are too many immigrants in Britain with the highest proportion – 68% – agreeing in 2007.[20] In 2006, 64% of respondents felt that immigration laws should be tougher and an additional 12% felt that immigration should be stopped altogether. However, almost two thirds were unable to say what a suitable limit on immigration would be. International comparisons indicate that immigration is a greater concern for the

British public than for populations of other countries. When asked which of 11 topics they found most worrying in their country, 44% of people in the UK answered 'immigration control' compared with 42% in Spain, 23% in the US, 18% in Italy, 11% in Germany and 24% on average for respondents to the survey.[21] Similarly, 81% in the UK agreed that many more people come to live in this country compared to other European countries of about the same size, whereas 70% of people in Germany, 62% in the Netherlands, 56% in Spain, 47% in Ireland and 15% in Finland felt this.[22]

It is clear that historically, and in political, media and public discourses over the last decade, immigration has been established as a problem. The claim that there is too much immigration and that an acceptable level can and must be enforced frames thinking about international migration. Statistics have been central to these immigration debates and claims. In the section that follows the quantitative evidence is reviewed. First we look at what immigration statistics tell us about patterns and trends in the scale of immigration to the UK. The UK experience is compared to that of other countries. Finally, evidence about the economic impact of immigration is reviewed.

How is immigration changing in Britain and worldwide?

The claims about the scale of immigration to Britain are based on the number of immigrants. But how is the number of immigrants measured? The debates about what constitutes immigration and how best it can be measured, which rage in the Office for National Statistics[23] and among those researchers whose ideas depend on these measures, rarely spill into mainstream discussions about the scale of immigration. As we have seen, headlines and anti-immigration arguments are littered with claims about how many immigrants there are. It is partly because of the difficulty of measuring migration that myths around immigration can grow and be sustained. The first point to make in reviewing these claims, therefore, is that none of the statistics can be taken at face value.[24]

Concepts and definitions of migrants and migration vary widely in measures of migration and this has implications for the results that the different measures produce. There is no legal definition of 'immigrant' in the UK and different measures and debates understand the concept in slightly different ways. In particular, the distinction between a short-term visitor and an immigrant is not easy to make unambiguously. The definition used officially in government migration statistics comes from the UN: 'A migrant into the UK is a person who has resided abroad for a year or more who states on arrival the intention to stay in the UK for a year or more, and vice versa for a migrant from the UK'.[25]

There are many sources of data on international migration, based on household surveys, passenger surveys, the decennial census and administrative data. However, they each paint incomplete pictures and the degree to which they can be used in conjunction is very limited.[26] They serve different purposes and measure different aspects of migration. As a result, they provide quite different estimates of immigration. For example, estimates of the flow of immigrants to the UK in 2001 ranged from 342,000 to 402,000 when reported from the International Passenger Survey, while 407,000 immigrants were counted in the year before the 2001 Census and the government's final estimate of immigration in 2001 was 480,000.[27] It is therefore essential when discussing the scale and impacts of international migration to be precise about what and who is being measured and how, and to approach immigration statistics with caution.

Given this large caveat about the difficulties of measuring migration, the best available evidence does provide an overview of the patterns and trends in international migration for the UK. Proponents of anti-immigration arguments are not wrong that immigration has increased: absolutely and in relation to population size immigration to the UK has increased in the past half-century and particularly since the mid-1990s. The same trend is evident for emigration and for the net impact of migration (immigration minus emigration). In 2005, 380,000 people emigrated from and 565,000 people immigrated to the UK. There is a pattern of net outflow made up mainly of British citizens and net inflow made up mainly of non-British citizens. Large foreign-citizenship immigrant groups are currently from Western and Eastern Europe, Africa, Australasia and the Indian subcontinent, demonstrating the diversity of immigration.[28] However, increased international population movement is not unique to the UK: the UN Population Division's latest review found that the UK experience mirrors that of international migrants worldwide. Those living in a country different from where they were born increased worldwide from 75 million in 1960 to 191 million in 2005.[29] Twenty-seven million of this increase was due to the creation of new countries after the fall of the Soviet Union and Yugoslavia. Nonetheless, the number of international migrants worldwide more than doubled between 1960 and 2005, an increase from 75 million to 164 million, or of 119%.

In the same period – that of major immigration to the UK – the number of UK residents born abroad increased from 2.57 million to 4.89 million in the censuses of 1961 and 2001, and further to 5.41 million in 2005. This is also a doubling, an increase of 110%, very similar to the worldwide increase of migrants.[30]

The nature of international migration has changed considerably over this period. Recently a number of new migration patterns have been identified that are partly a result of policy changes. In particular, accession to the European Union (EU) by a number of countries in 2004 and 2006 was accompanied by increased migration to Britain of migrants from these countries. In addition, the Sectors Based Scheme for migration and the Seasonal Agricultural Workers Scheme have actively recruited immigrants to particular labour market shortages including hospitality and food processing. As a result, short-term movement is gaining significance and there has been a relative increase in manual and clerical workers. The rate of increase in short-term immigration – here defined as one to two years – has been greater than the rate of increase in long-term immigration.[31]

In recent years, asylum seekers, refugees, migrants from Eastern Europe and undocumented (or, more commonly, 'illegal') immigrants have come to represent what is negative about immigration and have come to be what is meant when 'immigration' and the 'problem of immigration' are talked about. In much the same way as 'the problem of immigration' in the late 1950 and 1960s in the UK was more precisely a problem of 'coloured' immigration,[32] immigration is once again perceived as a problem on the basis of prejudices about certain groups of people. Just as the scale and pace of immigration overall has been exaggerated, the groups of 'problem' migrants have reached a status in immigration debates that belies their significance in terms of numbers.

In fact, the 'problem' migrants make up a small proportion of total immigration. Asylum applications as a percentage of non–British immigration have dropped from a decade high of 27% in 1999 to 6.5% in 2005.[33] The numbers of migrants from EU accession countries are larger. In 2005, 204,970 applications were made for workers registration by people from EU A8 accession countries (those that joined the EU in May 2004, including Poland). This can be compared with the total immigration figure for 2005 of 565,000. The number of applicants was slightly higher in 2007, at 210,575.[34] However, 60% of A8 migrants intended to stay for less than three months and only 12% stated an intention to remain in Britain for one year or more, thereby qualifying them as immigrants under the official definition.

—

Undocumented immigration perpetuates the myth of too much immigration most easily because there is an added deviance of illegality associated with these migrants. Less is known about this type of migration than others because of the inherent difficulties in measuring undocumented movements.[35] The volume of undocumented migration is usually estimated from documenting procedures, primarily amnesties, which have been used as management strategies in the US, Spain and elsewhere but not in the UK. In the UK, the best available estimate of the total unauthorised migrant population is 430,000, based on a comparison of those born overseas as recorded in the 2001 census with records of those given the legal right to stay in the UK.[36]

Despite increased immigration, immigrants make up a small fraction of the UK population, whether looked at in terms of nationality, birthplace or ethnic group, which are all ways that immigrants are directly and indirectly measured. Although people of ethnic groups other than White are often seen as immigrants, ethnic group is actually a poor indication of immigration. Half of all people in minority ethnic groups in the UK are born in the UK and two thirds of immigrants are White.[37] In 2006, 3.35 million UK residents were foreign nationals, or 5.7% of the population, a slight rise from 4.5% in 2002. Of these foreign residents, 43% were European, around 25% Asian, 16% African, 10% from the Americas and 3% from Oceania. In 2006 there were 5.76 million people living in the UK who were born elsewhere (or 9.8% of the population). A third were born elsewhere in Europe, just under a third in Asia, 10% in the Americas and around 3% in Oceania.[38] At the last census in 2001, 4.62 million (8.1% of the population of Britain) classed themselves as not being 'White'. If we consider immigration in the year prior to that census, less than 1% of the population are recent immigrants. Immigration is more common for some ethnic groups than others (Table 3.1). In particular, the 'Other' and 'Chinese' ethnic groups have relatively high proportions of recent immigrants but the figures are low for traditional immigrant groups from the Indian subcontinent and the Caribbean. This is an indication of changing routes of international migration.

So, UK international migration is growing in line with global trends. Immigrants, if defined as all those born outside the UK but now living there, make up about 10% of the population. How does this compare with the situation in other countries?

Table 3.1: Immigration rates by ethnic group, Britain, 2000-01

Britain	Number of British residents in the 2001 Census	Number of residents arriving in Britain in the year before the census	Immigrants in the year before the census (% of all residents)
All people	57,103,900	399,300	0.7
White: all	52,481,200	279,800	0.5
Minorities: all	4,622,700	119,500	2.6
Mixed	673,800	12,600	1.9
Indian	1,051,800	21,000	2.0
Pakistani	746,600	9,500	1.3
Bangladeshi	282,800	2,400	0.9
Chinese	243,300	14,500	6.0
Other Asian	247,500	9,400	3.8
Caribbean	565,600	4,400	0.8
African	484,800	17,500	3.6
Other Black	97,200	1,100	1.1
Other	229,300	27,100	11.8

Note: Immigrants are to Britain from outside the UK (excludes immigrants to Northern Ireland).

Source: 2001 Census, commissioned table M816g

Does Britain have more immigration than other countries?

Comparing international migration between countries is challenging given the measurement difficulties discussed above. The most comprehensive compilation of data comes from the UN. Table 3.2 uses this resource to compare the UK with selected other countries, including the top 10 in terms of the proportion of the world's international migrants resident there, for which the UK is eighth. It also shows migrants as a proportion of the total population of each country; and the annual balance of international migration in recent years as a rate per thousand of the population. The UN uses official data sources from each country (censuses, population registers and surveys) and defines immigrants as people born overseas or with overseas citizenship if birthplace information is unavailable. The countries are ordered from highest to lowest in the first column: the country's share of the world's migrants.

The significance of the United States as a home for migrants is striking: one fifth of the world's migrants live in the US, and the US has ranked top on this indicator at least since 1990. It is clear that the UK, with 2.8% of the world's migrants, is not exceptional and in fact

Table 3.2: UK immigration compared with other countries, 2000-05

Country	% of world's migrants (2005)	Migrants as % of population (2005)	Net migration rate per 1,000 population (annual average 2000-05)
US	20.2	12.9	4.0
Russia	6.4	8.4	1.6
Germany	5.3	12.3	2.7
Ukraine	3.6	14.7	−2.9
France	3.4	10.7	1.0
Saudi Arabia	3.3	25.9	2.2
Canada	3.2	18.9	6.7
UK	2.8	9.1	2.3
India	3.0	0.5	−0.3
Spain	2.5	11.1	9.7
Australia	2.2	20.3	5.1
Pakistan	1.7	2.1	−2.4
United Arab Emirates	1.7	71.4	49.6
Hong Kong	1.6	42.6	8.8
Kazakhstan	1.3	16.9	−8.0
Sweden	0.6	12.4	3.5
Sierra Leone	0.1	2.2	17.5
Gambia	0.1	15.3	4.4

Note: Migrants in the second and third columns refer to all those born outside the listed country.

Source: Compiled from UN (2006)

has a smaller proportion of the world's migrants than several other European countries. In 2005 international migrants constituted 3.0% of the world's population, so the UK is much nearer the average on this indicator than most countries.

International migrants are not evenly distributed, and their distribution has changed over the last few decades. From 1960 to 1995 there were more international migrants in developing countries (57%) than in developed countries; since 1995 there have been more international migrants in developed countries (63%). If we consider continents, Europe hosts the largest number of international migrants (64 million), followed by Asia (53 million), North America (44 million), Africa (17 million), Latin America and the Caribbean (7 million) and Oceania (5 million). As Table 3.2 shows, however, the distribution between individual countries within these continents is very uneven. In 2005 the countries hosting the largest number of international migrants were the US (38 million), the Russian

Federation (12 million), Germany (10 million), the Ukraine, France and Saudi Arabia (6 million each).

The third column of Table 3.2 shows the migrant stock as a percentage of each country's population. The continental values for migrants as a proportion of residents are 15% in Oceania and 13% in North America, 9% in Europe and 2% each in Africa, Asia, Latin America and the Caribbean. The range for individual countries is again remarkable; and the UK has a relatively low value of 9.1%, a value that equals the European average and is less than that for the following European countries: Andorra, Austria, Belarus, Croatia, Denmark, Estonia, France, Germany, Gibraltar, Iceland, Latvia, Luxembourg, Moldova, Netherlands, Spain, Sweden, Switzerland and the Ukraine.[39] The figure for the UK is also less than that for non-European countries to which it is often compared, including Australia (20.3%), Canada (18.9%), New Zealand (15.9%) and the US (12.9%); and far less than the countries that have the largest proportions of migrants including Qatar (78.3%) and Singapore (42.6%).

The final column of the Table 3.2 shows net migration. This is immigration minus emigration averaged over the five years 2000–05, expressed as a rate per thousand of the population. Again, the rate for the UK is not extraordinary. It is lower than, for example, Spain, Canada, Australia, the US, Sweden and Germany. The UK net migration rate of 2.3 per 1,000 of the population is less than that for the following European countries: Austria, Croatia, Denmark, Germany, Greece, Ireland, Italy, Luxembourg, Malta, Norway, Portugal, Spain and Sweden.

It is quite clear that the UK experience of international migration is not remarkable when set in a global context. Not only has the UK's immigration grown in line with world migration, but the UK has a smaller proportion of immigrants and lower rates of net immigration than Australia, Canada, the US and several large European countries. The UK experience is close to the average both in Europe and in the world.

Does immigration cost Britain money?

Control of immigration is often perceived to be an economic concern. Immigration debates are characterised by claims and counterclaims about the costs and benefits that immigrants bring. Anti-immigration lobbies rely on economic concerns to make their case, claiming that immigrants increase competition for jobs and thus depress wages, that immigrants are more likely to be a burden on the state and that they do not invest in Britain but send their earnings to their home countries. The counterclaims are that immigrants do jobs that need to be done, create businesses and demand, are less likely than others to be a burden on health and social services, and that more earnings are sent to Britain than leave.

A large body of work has taken a variety of approaches to measure the economic impact of immigration. Studies by the British government and by others independent of it have repeatedly found that the impact of immigration is positive and that migration has tended to promote economic growth.[40] Indeed, there

> is little evidence that native workers are harmed by migration. There is considerable support for the view that migrants create new businesses and jobs and fill labour market gaps, improving productivity and reducing inflationary pressures.... The broader fiscal impact of migration is likely to be positive, because of migrants' age distribution and higher average wages.[41]

A more neutral impact was found by a House of Lords investigation in 2008 that was largely sympathetic to arguments against immigration. It made 'the overall conclusion from existing evidence ... that immigration has very small impacts on GDP [Gross Domestic Product] per capita, whether these impacts are positive or negative. This conclusion is in line with findings of studies of the economic impacts of immigration in other countries'.[42]

An argument commonly made is that immigration depresses wages because the supply of labour is increased. There is general agreement that a drive to lower wages would pose the greatest economic threat, both to those who accept the poorer conditions and those who do not. However, research at the Centre for Research and Analysis of Migration for the Home Office and the Low Pay Commission has found that the impact of immigration on wages is less straightforward. Immigration is associated with suppressed growth of wages at the lower end of the wage scale but wages in the middle range benefit from immigration. On average, wage growth nationally is modestly encouraged by immigration.[43] There is, however, the additional concern, noted by the House of Lords investigation, with 'employers who illegally employ immigrants or who employ immigrants at wages and employment conditions that do not meet minimum standards'.[44]

An extensive review of migration in 2006 also concluded that 'the UK economy is a substantial net gainer from remittances':[45] money sent to the UK from abroad is greater than that sent by UK residents to other countries.

The economic benefit of immigration to Britain is positive partly because, since the mid–1980s, inflows of professionals and managers have exceeded outflows, and citizens of the developed world have formed a high and increasing proportion of workers entering the UK.[46] Refugees, often assumed to be a burden economically, are also disproportionately skilled. Home Office research has found that 23% of refugees have a skilled trade compared to 12% of the rest of the UK population and 22% of refugees are managers or senior officials compared to 15% of the rest of the UK population.[47]

The entrepreneurialism of immigrants is also well documented and has been noted as a feature of economic adaptation and integration for several decades throughout Europe and North America.[48] Generally, the generation of small businesses and self-employment in select niches, sometimes ethnic niches, has been a successful strategy for immigrants. Well-known examples include Koreans in Los Angeles and Chinese in New York[49] but migrants whose stories are less well known, such as Turkish in Finland, have also experienced self-employment and entrepreneurialism as a means to successful economic integration.[50]

Such entrepreneurialism may well be expected in North America, where the focus is on free-enterprise economies and welfare states are weak, yet the same has been seen in European countries with strong welfare states and traditions of state involvement in the economy. In fact, ethnic fragmentation of economies is a pattern recognised in large cities across the world. In Britain, South Asians have become established in retailing, catering and clothing sectors, and Chinese in the food sector. These businesses are supported by social networks and represent strategies to negotiate legal, economic and institutional structures in the new country. Immigrant businesses may also be able to benefit from transnational connections, for example for produce supply. Long-term success of ethnic businesses, however, depends on break-out from internal ethnic markets. This is evident in the UK: Indian and Chinese eateries have become a staple of town centres across the country.

Ethnic businesses may be partly a success because they circumvent discrimination and make good use of immigrants' own experience. But in fact ethnic businesses account for a small part of the employment of ethnic minorities in the UK, which extends well beyond these niches and the service, industrial and agricultural jobs that have directly recruited from abroad in the past 60 years.

Demographic considerations are important when reviewing the economic impact of migration. The population of Britain is ageing, which increases the population not working who are dependent on those who are working. Immigration is one way to redress this balance as immigrants tend to be young: in 2004, of 582,000 immigrants 91.4% were of working age. Whether immigration is a solution to an ageing population in the long term, when the whole world will be more aged, is as hotly debated as other economic impacts of international migration.[51]

MigrationWatchUK and the myth of too much immigration

In this chapter so far we have questioned the evidence for the claim that Britain has too much immigration on the basis that the UK's experience is unexceptional in an international context and that immigration has positive economic benefits. We want to extend our argument with an examination of the anti-immigration case made by MigrationWatchUK. MigrationWatchUK is a 'voluntary, non-political body which is concerned about the present scale of immigration into the UK'.[52] We have chosen to explore MigrationWatchUK's position because we believe that the evidence used by MigrationWatchUK is questionable, yet the organisation and its arguments have received prominence in migration debates and have assumed an authority – not least because of the profiles of its highly connected chair and advisory council – which we consider to be dangerous if there is no similar authority presenting counterarguments.

MigrationWatchUK's perspective on the problem of immigration was outlined in January 2007: 'The question is about scale and pace. How many more immigrants should be admitted to the UK and how rapidly can they be integrated?'. For MigrationWatchUK, recent and current levels of immigration are too high: '[a] major step must be to limit the scale and pace of further immigration.... The ideal would be to achieve a position where the number of people entering Britain was similar to the number emigrating'.[53]

As MigrationWatchUK sees it, there are a number of problems that result from the scale and pace of immigration. These can be divided into three main categories: population growth (and its impact on housing, infrastructure and the landscape); economic impact; and changes to 'British' culture (including as a result of changes to ethnic composition). The impact of immigration on housing is considered in Chapter Four, and the issues of ethnic composition are discussed in Chapters Five to Seven. Here we focus on MigrationWatchUK's claims about population growth and the economic impact of immigration.

Some general points must be made about MigrationWatchUK's role in the immigration debates, where it instils a sense of urgency, claims that current trends are exceptional and unacceptable, and misleads via its inaccurate use of statistics. The urgency of its language promotes fear, as illustrated in the following extract from the document in which MigrationWatchUK outlines 'the problem'.

> Immigration is now on an unprecedented scale ... immigration will result in an increase in the population of the UK of 6 million in the 27 years from 2004 ... this will lead to a requirement of about 1.5 million houses in the period 2003-2026. England is now nearly twice as crowded as Germany, four times France and twelve times the US ... the pressure on our borders continues ... immigration holds wages down ... Britain is losing its own culture ... leading to the formation of parallel communities ... [and] frictions between different communities.[54]

MigrationWatchUK's use of statistics side by side with fearful consequences without explanation or context leaves the reader to assume that the figures indicate exceptional and unacceptable trends. For example, its 'outline of the problem' continues with 'net foreign immigration reached 292,000 in 2005', '510,000 applicants have registered under the Workers Registration Scheme', 'Immigration (immigrants and their descendants) will now account for 83% of future population growth in the UK', 'About 50,000 illegal entrants are detected every year', and 'Demand for visas has risen by 33% in 5 years'. But as we have seen, immigration to the UK is not exceptional.

The accuracy of MigrationWatchUK's use of statistics must also be scrutinised. Its 'Key Facts about Immigration' states that '[i]n 2005 11.8 million non-EU nationals arrived in the UK'.[55] There are problems with the promotion of this statement as a key fact about immigration. First, the vast majority of these arrivals are not immigrants. Of the arrivals, 6.9 million (or 58%) were visitors and a further 4.1 million (a further 35%) were passengers in transit or passengers returning after a temporary absence abroad. This means that a maximum of only 7% of the 11.8 million quoted were potential immigrants. Second, these statistics refer to journeys rather than people.[56] People who arrived in the UK more than once during the year will be double-counted.

MigrationWatchUK's claim that 'In the 1990s, immigration became the most important component of population growth (accounting for 83%)'[57] is both false and peculiar. Government figures, which MigrationWatchUK generally uses in its statements, show that in the 1990s the UK population grew each year both naturally (from more births than deaths) and from international migration. Over the whole decade there was a net gain of 676,000 people from migration and 999,000 from natural change, adding to a total of 1.7 million of which 40% was the net gain from migration. The contribution from migration did rise during the 1990s but in no year did it reach 70%, let alone 83%.[58] It turns out that the source for MigrationWatchUK's 83% refers not to the 1990s but to a *projection* by the Government Actuary's Department for the period 2003-31.[59] Population change according to the main government projection, when compared to what would happen if there was no migration at all, yields a difference of 5.2 million, which is 84% of the projected total change and close enough to the MigrationWatchUK claim. Elsewhere, the MigrationWatchUK claim is indeed that immigration will account for 83% of *future* population growth in the UK.

Perhaps the false claim for the 1990s is a slip of the MigrationWatchUK pen. But even when applied to the future, the statement that the equivalent of 84% (or 83%) of population growth can be attributed to migrants and their children is decidedly peculiar. Population growth is made up from migration and natural change, but both are themselves balances of much larger flows. Migration is the balance of all immigrants minus all emigrants. Natural change is the balance of all births minus all deaths. Both these balances are very much smaller than the total number of in- or out-migrants, and the total number of births or deaths. One or both balances can be negative as well as positive. Thus, the MigrationWatchUK calculation can lead to odd statements such as 'natural change was responsible for 164% of all population change' – which is exactly the result of applying this indicator to the 1970s when the net impact of migration was to reduce the population.[60] One can extend the MigrationWatchUK calculation by taking immigration on its own, which was 3.5 million between 1991 and 2001, compared to the total population change of 1.7 million. One could say that immigration accounted for 211% of the population change, which is clearly ludicrous. MigrationWatchUK is playing with the figures to find a large but believable number to quote.

One of the characteristics of calculations about the marginal change in population (or in anything else) is that the results are likely to change quite drastically from one year to another. UK population projections have been revised twice since MigrationWatchUK published its figure of 83%; recent projections reduce their indicator downwards, showing that migration (and the children of migrants) might account for 69% of population growth during the period 2006–31.[61] If one takes each five-year period, the projected population growth due to migration is less than 50% of the total growth, in other words less than that due to births and deaths, for three of the five five-year periods between 2006 and 2031. The current increase in emigration, particularly of returning Eastern European migrants, will no doubt affect the next round of official projections.

Babies cause a headache for those like MigrationWatchUK who claim not to be anti-immigrant but who feel that Britain is too full. More babies in recent years mean that Britain is becoming more crowded, and at the same time reduces the relative contribution of migration to growth. Of course, MigrationWatchUK does not advocate restrictions on childbirth. It is population growth through immigration that exclusively concerns MigrationWatchUK.

Although it claims that it is only the *balance* of international migration that matters, MigrationWatchUK briefings lament the 'massive levels of immigration' and the difficulties that non-Western immigrants supposedly bring for themselves and for those already in Britain, which 'is losing its own culture' while those who are not 'native' to Britain suffer 'frictions between different communities, sometimes encouraged by satellite television from their home areas. E.g. Pakistani/Indian. Caribbean/Somali. Pakistani/Kurd'.[62] These nationalist prejudices of MigrationWatchUK briefings make it difficult to have a reasoned debate on immigration.

A key component of MigrationWatchUK's anti-immigration argument is immigration's detrimental effect on the economy. The organisation makes several points: that immigrants will not help to pay the nation's pensions in the future; that immigration holds down wage levels and interest rates and so is beneficial to employers but not to taxpayers; that immigrants do jobs that British people want to do. We have already seen that several of these claims are not supported by the evidence.

The crux of MigrationWatchUK's economic argument, however, is that although immigration results in economic growth it is cancelled out by the increase in population caused by immigration. Using this reasoning, MigrationWatchUK has challenged official statistics on the economic impact of immigration. It does this by setting any benefits against the assumed costs of increased population growth. MigrationWatchUK tells us that:

> '[t]he government claim that immigrants add £4 billion to production is very misleading as it does not take account of their addition to the population. Allowing for this brings the benefit to the host population down to 0.01% of GDP – or about 4 pence a week for the host community each year.[63]

In a later publication, the figure has changed to 28p per week (at that time the cost of a Mars chocolate bar, hence headlines referring to the 'Mars Bar' result), and later still to 62p.[64] It is calculated straightforwardly using government population projections and Treasury assumptions as shown in Box 3.2.[65] MigrationWatchUK describes 28p per person per week as 'largely neutral', but one could equally say that this contribution of immigration to the pocket of every resident on a weekly basis is a remarkable benefit of immigration. Since immigration is economically beneficial but is still seen by MigrationWatchUK as undesirable, the implication is that immigrants must put pressure on the space or well-being of others, claims that are indeed made by MigrationWatchUK and are addressed later in Chapters Four and Five.

Box 3.2: The MigrationWatchUK calculation of the economic benefit of immigration

- Step 1: 0.42% is the annual growth in the working-age population due to immigration projected by government for the period 2004-2031, and is therefore the annual growth in GDP contributed by immigration.
- Step 2: 0.35% is the annual growth in the overall population due to immigration during the same period, which is slightly less than the working-age population because immigrants tend to be of working age.
- Step 3: 0.07% – the difference – is therefore the contribution to the GDP made by immigrants, after taking into account the growth in population.
- Step 4: With a GDP of £1,234 billion, and 0.07% of it divided between the population of 60 million, the contribution of immigrants is £14 per annum or 28p per week.

The calculation is straightforward but perhaps too straightforward. Economists who have spent decades calculating the economic impact of immigration[66] would surely be unemployed if it were this simple! For example, the figure for overall population growth in Step 2 includes working age immigrants who have already been accounted for in Step 1. Conceptually this is difficult: on the one hand they contribute to GDP because of their age (which is a proxy for economic activity) yet on the other they decrease GDP because they add to the population. The relationship here would be easier to grasp were one side of the equation the contributions of immigrants and the other the costs of immigrants; or, if we are talking in populations, the 'economically active' immigrants versus the 'economically dependant' immigrants. But this is more tricky (and what economists spend decades figuring out). Again the critique comes back to the assumption made by MigrationWatchUK that population growth can easily be equated to 'cost of immigration'.

MigrationWatchUK does not stop there with its 'cost of population growth' approach. It believes that the children of immigrants should be factored into any calculations, as MigrationWatchUK does when measuring the contribution of immigration to population growth (see earlier in this chapter). It criticises the government's calculation of the proportion of GDP produced by immigrants, Step 1 in its calculation, because it 'takes no account of dependent children; when they are included the result is that migrants contribute slightly less to GDP than their population share'.[67] If MigrationWatchUK is concerned here with dependent children who are themselves immigrants (that is, they migrated with their parents or guardians), it is difficult to see how the result can be different from that in the box above. In this calculation, dependent child immigrants are taken into account in Step 2, as the assumed costs of their addition to population. If MigrationWatchUK is concerned with the children of immigrants born in the UK, its perspective is extremely problematic: if the definition of an immigrant is extended to descendents of immigrants, shouldn't the contributions from immigrants' children who have already been growing up during the period be considered as part of Step 1? If anyone of immigrant origin remains forever an immigrant, at what point, what generation, does the definition of immigrant stop? In this sense the vast majority of the British population are of immigrant origin, an observation that is addressed in more detail when we deal with population projections in Chapter Seven.

The macro-economic approach which compares inputs and outputs as if every person contributed and consumed the same amount is limited. Immigrants are more likely than others to be in poorly paid jobs, more often earning below the minimum legal wage, and more likely than others to suffer poor working and poor housing conditions. Whether from an economic or a humanitarian approach, the 'burden' of immigration is borne disproportionately by immigrants themselves, and the gains are disproportionately for others.

Conclusion

The claim that Britain has too many immigrants has its roots first in Malthusian concerns about the sustainability of an increasing population and second in a racialised history of immigration control. It has found renewed expression amid the new migration and super-diversity of the early 21st century. The claim is that immigration causes population growth that the country cannot manage.

This claim is problematic in many ways. UK immigration is quite unexceptional when considered in a global or in a European context. In economic terms, the evidence points to benefits that immigration brings to the UK. One of the key actors in these debates, MigrationWatchUK, sustains the myth that there is too much immigration by presenting evidence that is far from balanced, using claims that are factually inaccurate. Its use of immigration figures out of context promotes fear of immigration and of immigrants.

MigrationWatchUK accepts overall economic benefits of immigration, but pursues its fear by claiming that population growth is too much. MigrationWatchUK does not make clear why it is only population growth through immigration that it finds a problem. Serious concerns about the availability of housing and jobs are not well served by a focus on immigration. MigrationWatchUK holds political weight due to its acceptance by parts of the media and political elite, not because its logic and statistics hold water.

Notes
[1] 'Outline of the problem', 2 January 2007, available at www. migrationwatchuk.org/outline_of_the_problem.asp and 'Ten MigrationWatch contributions', 17 January 2007, available at www. migrationwatchuk.com/Briefingpapers/Achievments/13_2_10MW_contribute.asp
[2] The 2001 Census Small Area Microdata (5% sample) shows that over half of all immigrants (who arrived in the year before the census) were graduates with a degree, compared to under 20% of the population as a whole. Immigrants are more likely to be graduates for each ethnic

group, for example 68% of Indians, 48% of Africans and 32% of Pakistani immigrants were graduates. Only 10% of immigrants had no qualifications, compared to 30% of the population as a whole. See Chapter Four for more on this.

[3] Malthus (1798).

[4] These debates were heavily influenced by E.F. Schumacher, particularly his seminal work *Small is Beautiful* (1973).

[5] Minute 7 of a Cabinet meeting held on 3 November 1955, quoted in Carter et al (1987, p 1).

[6] Carter et al (1987, pp 1 and 3) use political documents from the period 1951 to 1955 to demonstrate the racialisation of immigration during that period. The administrative measures they refer to include alterations to the British Travel Certificate, tampering with shipping lists and delays to issuing of passports.

[7] Spencer (1997, p 43).

[8] Spencer (1997, p 43).

[9] Information is taken from the BNP 2006 Council Election Manifesto, BNP policies and BNP stance on issues, all available on the party website at www.bnp.org.uk/2008/02/bnp-policies/

[10] A selection of studies: Hall (1987), van Dijk (1991), Hargreaves (1996), Law (1997), Bromley and Sonnenberg (1998), Kaye (1998, 1999), EUMC (2002) and Stratham (2002).

[11] Stratham and Morrison (1999).

[12] Stratham (2002) undertook a content analysis of British newspapers. In 2002 he reviewed media coverage again, as part of a broader EU study (EUMC, 2002).

[13] *The Guardian*, 15 March 2008; Federation of Poles in Great Britain: www.zpwb.org.uk/en/3

[14] The concern about media coverage of asylum issues and the subsequent complaint to the Press Complaints Commission are documented in Finney (2003) and ICAR (2004, 2006).

[15] See Kaye (1998), Philo and Beattie (1999) and Pickering (2001) for elaboration of these arguments.

[16] For a summary of the legislation see the Information Centre about Asylum and Refugees navigation guide on UK asylum law and process, available at www.icar.org.uk/?lid=374

[17] See Robinson et al (2003).

[18] Beynon (2006).

[19] Independent Asylum Commission (2008, p 2).

[20] Surveys asked this question in 1989, 1994, 1997, 1999, 2000, 2002, 2007; results are summarised at www.ipsos-mori.com/polls/trends/immigration.shtml

[21] Ipsos MORI International Social Trends Monitor, November 2006.

[22] European Social Survey, 2002/03.

[23] In 2007 the Office for National Statistics launched the Improving Migration and Population Statistics (IMPS) project; see www.statistics. gov.uk/about/data/methodology/specific/population/future/imps/ default.asp

[24] See Dobson et al (2001, chapter 2) for an overview of these issues.

[25] Defined in Home Office (2006, p 95, table 8.1, note 2). Available at http://www.homeoffice.gov.uk/rds/immigration-asylum-publications. html

[26] Singleton (1999) and Rees and Boden (2006) provide reviews of international migration sources for UK subnational areas and for European countries respectively. Salt (2006) provides data for the UK from which many of the figures in this chapter are taken.

[27] ONS (2003, table 3.21); authors' calculations from UK census publications; ONS (2005a, figure 7.1).

[28] Salt (2006); figures based on International Passenger Survey (IPS) data.

[29] UN (2006); the summary sheet titled 'International migration 2006' has been used for most of the cited data.

[30] ONS (2005a, table 8.8); UN (2006).

[31] Key Population and Vital Statistics, 2005; Control of Immigration Statistics, 2005; both based on the IPS.

[32] See earlier discussion and also Layton-Henry (1992) and Paul (1997).

[33] From Salt (2006, p 109).

[34] Home Office (2008).

[35] Pinkerton et al (2004).

[36] Woodbridge, J. (2005).

[37] In Britain in 2001, 2.31 million non-White residents out of a total of 4.62 million non-White residents (50%) were born in the UK (2001 Census, Tables S102, S202). In the year prior to the 2001 Census, out of the total of 399,000 immigrants, 280,000 (70%) were White (2001 Census, Table M816g).

[38] Salt (2006, p 43), from the Labour Force Survey.

[39] The UN calculates migrant stock based on those born overseas and, if this is not available, citizenship.

[40] See, for example, the review in Glover et al (2001).

[41] Glover et al (2001, pp viii–ix).

[42] Select Committee on Economic Affairs (2008, para 66).

[43] See reports by Dustmann et al for the Home Office (Dustmann et al, 2003a, 2003b) and for the Low Pay Commission (Dustmann et al, 2007); all available online at www.econ.ucl.ac.uk/cream/

—

[44] Select Committee on Economic Affairs (2008, para 79).

[45] Salt (2006, p 90).

[46] Dobson et al (2001).

[47] Kirk (2004).

[48] Barrett et al (2001).

[49] Alba et al (2003).

[50] Wahlbeck (2005).

[51] For example, UN (2001); Harris and Coleman (2003).

[52] The MigrationWatchUK website can be found at www.migrationwatchuk.com/default.asp

[53] 'Outline of the problem', 2 January 2007, available at www.migrationwatchuk.org/outline_of_the_problem.asp

[54] 'Outline of the problem', 2 January 2007, available at www.migrationwatchuk.org/outline_of_the_problem.asp

[55] 'Key Facts about Immigration', available at http://www.migrationwatchuk.com/Briefingpapers/keyfacts/keyfacts_about_immigration.asp

[56] Home Office (2006, table 2.3).

[57] 'Overview of UK migration', 10 January 2007, available at www.migrationwatchuk.com/overview.asp

[58] ONS (2005a, table 9.1).

[59] Shaw (2004, p 11, table B).

[60] Calculations made from ONS (2007, table 1.6).

[61] Migration and population growth, www.gad.gov.uk/Demography_data/Population/2006/methodology/mignote.asp

[62] 'Outline of the problem, 2 January 2007, available at www.migrationwatchuk.org/outline_of_the_problem.asp

[63] 'Ten MigrationWatch contributions', 17 January 2007, available at www.migrationwatchuk.com/Briefingpapers/Achievments/13_2_10MW_contribute.asp

[64] MigrationWatch UK (2008). The changes result from government revisions to estimated GDP and future population, not to a change in MigrationWatchUK's approach to the calculation.

[65] From MigrationWatchUK (2007a, Annex A).

[66] The volumes by Chiswick (2005) and Chiswick and Miller (2007) represent decades of work on the economics of immigration.

[67] 'Ten MigrationWatch contributions', 17 January 2007, available at www.migrationwatchuk.com/Briefingpapers/Achievments/13_2_10MW_contribute.asp

4

Challenging the myth that 'So many minorities cannot be integrated'

The Government's own prediction shows our overcrowded island swelling by at least 2.1 million immigrants.... It could mean London ending up having Third World-style shanty towns springing up in the shadows of the City's gleaming skyscrapers ... the boom will put unbearable strain on schools, hospitals, roads and railways ... without controls on the numbers coming here we will face a future of public services struggling to cope. *The Sun newspaper*[1]

Introduction

The view that integration of immigrants is not possible is among the most prevalent and pervasive of the race and migration myths. It is at the heart of much anti-immigration and anti-minority sentiment in contemporary Britain. Like all persistent myths it benefits from poor definitions and imprecise concepts.

Chapter Three discussed claims that immigration is the main cause of population growth; that Britain takes more than its fair share of immigrants and that immigration is economically costly. This chapter investigates first the claim that immigrants cannot be integrated because they place too great a burden on space, housing and state resources. Second, it considers the claim that problems are caused not only by increased numbers of people but by increased ethnic diversity. The chapter argues that, on the contrary, immigrants and ethnic minorities take up less space and no more resources than others, and that ethnic diversity is not a burden but is one more dimension of difference that services handle democratically in the same way as gender and age.

In this chapter more than in others in this book, the distinction between immigrants and minorities is very blurred. The myth draws strength from the indistinct nature of these categories. For example, the extension of the concept of immigrants needing extra resources – which is easily associated with initial settlement in a new country – to ethnic minorities who have mostly been born and have lived all their lives in Britain and who therefore have no requirement for help in settlement, exaggerates the fear that the myth promotes. We talk about both recent immigrants and ethnic minorities in this chapter but we aim to specify who we are referring to at each point, and to point out when the myth conflates concepts of different populations.

The origins of the myth

The fear that immigrants will place a burden on the resources of society dates back at least to the middle of the 20th century. In the 1950s the Conservative government used the argument that Black people were unsuitable for work and therefore a drain on welfare in its efforts to introduce immigration controls.[2] The contemporary arguments are less overtly racialised but the sense that extra pressure is brought on services and resources by immigrants persists.

An example of the overt expression of the claim of the immigrant resource burden is the policy reaction to the immigration of asylum seekers and refugees in the late 1990s when migration for refuge reached a contemporary peak in Britain and elsewhere.[3] The response was the Dispersal Policy, which aimed to spread asylum seekers around Britain, thereby distributing the resource costs (and, it was implied, the social costs) evenly to authorities around the country. The policy as a whole received mixed responses but there was considerable consensus that the principle of 'spreading the burden' was in line with the government's aims of a 'firm but fair' immigration policy.[4]

The distinction between types of immigrants is important in this claim; only certain immigrants represent a resource burden. The journalist Anthony Browne distinguishes very clearly between wanted and unwanted immigrants, claiming that '[i]mmigrants from the Third World ... are on average less well educated, suffer higher unemployment, claim more of most forms of benefits, make more demands on public services such as schools and hospitals'.[5] While government reports disagree with this assessment, the government's defence of its managed migration policy is framed in terms of the detrimental effects that growth of immigrant communities could have on people and places suffering from deprivation. For immigration minister Liam Byrne '[i]t is true that a small number of schools have struggled to cope, that some local authorities have reported problems of overcrowding in private housing and that there have been cost pressures on English language training, but the answer is in action that is simultaneously firm and fair'.[6] His ministerial action is the points–based system for immigration, introduced in 2008, to ensure that those judged as a burden cannot establish lives in Britain.

For MigrationWatchUK, the immigrant resource burden results from the population growth due to immigration, as we discussed in Chapter Three. MigrationWatchUK also makes claims that pressure on land and housing is a result of immigration: 'Over the next twenty years, one in three new households will be down to immigration. Since brownfield sites provide two thirds of new homes, net immigration is the main reason for greenfield development'[7] ... 'New government household projections show an annual rate of household growth of 223,000 a year between 2004 and 2026. 73,000 (a third) of this increase is due to net migration into England. This amounts to a requirement for 200 new homes every day to house the additional immigrant population'.[8]

In its 2007 submission to the House of Lords Economic Affairs Select Committee Inquiry on the Economic Impact of Immigration (discussed previously in Chapter Three), the Local Government Association (LGA) expressed concerns along the same lines: 'population growth has resulted in some areas in pressures on services, and sometimes in resentment and tensions on the part of host communities. Particular demands vary depending on the demographic characteristics of the migrant – for example whether they have children and require children's services; whether they are relatively young and thus less likely to require health services'.[9] In contrast to MigrationWatchUK, however, the LGA does not call for limits on immigration but instead recommends better local information on immigration and place-specific targeting of funding and support.

The LGA's position reflects both the concern that immigrants place extra pressure on services and the claim that diversity itself is a threat to integrated, cohesive communities. Its submission to the House of Lords Committee was largely motivated by migration from European Union (EU) Accession states to parts of Britain that had previously experienced very little immigration. These areas have had to both support the settlement of new residents and react to a new diversity in their population by considering how to achieve integration.

As we saw in Chapter One, integration is a complex concept and one that is associated both with new immigrants and with ethnic minorities. Until recently, a general acceptance and indeed celebration of ethnic diversity was a characteristic of social policy in Britain. The 1976 Race Relations Act promoted public policy towards immigrants and their families, which unhitched integration from any expectation that immigrants would wholly adopt the customs and residential spread of the existing population. First, an anti-racist ethos took the emphasis away from concerns with geographical segregation and was prioritised for 25 years. School bussing was ended and the Commission for Racial Equality was created with powers to investigate public organisations accused of discriminatory activity. Second, recognition of the rights of all ethnic groups led to multiculturalism, a respect for and celebration of different groups' origins and cultural traditions. This dual priority was not welcomed by all who had argued for the need to outlaw race discrimination. Some radical activists saw the celebration of cultural traditions as a dilution and professionalisation of resistance to racism, emphasising difference in place of the common need to confront institutional discrimination.[10]

But both multiculturalism and anti-racism continued to be emphasised together, and 25 years later in 2000 the report of the Commission on the Future of Multi-Ethnic Britain (known as The

Parekh Report) advocated that social cohesion required the following two elements: the common understanding that society should be recognised as a community of communities as well as a community of individuals; and a challenge to all racisms and related structural inequalities.[11]

However, the hunt for discrimination and respect for a community of communities was abruptly challenged by two sets of dramatic events of 2001: the attacks on New York and other US cities that led to the 'war on terror' and, closer to home, urban disturbances – or 'race riots' – in English towns.[12] Since 2001 there has been fear of similar incidents, as well as increased immigration to Britain (and the rest of Western Europe), extension of the EU, and interventionist foreign policy. These events have together thrown into question the diversity policy strategies of the 1980s and 1990s, challenging although not overthrowing the twin gains of the 1970s.

First, there has been a return to concerns about geographies of segregation; to the assumption and fear that residential clustering or separation is an indication of social division (see Chapter Six). Second, official thinking has turned from philosophies that recognise the salience of group identities to ones that emphasise commonalities and shared values across ethnicities and religions, and which identify extreme behaviours and ideas as an indication of too much diversity.[13]

The 'project of multiculturalism' is now being held responsible for what is perceived to be fragmentation of Britain's communities, separation and division that fosters hostility and extremism. In particular, there has been

> widespread questioning about whether Muslims can be and are willing to be integrated into European society and its political values ... whether Muslims are committed to what are taken to be the core European values of freedom, tolerance, democracy, sexual equality and secularism.[14]

The Equality and Human Rights Commission, established in 2007, reinforces the position of failure of multiculturalism, problems of segregation and the need to build a national identity based on shared values. Where group identity was being evoked at the expense of common identity, government policy has supposedly become a 'benign form of exclusion and neglect' and has 'played a decisive role in the separateness of communities.... Separation feeds a dangerous tribalisation of communities'.[15]

The government's Commission on Integration and Cohesion (2007) report *Our Shared Future* situates diversity as a challenge that must be addressed alongside other social issues such as deprivation and discrimination; and where local specificities must be considered. The report found that:

> Diversity can have a negative impact on cohesion, but only in particular local circumstances. We suggest three types of local areas where this is true: urban areas that are just starting to experience diversity, such as some of the outer London Boroughs and Southern commuter towns; rural areas that are just starting to experience diversity, such as the areas around the Wash; and ethnically diverse urban areas experiencing new migration, such as inner cities in the major metropolitan areas.[16]

There are few places in Britain not included in one of its three types of area threatened by the 'negative impact' of diversity.

The cohesion and citizenship agenda gains support from all political colours, the Left differing from the Right in its greater optimism for the success of assertive integration strategies.[17] Most who support it see a problem of 'cultural separatism', particularly of Muslims, as was explicit in David Cameron's speech on the subject of integration in June 2007,[18] and had been in Prime Minister Blair's intervention on integration.[19] Their solutions are also familiar: to assert a sense of Britishness.

It is in the context of cohesion and citizenship agendas that claims are made about the need to curb immigration because more immigrants cannot possibly be integrated. Chapter Three has already demonstrated that claims about the scale and economic impact of immigration are exaggerations and misrepresentations of the evidence. Now we review the evidence for claims that immigration, and the diversity brought by immigration, place unmanageable pressure on space, housing, greenfield areas and public services.

Not enough space and not enough housing?

We first examine the mantra of anti-immigration and anti-diversity perspectives, that 'we're a small island bursting at the seams'. There are many reasons for increased housing demand and a focus on immigration is very misleading. Greater income and more people living on their own or in bigger houses is the major reason for new housing demand, while immigrants and their children tend to live in the more dense urban areas and with more people in each property. A focus on England is a misleading way of making international comparisons.

There is, certainly, a limit to Britain's habitable landmass and it is also true that the population has grown over recent decades, partly as a result of immigration. However, the issue of space can be looked at differently; we should consider not only the size of the population but the way that it lives, in terms of household size, property size and the number of homes that people own.

There has been an increase in the number of one-person households in the past half century.[20] In the 1950s the proportion of the population living alone was under 3%. In 2001 12.5% of the population lived alone, and these households with one usual resident made up 30% of all households.[21] In 2005 the number of people living alone in Britain had more than doubled since 1971, from three million to seven million.[22] This increase has demographic and economic causes. There are more people who are divorced or never marry, and more older people living alone as a result of an ageing population and the mortality differential between men and women. Rising incomes, higher education and an era of independence and individualism have led more people to live alone, particularly young people (although whether they feel this is desirable is a different matter). As a result of these changes, the increase in the number of households since the 1980s owes much more to single-person households than to the increase in the population.[23]

The increase in single-person households has led to a reduction in average household size. In 2006 the average number of people living in a household in England and Wales was 2.4, a reduction from 2.9 in 1971.[24] Not only is there a trend towards fewer people living in each property, but there is a trend towards larger properties, with increases in the proportions living in each of semi-detached and detached houses.[25]

In addition, there has been an increase in second-home ownership such as people owning 'commuter pads' in city centres, or countryside homes in addition to suburban residences. This has been a controversial issue, primarily because of its effect on rural areas, creating 'ghost villages' and causing property prices to rise out of reach of local residents.[26] Financially, the market has been favourable for second-home ownership over the last decade: mortgage rates have been low, the Council Tax system allows a reduction for properties used as second homes, and for unmarried couples two homes can be owned without being eligible for capital gains tax. Second-home ownership has become so significant that the Office for National Statistics is planning to measure this important social change in the 2011 Census.[27]

The effects of these trends on how many people can be accommodated can be simply illustrated with a hypothetical example. The land area of England currently taken up by domestic buildings is 1,507,704,910 square metres.[28] If we say that a detached house occupies on average 300 square metres, there is room for 5,025,683 houses. These could accommodate either 5,025,683 people living alone or 11,860,612 people living in households of average size (2.35 people). This is, clearly, far fewer people than the population of England, which is 49,138,831.[29] If we say that a block of 10 flats can occupy the same 300 square metres then there is room for 50,256,830 people living alone or 118,103,550 people living in households of average size (2.35 people). The straightforward point is that the amount of pressure on space and housing depends on how we live.

The claim is that immigrants are placing pressure on space and housing. However, immigrants and their children tend to live in larger households than average. Table 4.1 shows average household size for each ethnic group, an approximation for immigrants and their children. There are clear differences between ethnic groups. White, Caribbean and African groups have household sizes closest to the average while for the South Asian, Chinese and Other groups, households tend to consist of more people. This is particularly the case for Pakistani and Bangladeshi households, which, on average, have around four people. Table 4.2 confirms these patterns, showing that, taken together, a quarter of minority households contain one person, a little less than the 30% of White households. For the South Asian groups, the proportion of one-person households is lowest, and as low as 9% for the Bangladeshi group. If the whole population lived at four people to each house, 20,102,732 people could be accommodated in detached houses in England and 201,027,324 people in flats.

If it is not the case that immigrants and their children are living in spacious accommodation, perhaps immigrants and their children take up more land space than others? Of course, nothing could be further from the truth. Table 4.3 shows that White Britons, as they are measured in the census, take up three times as much space as Bangladeshis, on average.

Table 4.1: Mean household size by ethnic group, 2001

Ethnic group	Mean household size
All households	2.35
All minorities	2.96
Irish	2.15
Caribbean	2.29
White Briton	2.31
Other Black	2.39
Other White	2.42
Mixed	2.46
Chinese	2.59
African	2.75
Other	2.77
Other Asian	3.19
Indian	3.26
Pakistani	3.88
Bangladeshi	4.18

Source: 2001 Census, Sample of Anonymised Records, England and Wales.

Table 4.2: People living alone (% of all households) by ethnic group, 2001

Ethnic group	One-person households (% of all households)
All households	30.0
All minorities	24.2
Caribbean	38.0
Irish	37.5
Other Black	34.2
White Briton	30.4
Mixed	30.4
African	30.1
Other White	28.2
Chinese	27.8
Other	23.6
Other Asian	18.4
Indian	15.4
Pakistani	11.9
Bangladeshi	8.8

Source: 2001 Census, England and Wales, table S106

Note: Minorities in these tables and Table 4.3 are all census ethnic groups other than White.

Is the UK overcrowded? MigrationWatchUK is very careful to compare *England* with other countries in Europe when it talks of an overcrowded country. England has more than four fifths of the UK population but only a little over half of its land surface. England's density of 390 people per square kilometre is indeed higher than Germany or France, but it is also much higher than the density of the UK, which is 250 people per square kilometre, similar to Germany's density of 230. MigrationWatchUK could just as well achieve its target of lower density by encouraging northward migration, and particularly migration away from London where there are 4,700 people per square kilometre. It is a safe bet that those who shout the loudest about immigrants taking up too much space in Britain are among those who themselves take up a larger share than most.[30]

The claim that 'net immigration is the main reason for greenfield development' is equally disingenuous, because the great majority of those moving to less urban and to rural settings are not immigrants. Indeed, there is a far stronger case for saying that immigration is a *consequence* of movement of indigenous Britons out of cities and into the suburbs and rural areas, which began before the 1960s as a result of growing prosperity and car ownership that promoted

Table 4.3: Local living density, persons per hectare by ethnic group, 2001

Ethnic group	Local living density, persons per hectare
All people	51.6
All minorities	95.0
White Briton	46.2
Irish	70.0
Chinese	76.6
Mixed	77.0
Indian	78.3
White Other	81.0
Other Asian	87.2
Other	92.8
Pakistani	93.0
Caribbean	101.6
Other Black	108.1
African	130.7
Bangladeshi	148.1

Note: The average living density in the Census Output Areas in which each group lives. Since most people live in urban areas, the average living density is higher than a country's overall population density. 100 hectares = 1 sq km.

Source: 2001 Census, Key Statistics, England and Wales

commuting, and replacement of large heavy industrial workplaces with more dispersed lighter industry and service jobs. This dispersal during the past 60 years has freed up cheap housing and created demand for low-wage jobs in poor conditions to keep Britain's cities ticking over day and night. Chapter Six gives the evidence for Leicester, where out-migration preceded immigration and has since slowed.

Are immigrants a burden on the state?

In Chapter Three we saw that immigration is economically beneficial. Here we address the issue of immigrants placing strain on public services. The first point to make is that migrants are self-selective: migrants are most likely to be young, in good health and of high socioeconomic status.[31] Migration is demanding and an individual has to feel that the social and economic benefits of moving outweigh the costs and upheaval. For international migrants, these considerations are magnified because of the challenges of moving to an entirely different society where they may have limited destination-specific human capital and social networks. When migration is voluntary (we will come to forced migration below), it is shaped by the forces of the global market, by patterns of supply and demand of jobs, skills and labour.[32] Most international migrants move because they are more certain than not that they will find employment, and, indeed, many international moves are conditional on the migrant having secured employment or having skills that are in demand in the receiving country. Bank of England research has confirmed that recent immigrants to Britain are more educated than both UK-born workers and previous immigrant waves.[33]

Table 4.4 presents the percentage of immigrants and non-immigrants who are managers and professionals, who are university graduates and who are employed. The figures are taken from the 2001 Census and are given for the total population and for ethnic groups separately. For the whole population, immigrants are more likely than non-immigrants to be managers or professionals and to be university graduates. The same data source shows that they are less likely to have no qualifications and that these patterns are even stronger if only those who immigrated in the year prior to the census are considered. However, despite their higher qualifications and occupations, immigrants are less likely to be employed. This is surprising given their skills and education but represents the difficulties immigrants face, including language (a form of human capital), understanding the systems and cultures for recruitment and employment (a form of social capital) and discrimination, when entering employment in a new country. Only for the White group are immigrants more likely to be employed than non-immigrants.

For the African group, non-immigrants are more likely than immigrants to be university graduates. For all other ethnic groups the pattern is the opposite way round. However, the proportion of African graduates, of both immigrants and non-immigrants, is higher than

Table 4.4: Occupation, education and employment of immigrants and non-immigrants by ethnic group, 2001 (%)

Ethnic group	Managerial and professional occupations		University graduates		Employed	
	Immigrant	Non-immigrant	Immigrant	Non-immigrant	Immigrant	Non-immigrant
All people	22.0	11.0	43.3	18.2	64.9	66.0
White	29.6	14.2	50.1	24.8	72.6	64.1
Mixed	17.6	11.8	40.8	21.3	62.5	67.2
Indian	33.2	19.3	49.2	30.1	61.8	79.8
Pakistani	15.8	11.8	24.8	19.5	40.7	57.0
Bangladeshi	13.9	10.2	23.1	16.7	37.2	57.0
Other Asian	19.3	21.3	34.1	27.3	54.0	71.9
Caribbean	14.7	10.6	23.9	21.7	50.1	71.9
African	14.4	19.3	42.4	44.3	57.9	70.9
Chinese	27.9	24.0	43.8	34.4	62.7	81.6
Other	15.6	17.5	51.9	23.2	61.5	66.0

Note: Immigrant in this table refers to all residents in England and Wales who were born outside the UK.

Source: 2001 Census, Small Area Microdata (5% sample); England and Wales

—

for any other ethnic group. The proportion of immigrants who are graduates is particularly high for the White, Mixed, Indian, African and Chinese. In all these cases more than four in ten immigrants have a degree.

In terms of occupational status, for all ethnic groups apart from African, Other Asian and the residual Other group, immigrants are more likely to be managers and professionals than non-immigrants. Indian immigrants are most likely to be managers or professionals (one in three) and the figure is also high for Chinese and White immigrants. What these results clearly show is that immigrants have greater capacity to support themselves than lifetime residents, in terms of qualifications and occupational status. Why this is not transferred into employment rates, demonstrating an immigrant as well as an ethnic penalty,[34] is a serious issue of structural integration.

Anthony Browne's claims of a drain of third world immigrants on the state, referred to earlier, are based on a government report that he himself admits does not come to his conclusion.[35] The report clarified that immigrants make a clear fiscal contribution to the state – they contribute more in taxes than they use in benefits and public services. It also confirmed the higher qualifications of immigrants than existing residents, including the higher qualifications of immigrants from India and the Middle East. Immigrants are a very diverse group, and the report attempted to identify the kind of immigrant that may make a negative fiscal contribution, but it could not be done. There are no data of benefits and the labour market that identify immigrants' origins in each world region. There are other reasons why the calculation of fiscal balances is not easy that leave Browne's interpretations open to question. Many immigrants have legal status that limits their work and their benefits, including most asylum seekers. It could be argued that the impact of migrants whose residence is on humanitarian grounds, such as refugees, should not be economically evaluated because they have a legal right to refuge under international law. In any case, if asylum seekers and refugees are taken to have a negative economic and resource impact, as they often are, the overall positive benefit of immigration economically would be higher if they were excluded from the calculations.

What does this mean then for claims of benefits? As Browne himself suggests, 'the levels of British benefits are so low that there is little evidence that people are crossing the world simply to access them. It seems very unlikely that asylum seekers are paying people traffickers up to £5,000 and risking their lives getting into the UK simply to get benefits of around £50 a week'.[36] The proportion of migrants

—

claiming welfare benefits is small and decreasing. A case study of Manchester by Manchester City Council using National Insurance registration data showed that, in 2006, 5.8% of non-British nationals were claiming out-of-work benefits (Disability Living Allowance, Incapacity Benefit, Income Support or Jobseeker's Allowance).[37] For comparison, 19.6% of Manchester local authority's working-age population was claiming these benefits in 2006 (4.6% was claiming Disability Living Allowance, 8.1% was claiming Incapacity Benefit, 8.8% was claiming Income Support and 2.8% was claiming Jobseeker's Allowance). For England and Wales as a whole, 7.7% of the working-age population was claiming these benefits.[38]

For benefits that consider household income, many South Asian households in particular (extending the scope to migrants and their descendants) are less likely to be eligible due to their larger household size and extended family structures that give potential for greater total household income.[39] Although there is little work on differences in take-up rates for benefits by ethnicity, findings suggest that differences do exist. For example, minority ethnic groups are thought to be underclaiming Disability Living Allowance and Chinese people have been identified as particularly unlikely to claim benefits because of the stigma within this community of receiving state support.[40]

Two minorities that have particularly born the brunt of accusations of being a burden on the state are asylum seekers and refugees. It is important to distinguish between these groups of forced migrants. Asylum seekers are those seeking protection under the 1951 United Nations Refugee Convention because of a well-founded fear of persecution, while refugees are people who have had this application approved. Thus, refugees have the same rights as all British residents and are indistinguishable in official sources because the status of refugee is not recorded outside the refugee process. Asylum seekers, including those awaiting appeal, do not have the right to work. The only exception is a right to apply for permission to work under a European Directive if they have waited more than 12 months for an initial decision on their asylum application by the Home Office. They are eligible to apply for accommodation and subsistence support from the National Asylum Support Service but not for other benefits. Refugee organisations have argued that the legislation since 1993 that has reduced the rights of asylum seekers has led to considerable destitution among this population.[41]

The evidence does not support the claim that immigrants place an exceptional burden on the state because they are less capable than others of supporting themselves. Instead, it points in the opposite

—

direction and highlights the disadvantage suffered, particularly by forced migrants, as a result of anti-immigrant legislation.

Is diversity itself a burden?

There remains the question of ethnic diversity itself. If ethnicity is a marker of different choices, then maybe it signals a diversity of requirements from public services and employers, and therefore a greater expenditure in order to satisfy those diverse demands. Provision of halal meals in schools and prayer rooms in hospitals and at work all imply a cost. Put brutally, there are economies of scale if people can be treated not just equally but in the same way. These long-term considerations are different from the short-term costs to accommodate and integrate immigrants and their families into education and housing. These short-term needs have been expressed by local authorities in order to integrate immigrant labour into both rural and urban areas in recent years.[42]

Responding to diversity of requirements in service provision is a long-term project but it is also not limited to ethnic diversity associated with past immigration. Respect for more than one home language has long been understood in Wales. Provision of prayer facilities at work or halal meat at school recognises social differences in the same way as gender-specific toilet rooms, vegetarian options and disabled access. Responding to diversity of needs is nothing new, and there is no reason for the costs associated with service provision for ethnic diversity to be any more seen as a burden than costs associated with service provision for any other kind of diversity.

The costs of diversity are accepted as part of the normal working of democratic Britain. The question is not who pays but how are different needs met, who decides and how are different needs and demands represented in the decision-making processes. Mostly this is a matter for flexibility through the experience and professionalism of local government, the voluntary sector and commercial providers of services.

The proposal that diversity is costly restricts and represses because it suggests that those with new or unusual choices have somehow got it wrong at the expense of everyone else, with no understanding or tolerance of the rich diversity that makes up any human society. Whenever diversity is framed as competition, so that one person's demands are seen as a threat to others, then the minority easily becomes the scapegoat for more structural problems of scarcity of resources.[43]

Conclusion

The myth that so many immigrants and their descendants – ethnic minorities – cannot be integrated has taken hold in Britain in recent years. The myth combines the concerns that immigrants are a burden on space and resources and that increased diversity itself represents a burden on society. Fanciful footwork with figures gives rise to the claim, made most prominently by MigrationWatchUK, that pressure on housing would be vastly reduced if immigration were reduced, and that immigration accounts for the entire demand for new housing in greenspace. These powerful headlines are nonsensical when put against the evidence that clearly shows that minorities occupy much less space and less housing than the average. The housing crisis can just as easily be blamed on younger people for leaving home, on those who live in large properties, on those who live alone or on owners of second homes. Britain could accommodate many millions more people if there were fewer people living alone, or if more people lived in Wales and Scotland.

The argument that there are too many minorities to be integrated also relies on the assumption that minorities place an unmanageable burden on state resources and services. However, migrants are less likely than average to be claiming state support and forced migrants in particular are vulnerable to destitution. Immigrants contribute more in taxes than they use in public services. Immigrants are also more educated on average than the population.

The whole idea that there are too many minorities to be integrated is fed by the rhetoric that it is impossible to have successful ethnic diversity. But there are plenty of arguments, and plenty of people making them, in favour of diversity and its success in Britain. Furthermore, there is no reason for ethnic diversity to be seen as a burden any more than diversity by disability or age or gender. Ethnic diversity is not a burden but is one more dimension of difference that services are perfectly capable of handling democratically.

Notes
[1] Pascoe-Watson (2007).
[2] Carter et al (1987).
[3] Robinson (1993) and Koser and Lutz (1998) document the rise in significance of forced migration.
[4] Robinson et al (2003) provide an overview and critique of refugee dispersal policies in the UK, the Netherlands and Sweden. Finney and Robinson (2008) discuss local reactions to the policies.
[5] Browne (2002, p xii).

—

[6] www.dailymail.co.uk/pages/live/articles/news/news.html?in_article_id=449242&in_page_id=1770

[7] 'Outline of the problem', 2 January 2007, available at www.migrationwatchuk.org/outline_of_the_problem.asp

[8] MigrationWatchUK (2007b).

[9] T.D. Allen (no date) Local Government Association submission to the House of Lords Economic Affairs Select Committee Inquiry on the Economic Impact of Immigration, available at www.parliament.uk/documents/upload/EA249%20Norris.doc

[10] For example, Sivanandan (1985).

[11] Parekh (2000).

[12] Abbas (2007).

[13] Kalra and Kapoor (2008) compare these changed emphases of policy in Britain to similar changes in the US.

[14] Modood (2003, p 101).

[15] Trevor Phillips, guest lecture presented at the Manchester-Harvard Summer School, University of Manchester, 2 July 2007.

[16] Commission on Integration and Cohesion (2007, p 9).

[17] Modood (2005); Kundnani (2007a, p 29).

[18] For example, see the press report at www.dailymail.co.uk/pages/live/articles/news/news.html?in_article_id=460084&in_page_id=1770

[19] Blair (2006).

[20] Hall et al (1997).

[21] www.ccsr.ac.uk/sars/2001/indiv/variables/hnresdnt/

[22] www.statistics.gov.uk/downloads/theme_social/Social_Trends37/ST37_Ch02.pdf

[23] Hall et al (1997).

[24] www.statistics.gov.uk/downloads/theme_social/Social_Trends37/ST37_Ch02.pdf

[25] www.ccsr.ac.uk/sars/2001/indiv/variables/acctype/ gives the most recent proportions.

[26] For example, see 'Councils may be allowed to stop sales of second homes', *Daily Telegraph*, 19 May 2006, www.telegraph.co.uk/news/main.jhtml?xml=/news/2006/05/18/nhomes18.xml

[27] ONS (2005b).

[28] Generalised Land Use Database Statistics for England 2005 (2007), http://www.communities.gov.uk/publications/planningandbuilding/generalisedlanduse

[29] www.statistics.gov.uk/census2001/profiles/64.asp

[30] MigrationWatchUK's chairperson refused to provide information to the authors on the size and location of his advisory board's residences,

feeling it was not relevant. The authors live comfortably in terraced housing in Bradford and Bury.

[31] Hamnett (1991); Champion and Fielding (1992); Halfacree et al (1992); Owen and Green (1992); Brimblecombe et al (1999, 2000); Bailey and Livingstone (2005, 2006).

[32] See Massey et al (1993) for an overview of economic theories of international migration.

[33] Saleheen and Shadforth (2006).

[34] See Berthoud (2000) and Simpson et al (2006).

[35] Browne (2002, chapter 24). The report is Gott and Johnston (2002).

[36] Browne (2002, p 90).

[37] Frost (2006), a report for Manchester City Council.

[38] Data from the Department for Work and Pensions Work and Pensions Longitudinal Study, available at www.dwp.gov.uk/asd/tabtool.asp. Benefits data are for August 2006. Populations used are from National Statistics estimates for mid-2006.

[39] Platt (2007).

[40] Law et al (1994).

[41] See the Information Centre about Refugees and Asylum briefing about destitution, available at www.icar.org.uk/?lid=6575 and Refugee Council resources at www.refugeecouncil.org.uk/policy/

[42] These short-term costs were the focus of a local government inquiry including a survey reported by the Institute of Community Cohesion (2007).

[43] This is the danger that Trevor Phillips (2008) pointed to when he said that 'though there are benefits to migration, they aren't shared out equally. The problem is that though the inequality may actually be caused by a lack of public investment, it may be attributed to the presence of immigrants'.

5

Challenging the myth that 'Minorities do not want to integrate'

We have focused on the very worrying drift towards self-segregation, the necessity of arresting and reversing this process.... The Bradford District has witnessed growing division among its population along race, ethnic, religious and social class lines – and now finds itself in the grip of fear. *Sir Herman Ouseley*[1]

Introduction

This chapter addresses a fear that there is an unwillingness to integrate among minority ethnic populations. The fear is that this 'self-segregation' maintains and exacerbates geographical and social segregation and is a source of potential conflict.

As Chapter Six will show there are no ghettos in Britain, and migration patterns are not ones of retreat or flight but rather of suburbanisation and moves out of cities, which are being experienced irrespective of ethnicity. This migration is resulting in increasing numbers of areas that are ethnically mixed. Nevertheless, the fear of minority self-segregation persists and five aspects of it will be addressed in this chapter.

First, the chapter asks whether there is a trend towards more same-ethnicity friendship groups and discusses what this can tell us about desire for ethnic mixing. Second, we consider housing aspirations of people from different ethnic groups to uncover the extent to which there is unwillingness to mix residentially. Third, we consider social attitudes and particularly whether there is fear of mixing and fear of ethnic difference. Fourth, we tackle the issue of whether school choice is creating ethnic segregation.

The final aspect of the myth of self-segregation that is challenged relates specifically to one minority group, defined by religion rather than race. This is the claim that clusters of Muslim population act as a 'breeding ground' for terrorism. As we saw in Chapter One, Muslim terrorism has become one of the defining issues of British politics and social policy in the first decade of the 21st century. In the environment of a Western 'global war against terrorism' the claims are made that Muslim communities isolate themselves from the rest of society thereby protecting terrorists who threaten Britain's social fabric. We assess the extent to which residential segregation is associated with terrorism.

This chapter is not disputing the need to reduce social conflict where it exists, but seeks to challenge the identification of segregation as a cause of conflict, and inward-looking retreat by minorities as a cause of segregation.

Origins and contemporary expressions of the myth

Before we present evidence to challenge the claims of self-segregation, this section defines those claims more precisely and sets them in context by considering their origins. Concern about incomers' commitment to integration is certainly not new. It accompanies the fears of the burden of immigration and the danger of ghettos that are illustrated in other chapters. At the beginning of the 20th century when legislation was first introduced to control immigration to Britain, these fears were tackled by an assimilationist approach: it was expected that newcomers fit in with and adapt to life in Britain, with no concern for the maintenance or preservation of their customs and traditions.

The association between residential segregation and physical conflict is also well established in academic writing on race relations. In contrast to the 'contact hypothesis', which posits that understanding and tolerance develop when different social groups come into contact, the 'conflict hypothesis' suggests that contact brings clashes, sometimes violent, which emphasise the separation of groups. The geographer Frederick Boal suggested in 1976 that 'spatial concentrations of an ethnic group can provide it with a base for action in the struggle of its members with society in general. This struggle may take a peaceful political form or may become violent'.[2] He refers to the protection of Cosa Nostra criminals in American-Italian communities in US cities, as well as to insurrectionary guerrilla warfare in the Northern Ireland conflict. From the perspective of the 'host society', argues Boal, this resistance offers nothing good, only threats and dangers. Boal has repeated the view that conflict is an inevitable consequence of ethnic difference in his more recent writing: 'conflict occurs when racial and ethnic groups come into contact'. The conflict is only eliminated when differences between ethnic groups no longer exist, as in assimilation, or are eliminated, as in ethnic cleansing.[3]

As previous chapters have pointed out, for two decades at the end of the 20th century, race relations were governed by a viewpoint that valued diversity and understood integration as a process of adaptation that involved all members of society. Discrimination and disadvantage rather than cultural differences were the major source of tensions. The shift back to cultural and geographical explanations of disadvantage and conflict occurred in 2001, coinciding with 'riots' in northern English towns and the 'war on terrorism'.

The tone of official reports published at the time of the riots and later in the year talked of the communities' own responsibility for segregation.[4] Although detailed and nuanced in their study of each town, the summaries and the unchallenged media headlines that followed the reports changed the language of race relations to talk of 'self-segregation', 'parallel lives', lack of 'meaningful exchanges', 'isolationist attitudes' of community leaders, and 'cities gripped by fear'. The reports held minority ethnic communities responsible for the inner-city problems. Referring to these reports, one observer with a long record of research in housing and ethnicity concluded that '[t]he subtext of the debate about minority ethnic clustering is that self-segregating British Muslim communities are endangering the security, ordered stability, and national identity of (White) Britain'.[5] The responsibility for integration had been firmly placed with minorities and removed from the White majority.

This concern with minorities' own responsibility for segregation and for race tensions parallels government demands that poor local communities take responsibility for their social conditions, as we noted in Chapter Two. The New Labour government at the turn of the millennium has been identified with a localist philosophy that demands local partnerships to work on community cohesion, social capital and civic responsibility.[6] The combination of cultural focus and local responsibility has created government policies of community cohesion that aim to break down 'self-segregation' and 'parallel lives'. Community cohesion is an antidote and preventative to ethnic conflict and is more prominent now than concerns about social inequality.

The post-riot reports and their language were adopted politically at the highest level, such that local authorities in Britain are now required to produce strategies to increase community cohesion. That they have made such impact is in no small part a result of strong backing from Trevor Phillips, from 2003 the chair of the Commission for Racial Equality and then its broader successor the Equality and Human Rights Commission. He was also the first to make a link between so-called self-segregation and terrorism.

The reports following the riots of 2001 made no direct link with terrorism.[7] The riots preceded the September 2001 Twin Towers atrocity by several months. Only after the London bombings of July 2005 was that connection claimed, in a very high-profile intervention by Trevor Phillips. The bombings and loss of life were the starting point for his speech already referred to in this book and headlined in the days before its delivery as 'Sleepwalking to segregation'. He claimed that 'crime, no-go areas and chronic cultural conflict' were outcomes of 'marooned communities … we have allowed tolerance of diversity to harden into the effective isolation of communities'. The resulting 'fragmentation of society' was endangering key British values of respect for individuality, free speech, equality, democracy and freedom. As well as specific extreme cases such as the bombings and intolerance against criticism of specific religions, Phillips illustrated fragmentation and segregation through the geography of residence, the ethnic composition of schools and the lack of balance in friendship groups.[8] While the speech was also wide-ranging in its criticism of racism and poverty, it dismissed suggestions that integration would come through economic and political means alone. The clear message, taken up by the media and the government and repeated by Phillips in further hard-hitting interventions, was that Britain's minorities were wilfully separating and that this had led to conflict and would continue to do so if it was not reversed.

The recommendations that arise from the view that minorities are to blame for their own lack of integration vary from their education (to gain better understanding) to security surveillance of students from diverse areas. All the proposed solutions are concerned with the supposed incompatibility of the behaviours and beliefs of minority groups with the civic duties of a British citizen. Prime Minister Tony Blair in his last year of office proclaimed that integration requires defeat of racism as well as extremism, but his examples of what needed to happen to ensure integration were directed at minorities, particularly Muslims; they related to young marriages, uncontrolled religious teaching and the wearing of the veil.[9] Similar issues have been raised by other politicians: Labour minister David Blunkett appealed to Muslims to speak English not only in public but at home;[10] Jack Straw stirred a debate when he suggested in 2006 that he could better communicate with his Muslim women constituents if they did not wear the *niqab*; Lord Stevens, the former head of London's Metropolitan Police force, a Crossbench peer and an advisor to Prime Minister Gordon Brown, has vociferously demanded that 'the Muslim community in this country accept an absolute undeniable, total truth: that Islamic terrorism is their problem'.[11] The point here is not that there is debate about diverse practices but that minorities, and particularly Muslims, are singled out as having behaviours potentially undesirable for British society, and that the responsibility for ensuring that they 'fit in' lies with the minorities themselves. This thinking bears little trace of previous philosophies of equality and celebration of diversity and instead blames specific transgressions of the few on the behaviour of whole minority groups. By requiring behavioural change as the measure of integration, the 'new' approach harks back to assimilationist ideologies and societies ordered through White indigenous supremacy.

Is there an increase in same-ethnicity friendship groups?

One of the themes of the discourse of parallel lives and isolation is the lack of friendships that cross ethnic barriers. Having commissioned a survey from YouGov in 2004 and 2005, Trevor Phillips, the chair of the Commission for Racial Equality, reported in a speech that 'alarmingly, we showed that young people from ethnic minorities were twice as likely to have a circle of pals exclusively from their own community as were older ethnic minority folk.... It must surely be the most worrying fact of all that younger Britons appear to be integrating less well than their parents'.[12] Phillips' speech continued to paint a dismal picture from the YouGov surveys of friendships:

> Behaviour in white Britain has not changed a bit. Last year, 94% of white Britons said that all or most of their friends are white. This year it is 95%.... What the figures tell us about the behaviour of ethnic minority Britons is even bleaker.... This year the figures show a marked turn for the worse. The 47% of ethnic minority Britons who last year said that most or all of their friends were white has now shrunk to 37%; and the proportion who have mainly or exclusively ethnic minority friends has grown from 31% to 37%. This is way beyond any statistical fluctuation.[13]

The language used here is intemperate at least. The survey asked 816 minority ethnic Britons in 2004 and 470 in 2005 whether their friends were all or mainly White, all or mainly ethnic minorities, or roughly half White. The proportions with roughly half White friends were 23% in 2004 and 26% in 2005. If these figures are added to those in the quote above, for the majority of minority ethnic Britons in both years half or more of their friends were White. Descriptions of 'even bleaker' and 'marked turn for the worse' to describe a situation where most minority ethnic Britons have either about half or more than half White friends, is again exaggerating the evidence. What of the claim that the change in one year is 'way beyond any statistical fluctuation'? A change from 31% to 37% based on separate samples of 470 and 870 people would be considered by statisticians as only just significant. Samples of those sizes could have produced such a difference when the real population proportions had not changed at all. This is so if the survey were what statisticians call a probability sample, where everyone has a known chance of being included. But YouGov is an online survey of a self-selected panel, which is 'quota sampled' to ensure appropriate numbers at each age and sex. YouGov does not use standard sample design methods to ensure a set of people or views representative of the population.

One should be especially suspicious of the Commission for Racial Equality friendship survey results because they are contradicted by better-designed studies. Standard methods to ensure representative samples are used in the government's Citizenship Survey. It asked similar questions in both 2003 and 2005 and the results suggest that minorities born in Britain are *less* likely to have exclusively minority friends than those born outside Britain.[14] Furthermore the survey reported that:

> As might be expected, people who lived in areas with higher minority ethnic populations were more likely to have friends from different ethnic groups to themselves. Eighty-three per cent of people who lived in the ten per cent highest minority ethnic density areas had friends from different ethnic groups to themselves compared to 31 per cent from the ten per cent lowest density areas.[15]

Narrow friendship groups (in the sense of within the same ethnicity) are less likely in ethically diverse areas than in the monolithically White areas. There were no changes in composition of friendship groups between 2003 and 2005 for the White, Asian or Black groups, in spite of samples much bigger than those used by YouGov. It is debatable whether the leading servant of a public body should make a high-profile alarming media message from statistics that reflect unexceptional population change.

The Citizenship Survey report has a tone quite different from the Commission for Racial Equality speech (although both were publicly funded). The Citizenship Survey report is based on large samples and has a measured account of its important findings. An academic analysis of the same data finds similar results – that over half of the White population have friends exclusively among the White population, while less than 20% of minorities born in Britain have friends only from their own group, including the Pakistani and Bangladeshi groups that make up most of the Muslim population in Britain.

> It is in fact the Whites who are by far the most likely to have friends only from their own race – that is, other Whites. Given the much larger number of Whites in Britain, and the geographical concentration of ethnic

minorities in large conurbations, many Whites will not have opportunity to meet ethnic minorities. However, the very high proportions of the ethnic minorities who report having some friends from other races are quite striking.[16]

The 'worrying' proportion of young people with 'pals exclusively from their own community' has not been released by the Commission for Racial Equality, but is less than 20% according to that alternative analysis. How worrying is this? How worrying is the much higher figure of 56% for the White population? Perhaps neither figure is surprising given the demographics and geographies of Britain's ethnic group populations.

That 'most worrying fact of all' is put in context by some simple demographics, presented in Table 5.1. Even if there were increasingly mono-ethnic friendship groups, this may well be a result of demographic shifts rather than self-segregation. There are twice as many Black and Asian people aged in their twenties than aged in their fifties: for example 18% of England and Wales' Indian population is aged 20-29 but only 9% are aged 50-59. The Pakistani and Bangladeshi populations are still more youthful with only 5% or less aged in their fifties and more than three times this number aged in their twenties.[17] That young age structure is typical of immigrant-origin populations and demographers expect the age structure to 'settle down' only after several generations have been born in Britain. The youthfulness is greatest for the African and Bangladeshi groups who immigrated to Britain most recently and less pronounced for the Indian and Caribbean groups, with Pakistani youthfulness somewhere between. But all have much younger populations than the White British where the number of older and younger people is approximately in balance.

A potential consequence of these differing age structures for friendship patterns is that older pioneer immigrants could have been

Table 5.1: Percentage of the population in their twenties, thirties, forties and fifties

Age range	White Briton	Indian	Pakistani	Bangladeshi	Caribbean	African	Chinese
20-29	12	18	20	21	12	18	23
30-39	15	17	14	13	23	24	17
40-49	13	15	10	8	15	13	16
50-59	13	9	5	4	8	5	8

Source: 2001 Census, table ST101

exposed to more White friends and neighbours than their children and grandchildren. Young Black and Asian adults may speak with a Yorkshire, Midlands or London accent that their elders never acquired, but their family and neighbourhood environment from which friends are drawn is more populated by their own ethnic group than was the case for their elders. In this context, the reliable findings of the Citizenship Survey, of increased ethnic mixing in friendship groups of minorities born in Britain, are an even greater challenge to the claim of self-segregation.

In addition to survey results and demographic changes, there is one vivid indicator of how Britain is increasingly becoming a place of friendship across ethnic groups: the growth of the Mixed ethnic group. Someone of Mixed ethnicity has parents of different ethnicities from each other. The size and growth of the Mixed group therefore indicates the most intimate form of friendship. There are 650,000 people of Mixed ethnic group in England alone, making it the third largest minority after Indian and Pakistani groups. It is one of the fastest-growing ethnic groups.[18] Similarly, there is growth in marriage between people of different ethnic groups. Asian Muslims, Sikhs and Hindus all marry out of their own groups just as often as do White Christians.[19]

The claim that friendship groups are increasingly within rather than across ethnic groups is therefore highly questionable. Through a judicious compound of alarmist language and false claim to scientific rigour, the Commission for Racial Equality created a striking message about friendship groups, unsupported by the evidence, of dangerous inward-looking communities, harbingers of a bleak future for Britain.

Is there desire for residential segregation?

The kindest claims of isolationism paint a picture of minorities feeling content but in fact marooned in separated residential areas, unaware of the detrimental consequences for themselves and for integration. We will see in Chapter Six that the separateness of minorities is overstated. Minority ethnic residents in Britain are far more likely to live in diverse areas than are White residents. For each minority ethnic group there is dispersal from areas where immigrants have settled. Might there be barriers limiting dispersal, and might those barriers include an inward-looking complacent attitude of self-sufficiency? Statistics of migration cannot help much, first because there is no norm to suggest when dispersal has reached a supposedly satisfactory level, and second because these data do not tell us about the aspirations of migrants or non-migrants.

Instead, we can learn directly from young people from minority ethnic groups about their aspirations. There have been several qualitative studies that investigate housing preferences in northern towns including Bradford and Oldham, two of the towns directly affected by disturbances in 2001 and caricatured as segregated cities.[20] From the reports of these studies we can understand the attitudes of young minorities to racially mixed areas, and the nature of the barriers to movement.

A cross-cultural study in Oldham and Rochdale concluded that:

> The housing aspirations and expectations of White and Asian young people are remarkably similar. High priority is placed on safe neighbourhoods with a good environment, an absence of anti-social behaviour and proximity to other family members and friends. General concerns about anti-social behaviour and the desire for neighbourly communities were not expressed in racial terms.[21]

Better housing, a safe environment and a lack of anti-social behaviour are all prized by minority and White young people alike. Similarly, escape from the claustrophobia of the family home was expressed by young people from different groups. For young Asians in Bradford,

> This expansion is not simply a response to population growth or the search for better housing (although this was part of the incentive for movement), it is also symbolically important, especially for some younger women. The newly acquired spaces enable them to occupy a social, cultural, and spatial position on the margins of the community, which affords some freedom from perceived social strictures and conventions. Family links, interdependencies, and obligations nevertheless generally translated into an expressed desire to move 'not too far' away from the family home.[22]

For older Asians, the comfort of remaining within familiar neighbourhoods with familiar institutions, shops and acquaintances all within walking distance was more important than for the young Asians interviewed. For them, mixed areas were the expected and desired outcome. A young Pakistani woman in Rochdale expressed advantages of mixed areas and warned against the isolation of the most Asian areas, recognising that 'your life's a lot more richer because you obviously learn things that you just wouldn't in predominantly Asian areas', while a Pakistani man in Oldham felt the interviewer wrongly suggested he might not be capable of living in a White area: 'We don't have a problem moving into a White area, we can speak the language'.

Nonetheless, movement away from clusters of Asian population is constrained. One young Asian man in Bradford indicated that the constraints are partly economic but also intimated that he would not wish to be the first Asian in a White area: 'They [Pakistanis] will probably not move to a strictly white area. As you earn more you want to move into better area, but will always look for an ethnic or Asian mix'.[23] The experience of hostility in areas that are mainly White is not pervasive, but has been relatively common in the experience of those interviewed in Britain, or their families, to the extent that they do not wish to be the first to move into a new area. A young Pakistani woman in Rochdale said: '[i]f it means that you have to compromise on getting abused and having all these problems ... we won't touch that', and an elderly man in Bradford was thankful for the safety of Manningham in inner Bradford: 'Everything is here, our culture, our shops, mosque ... and the best thing about this area: no racism'. Two comments should be made about abusive behaviour. First that the nature of the abuse reported by Asians in White areas includes broken windows, faeces through the letterbox, vandalised property and sustained verbal attacks, all of which are recognised as unlawful, and are quite different from cultural shyness or disinterest, which are described as hurtful in focus groups but are not perceived as barriers to movement. Second, although not on the same scale, there is undoubtedly hostility towards White people in some predominantly Asian areas.

Another clear barrier is income. As one might expect, families and individuals with higher incomes are a lot more likely to move from inner urban housing than those on lower incomes. In fact, the slowly decreasing ethnic segregation that we shall see in the next chapter is in the opposite direction to the slowly increasing segregation between areas on lines of income, education, health and employment.[24] Lack of income is a barrier to ethnically mixed suburbs because it keeps people from moving out of cheaper housing. But such movement when it does happen may just leave the most vulnerable behind. It is arguable whether faster de-segregation is the right thing to promote if it exacerbates the poverty of the neighbourhood left behind.[25]

Structures of the housing market may also create barriers to ethnically mixed neighbourhoods. Procedures of housing authorities and estate agents, together with perceptions of place in terms of ethnicity, can result in different ethnic groups being steered towards or placed in housing in particular neighbourhoods.[26]

Nonetheless, demographic pressures and young minorities' own aspirations are pushing for further ethnic diversity on the edges of existing minority concentrations, and new clusters further from them. As these suburban White areas are the very neighbourhoods where xenophobic political parties target their activity, playing on fears of cultural difference and competition, these are the areas where effective support for new tenants and residents is needed regardless of ethnicity. Lack of affordable housing, poor environments and anti-social behaviour are the factors that limit spatial integration, not the willingness of young minorities to move to new independent spaces.

Are cities 'gripped by fear'?

Opinion surveys have become common, and some have a long history that can track changes in attitudes over time. If cities were increasingly gripped by the fear of ethnic tensions then a significant level and increase of mistrust would show up in these surveys, which we review in this section.

The British Social Attitudes survey has been conducted annually since 1983 with a standard probability sample. A careful study of that survey has noted that more than one author finds a reduction in self-rated prejudice over time, but warns that individuals tend to rate their own prejudice in relation to that of their peers, making it difficult to compare different generations' attitudes. This study instead measures social distance of White respondents to minorities by the question 'Would you mind or not mind if a suitably qualified person of Black or West Indian/Asian origin were appointed as your boss?'. A similar question asks whether the White respondent 'would mind or not mind if one of your close relatives were to marry a person of Black or West Indian/Asian origin?'. Offensive though these questions might be to readers of Black or West Indian/Asian origin, they measure White prejudice fairly well over a period of 13 years from the early 1980s to the late 1990s. The results suggest that younger generations were more tolerant, and also that the more tolerant groups, which tended to be those most educated, grew in size. There was also growing general tolerance during the period, additional to the influence of generation and social groups. White people have become more accepting of minorities having higher social status than them and of racial intermarriage. Thus, the attitude towards diversity has become more tolerant and although the events and debates of the 2000s could wind back that tolerance, 'the shift would need to be large and lasting in order to offset the continuing liberalizing effects of generational replacement'.[27]

Barometers of social attitudes also suggest that opinion in Britain is more tolerant than in many other countries of Europe. Although a quarter of UK residents wished to 'live in an area where almost nobody is of a different race, colour or ethnic group from most people living in this country', this is similar to the 22% in Germany and considerably lower than the values for Greece (44%), Ireland (34%) and the Netherlands (32%).[28] Survey results show that minorities in Britain do not feel that retaining their own cultural way of life is at odds with adopting White lifestyles: 80% felt their culture should be preserved but a third also felt that White lifestyles should be adopted.[29]

The 2005 Pew Global Attitudes Survey found a tolerant view of wearing headscarves. Twenty-nine per cent of respondents in Britain thought that 'banning the wearing of headscarves by Muslim women in public places' is a good idea, far fewer than in France (78%) and lower than all other countries polled in Europe, as well as Canada and the US, and in fact not much more than the 17% in Pakistan.[30] The same survey found fewest in Britain with an unfavourable view of Muslims out of all countries of Europe (14% in Britain compared to 45% in Germany). A majority in Britain as in other European countries felt that Muslims in their country felt a strong sense of Islamic identity. In Britain relatively few felt that this led to conflict although more felt that it impeded integration.

Wide-ranging analyses of European Social Survey data on Muslim communities in Europe find that the analyses 'support a socio-liberal view of "migration" and "integration" ... and contradict the very extended current alarmist political discourse in Western Europe'. Muslims in Europe are willing to engage with the Western democratic and secular structures.[31] Indeed, a Muslims in Europe study found that 98% of Bangladeshis in London compared with around 75% of Moroccans in Madrid and Turkish in Berlin feel at home in their country.[32]

If there is a positive desire for integration among ethnic minorities, concern may be switched to some extent to the White heartlands where both intolerance and fears of changing Britain are greatest, as has been shown in the districts affected by riots in 2001. Fifteen-year-old Asian Muslim pupils in both mixed and mainly Muslim schools in Blackburn and Burnley were found to be more tolerant than their White peers, especially those in all-White schools. Four in ten Asians were interested in learning about religions other than Muslim, compared to one in ten of their White counterparts being interested in learning about religions other than Christianity.[33] In Oldham, the social networks of minorities are more diverse than of their White counterparts.[34] Adults were progressively more optimistic 'that people from different ethnic backgrounds could get on well together' the younger they were, ranging from 82% of those aged under 25 to 52% of those aged 75 and older, and the proportions had increased between 2003 and 2005. A similar opinion survey in Bradford found that one quarter of respondents (representative of the district by age, sex and ethnic group) felt that residents from different backgrounds were antagonistic in Bradford as a whole, but only 3% felt that that was the case in their own neighbourhood, a case of the grass being greener at home. The top changes hoped for by respondents in Bradford, who were 80% White matching the district's adult diversity, were first, 'a rejuvenated city centre with quality shops' and second, 'racial harmony and integration'.[35] In the areas of the worst violence in the 2001 riots there is more optimism and willingness to engage than many pundits lead us to expect.

Is school choice creating segregation?

One of the strongest assumptions in British race relations is that school segregation is high and increasing, and that where there is a choice of school then parents will choose on the basis of ethnicity and by so doing create mono-ethnic schools. Rarely is any evidence used to discuss the claim. There are two claims mixed in here. First that some schools have a very different ethnic mix than others, and second that parental choice divides schools by ethnicity even when their neighbourhoods are mixed.

The first claim is undisputed: some schools do have a very different mix than others. Of Bradford's 24 secondary schools, 10 have either more than 90% or less than 10% White pupils. The same can be said of most other metropolitan districts, simply because the White population makes up the vast majority of the population. It is also simply a reflection of the clustered patterns of residence, which are discussed in the next chapter and are largely a result of a sequence of labour shortages, immigration, natural growth and suburbanisation. This type of unremarkable 'school segregation', measured by very varied ethnic composition of schools, was evident again when the government published statistics of pupil ethnicity in May 2007. Nonetheless, those statistics and no others were the basis of front-page headlines with an interpretation far beyond this simple picture. The main story in *The Observer* headlined 'Revealed: UK schools dividing on race lines' declared that 'A majority of pupils in many areas of the country ... have little contact with children from different ethnic backgrounds, even though they live in close proximity'. But the statistics had given no information at all on living patterns, and therefore no evidence to support that key phrase 'even though they live in close proximity'. There was no evidence in the government or journalist's reports from which to draw the conclusion that schools were any more 'divided' than neighbourhoods. Rather, the piece was an opportunity for the Conservative Party to announce a new policy:

> David Willets, the shadow education secretary, told *The Observer*: 'There are towns which have been divided into two where social, ethnic and religious divisions are all aligned and create enormous tensions. Schools in these towns are becoming more and more segregated. One way to tackle them is, if you're creating an academy, you set a target that it should take its students from both communities'.[36]

Thus, the claim that schools are divided more than their neighbourhoods has such momentum that it can be front-page news, hooked on evidence that does not support it, in order to trumpet a new policy platform for a political party. *The Observer* subtitles its front page with 'A remarkable picture of how Britain is "sleepwalking" towards US-style segregation', and adds comments about 'increased racial tensions' created by segregation, in order to emphasise its message.[37] The article gives no evidence at all that schools 'are becoming more and more segregated', or that 'schools are dividing on race lines' but these claims are the headline news. It would be surprising if schools were becoming more segregated, since (as we will see in the next chapter) neighbourhoods are becoming less segregated and more diverse. Nonetheless, in January 2008 the head of the Equality and

Human Rights Commission went a little further by claiming that 'We all know that schools are becoming more segregated than the areas they sit in'.[38] So now we turn to ask, what do we know?

School social segregation has been studied most recently through the national database of school pupils in England, which contains each young person's ethnicity, home address and school. One can use the database to compare actual school ethnic diversity over time, and to compare it with the outcome if every pupil went to their nearest school.

If one measures the average proportion of an ethnic group in the schools where it is found, then it has been increasing slightly for those groups whose share of the population has been increasing. But the evidence is clear that for primary and secondary schools in England over the period 1997/98 to 2003, 'there has been some increase in segregation levels in some cities, but only to the expected extent given the changing relative size of the ethnic minority populations there'.[39] Does this lay to rest the claim that 'schools are becoming more segregated than the areas they sit in'? It certainly suggests that the difference between schools and their neighbourhoods has not been increasing, but is there a difference at all?

School sorting by income and ethnicity does occur, and this is not surprising. Some families choose schools that are not nearest to their homes, and are schools that have a greater proportion of their own ethnic group.[40] The Department for Children, Schools and Families has published a comparison of how pupils from families on a low income are spread between schools. Using the home addresses of all pupils in state schools in England, it allocates them to their closest school, keeping the same number of schools and their same capacity. There is a considerable degree of segregation even when children are allocated to their closest school, because Britain is socially segregated, especially through the housing market. The government report then finds that schools and parents have managed to sort themselves by income even more than in their 'natural' catchment areas, raising their 'index of dissimilarity' by 0.06, or 18%. This demonstrates that school choice tends to create a lower diversity of income within school populations than if pupils went to their nearest school. The report shows that sorting also occurs by ethnicity, creating more school concentrations of minority pupils than in neighbourhoods, but the increase in sorting by ethnicity is less than the increase in sorting by income: it varies for each ethnic group but in no case is it more than 0.03, or 5%, half the additional sorting by income.[41] Thus, there is definitely selection of schools that increases the concentrations of White and minority pupils, but it is less than the social selection by income. It may be that the two types of school selection are confounded: because income (or class) and ethnicity are correlated, when pupils bypass their local school one cannot distinguish whether it is their ethnicity or their income that is associated with that behaviour.

If school choice is leading to less heterogeneous, less mixed schools than is thought to be desirable, it is important to consider how that system of choice operates. Research by the Runnymede Trust has asked exactly this question, revealing the complexities of school choice decision making and the discrepancies between choice and outcome.[42] Ability to negotiate the school system is not equal across social groups: groups that are socioeconomically disadvantaged – among which ethnic minorities are disproportionately represented – have less capacity to achieve the school place that they most desire. What was clear in this research was that there were overall preferences among minority ethnic parents for their children to attend ethnically mixed schools. As the following Pakistani parent comments, mixed schools were seen as important both in terms of providing a context for education about ethnic diversity and having a smaller risk of racial bullying: 'I believe mixed multicultural schools are very good because children learn about different cultures and interact with children [from] a variety of ethnic backgrounds'.

Other authors have also stressed the importance of not assuming racial explanations for school sorting:

> It should not be concluded that ethnic groups actively avoid each other. A preference to be schooled with children of the same ethnicity (if that is what we are observing) is not, in itself, a process of avoidance but of seeking ethnic peers, or of seeking a particular type of education in particular types of school.[43]

Schooling of our children is of prime and personal importance. Many schools have an entirely White roll, but schools in urban areas often have a diverse roll and some have very few White pupils. There is evidence that pupils and parents choose schools in a way that increases the concentrations of White pupils in some schools and minority pupils in other schools, and possibly of particular minorities. But this ethnic sorting is less than the sorting by family income and both may be a symptom of greater effective choice by those with more resources. The system of school choice does not operate equally across social groups and arguably prevents schools from meeting their responsibilities for promoting good race relations and community cohesion. For those who favour community schools drawing all children from the same locality, then a range of school ethnic compositions is a consequence and need not be a concern. For those who feel that ethnic mixes at school must be engineered as a positive policy for integration, then a very great amount of bussing would be involved with potentially detrimental effects. For those who accept the current system of market choice in schooling, social selection by income and ethnicity are an expected consequence.

Does segregation breed terrorism?

In launching the Labour Party's 2006 debate on community cohesion, Baroness Valerie Amos lamented 'Suicide bombers with broad Yorkshire accents' and continued: 'Our challenge is to engage with and encourage the debate within the Muslim community'.[44] She clearly signalled that the community cohesion agenda extends into national security, accepting that 'of course, in part, it is about our foreign policy'. Baroness Amos has been a Labour minister of government and in 2006 was the Leader of the House of Lords. In linking the 'fragmentation and differences emerging within and between our communities' to indiscriminate taking of innocent lives, her agenda is given an urgency that is hard to ignore. In fact, the lethal link she made had been made repeatedly by others since the London bombings the previous July. 'The disastrous doctrine of multiculturalism ... has promoted a lethally divisive culture of separateness, in which minority cultures are held to be equal if not superior to the values and traditions of the indigenous majority'[45] and 'The real suicide bomb is "multiculturalism"'[46] has been a common view among the commentators, although others, including London's mayor until 2008 and its chief of police, refused to blame terrorism on either religion or diversity policies.

The claim that neighbourhood concentrations of Muslims encourage and indeed 'breed' terrorism, at the very least by harbouring potential terrorists, was made clearly by Trevor Phillips in his speech quoted earlier in this chapter. Security advice also suggests that 'extreme violence in the name of Islam' is more likely to be adopted by Muslims who live, study and socialise with other Muslims in isolation from the mainstream.[47] In February 2008 it was reported that a new counter-terrorism strategy produced by the Association of Chief Police Officers involved mapping every area of the country 'for its potential to produce extremists and supporters for al-Qaida'.[48] Neighbourhood profiling is central to these procedures to prevent terrorist recruitment. If it were true that neighbourhoods with Muslim concentrations breed terrorists then one would expect the proportion of Muslims charged with terrorism to be higher in areas where there are many Muslims than areas where there are not.

It is this claim that we have examined in Table 5.2. Records including the place of last residence of each person charged with terrorism are kept by the Crown Prosecution Service (CPS) but are not available for confidentiality reasons, and were too extensive on paper records for the CPS itself to collate.[49] Instead, we have identified the persons charged with terrorism as reported in *The Guardian* and BBC online archives for the two years between August 2004 and October 2006. Seventy-five were also identifiable as of Muslim origin by their name, with a place of residence stated closely enough to place in a local district. The table divides all the districts in England and Wales according to their concentration of Muslims, such that a quarter of Muslims live in each group of districts.

If 'segregated areas', where there are the largest concentrations of Muslims, were hotbeds of terrorism, especially if this is where security services sought them most, then one would expect more to be charged in these areas. Seventeen of those charged in the period August 2004 to October 2006 were residents of Bradford, Luton, Newham or Wandsworth, four of the seven most Muslim districts where 18% of the population is Muslim. But just as many lived in other areas; for example, 16 lived in the districts with on average only 1% Muslims, coming from Breckland in Norfolk, Doncaster, Bournemouth, Reigate in Surrey, Bexley, Brighton and Hove, Aylesbury Vale and Greenwich. The only set of districts where

Table 5.2: Proportion of Muslims charged with terrorism according to local concentration of Muslims

District type	Number of local authority districts	Muslim population	Concentration of Muslims (% of local population)	Number of Muslims charged with terrorism
Lowest concentrations of Muslims	325	391,344	1%	16
Low concentrations of Muslims	30	381,933	6%	26
High concentrations of Muslims	14	356,025	11%	16
Highest concentrations of Muslims	7	432,418	18%	17

Source: Census 2001 and media reports (see text)

more Muslims were charged than others was those with the second-lowest concentrations, including Crawley, Lambeth, Wycombe and Manchester. So, Muslims living in highest concentration Muslim areas are not more likely to be terrorists than Muslims living in any other type of area. There is no reason to link particular levels of concentration with terrorism.[50]

The overall message is clear – that concentrations of Muslims are not after all associated with terrorism. Indeed, following the news reports many of those charged with terrorism in Britain give the impression of well-educated, integrated individuals, whose friends and associates are shocked to hear of their activities. It is neither segregation nor neighbourly sympathy from segregated neighbourhoods that produces or characterises someone committed to acts of terrorism.

Conclusion

This chapter has addressed claims that minorities are unwilling to engage with the mainstream of British society, that self-segregation is the cause of separation, discord and conflict. Unwillingness to engage leads to parallel lives and physical segregation, it is said, and physical segregation leads not only to further disengagement but also to conflict and violence.

If one turns 'unwillingness to engage with others' on its head and talks of positive engagement with those like ourselves, then undoubtedly we all enjoy the comfort zones of family, friends and the neighbourhoods we know best. That social networks are mostly with our own social and ethnic groups is not surprising. On the contrary, it is surprising that it is not more so than we have found to be the case. The majority of minority residents have half or more of their friends from other groups, and this is a far higher proportion than for White residents. White and Asian young adults living in northern cities share similar housing aspirations: better environments, well-built housing, not too far from family and friends and free from anti-social behaviour. Asian young women in particular want their children to grow up in mixed areas, and the migration statistics show this is exactly what they do: seek houses in the suburbs. School ethnic composition is a little more polarised than residential polarisation, but the difference is not more than one would expect from social selection by income, and is not growing over time. Muslims are no more likely to be terrorists in Muslim areas than in other areas. Other research shows that Muslim political engagement with the British electoral system is greater than White engagement, and greater still in areas of

Asian concentration.[51] All this says that minority residents by and large are perfectly willing to integrate and do engage. Although diversity and conflict are associated in political and academic literature, the evidence of a causal link is hard to find in practice.

Opinion polls would suggest that rather than minorities having a problem with engagement it is the majority White populations that are most isolated and least engaged with communities other than their own. However at odds with the ruling myths of minority isolation and self-segregation, at one level this is an overwhelmingly self-evident observation: as it is by far the largest group, the White population will be naturally more likely to bump into its own than the smaller groups who tend to live in much more diverse areas. But there is a more worrying level to the isolation of the White population. It is they who on average are less tolerant, more suspicious and less willing to engage with the diversity of democratic Britain as it is emerging after 60 years of state-sponsored and worldwide international migration. An assimilationist agenda placing responsibility for integration exclusively on the shoulders of minorities is clearly not a viable option.

Notes
[1] Ouseley (2001), Foreword. The report was prepared before the riots in Bradford but published days after them.
[2] Boal (1976, p 49).
[3] Boal (1999). The quote is from p 587.
[4] Cantle (2001); Denham (2001); Ouseley (2001). The reports and theories of integration have been further discussed in Chapter One.
[5] Phillips, D. (2006, p 29).
[6] Amin (2005).
[7] Cantle (2001); Denham (2001); Ouseley (2001).
[8] Phillips (2005).
[9] Blair (2006)
[10] *The Observer*, 15 September 2002.
[11] 'The Stevens Plan: if you're a Muslim – it's your problem', *News of the World*, 13 August, 2006.
[12] Phillips (2005).
[13] Phillips (2005).
[14] Heath and Li (2007, p 22).
[15] Kitchen et al (2006, p 20).
[16] Heath and Li (2007, p 22).
[17] The figures are for 2001, from Census data.
[18] ONS statistics for England, 2001-05, from www.statistics.gov.uk/downloads/theme_population/PEEGCommentary.pdf

[19] Census 2001 in Voas (2008).

[20] In particular, Harrison et al (2005), Phillips, D. (2006), Alam (2007), Simpson et al (2007) and Phillips et al (2008).

[21] Simpson et al (2007, p 4). Quotes from Oldham and Rochdale are taken from this report.

[22] Phillips, D. (2006, p 35). Quotes from Bradford are taken from this article unless otherwise attributed.

[23] All quotes in this paragraph are from Phillips, D. (2006).

[24] Dorling and Rees (2003) show social segregation over four censuses (1971-2001).

[25] For general discussion of housing market polarisation and residualisation, see Burrows (1999) and Lee and Murie (1999).

[26] See Phillips (1998, 2006).

[27] Ford (2008a, 2008b).

[28] European Social Survey, 2002/03.

[29] From the EMPIRIC study, see Sproston and Nazroo (2002).

[30] Pew Global Attitudes Project 2005, http://pewglobal.org/reports/display.php?ReportID=248

[31] Tausch et al (2006, p 2).

[32] European Social Survey, 2002/03.

[33] Lancaster University's report to the Home Office based on schools in Blackburn and Burnley, reported in *The Guardian*, 21 October 2006.

[34] Community relations in Oldham 2005, findings from the 'You and your community' survey, Oldham Metropolitan Borough Council, 2006.

[35] Results from the Community Cohesion questions in 'Speak out!' surveys, City of Bradford Metropolitan District Council, 2003. See www.bradfordinfo.com/CroosCutting/datasets.cfm

[36] Watt (2007).

[37] *The Observer* article draws on research by Simon Burgess and Deborah Wilson at the Centre for Market and Public Organisation (CMPO), University of Bristol.

[38] Trevor Phillips, *Today* programme, BBC Radio 4, 14 January 2008.

[39] Johnston et al (2006, p 1).

[40] Harris and Johnston (2008).

[41] DCSF (2008, table 6.3 on ethnicity, for example showing an increased segregation for Bangladeshi pupils from 0.73 to 0.76 in school attended), and personal communication from DCSF, 2 August 2008 ('The Attended school D index for FSM pupils is 0.39 compared to the allocated school D index of 0.33. The difference between the two is bigger than that observed for the ethnic groups in table 6.3').

[42] Weekes-Bernard (2007).

[43] Harris and Johnston (2008, p 82).

[44] Baroness Valerie Amos, Labour Party Conference, 26 September 2006.

[45] Melanie Phillips, *Daily Mail*, 14 July 2005.

[46] Mark Steyn, *Daily Telegraph*, 19 July 2005.

[46] For example, *Promoting good campus relations, fostering shared values and preventing violent extremism in universities and higher education colleges* (DIUS, 2008), which has provoked criticism among staff who felt that they were being asked to spy on students.

[48] Dodd (2008).

[49] In response to a Freedom of Information request by the authors.

[50] This is confirmed by a chi-squared test: there is no statistical association between concentration of Muslims and charges of terrorism.

[51] Fieldhouse and Cutts (2008).

6

Challenging the myth that 'Britain is becoming a country of ghettos'

Some districts are on their way to becoming fully fledged ghettoes ... *Trevor Phillips, Commission for Racial Equality*[1]

Some districts are on their way to becoming fully fledged ghettoes – black holes into which no-one goes without fear and trepidation, and from which no-one ever escapes undamaged. The walls are going up around many of our communities, and the bridges ... are crumbling.

The aftermath of 7/7 forces us to assess where we are. And here is where I think we are: we are sleepwalking our way to segregation. We are becoming strangers to each other, and we are leaving communities to be marooned outside the mainstream.... These marooned communities will steadily drift away from the rest of us, evolving their own lifestyles, playing by their own rules and increasingly regarding the codes of behaviour, loyalty and respect that the rest of us take for granted as outdated behaviour that no longer applies to them. We know what follows then: crime, no-go areas and chronic cultural conflict. *Trevor Phillips, Commission for Racial Equality*[1]

Introduction

This chilling evaluation from Trevor Phillips in 2005, then the head of Britain's government race relations body, instils a sense of fear about the nature of minority ethnic residential concentrations, 'marooned outside the mainstream'. His comments made international headlines when they were released ahead of their delivery at a speech to the Manchester Council for Community Relations, and stoked debate about segregation and diversity. The debate had begun in 2001 when reports into riots in northern English cities talked of 'self-segregated' cities 'gripped by fear', and pointed to isolation and competition between ethnic communities, so segregated that an Asian interviewee 'would not see another white face until I see you again next week'.[2] The result of those reports was a government focus on 'community cohesion' to bridge what were seen as gulfs between communities. Phillips gave a national security edge to government policies by blaming segregation not only for social disadvantage but also for violence and terrorism in the reference to the 7 July 2005 bombings in London. The desire or otherwise for ethnic diversity and the claimed link between segregation and terrorism were examined in Chapter Five. Residential segregation is the subject of this chapter.

Since 2001, residential concentrations of minority population have often been labelled in the media as problematic, dangerous areas in the way that Trevor Phillips outlined, a product of flight of White residents from areas that have become alien to them after disproportionate minority in-migration. The evidence for White flight and minority retreat is often no more than the changing composition of many urban local authorities. For example, when the head of policy at the Commission for Racial Equality claimed that '[w]e are also living in a society that is becoming more [residentially] segregated by ethnic group' the evidence given was that '[t]he census shows us that 80 local authority areas saw both a decrease in white population and an increase in the ethnic minority population between 1991 and 2001'.[3] Similarly for MigrationWatchUK, which adds immigration to the picture: 'A comparison of the censuses of 1991 and 2001 shows a clear pattern of decline in the white population of the more highly ethnic local authorities in the metropolitan areas of Greater Manchester, West Midlands and West Yorkshire, ... accompanied by a rapid increase in the Pakistani population.... A major factor is the high rate of marriage to partners on the Indian sub-continent'.[4] In its final report in 2004, the government's Community Cohesion Panel was also convinced that residential segregation is a major problem: 'we recommend that a suite of policies be developed in response to segregated neighbourhoods to try to ensure that the choice of a mixed environment is seen as both desirable and attainable'.[5]

This chapter shows that residential clustering is a result of neither White flight nor minority retreat, but much more benign demographic change, mostly non-racial in character. We ask, what is residential segregation and how does it come about? Is it bad? To what extent does White flight exist? Is segregation so accentuated in some areas in Britain that one may fairly name them ghettos? Does segregation lead to isolation and poverty?

Origins and assumptions of the myth

In the period between the 1920s and the 1960s, amid extensive migration from Europe to the US, the Chicago School of Sociology promoted a theory in which initial spatial concentration of immigrants within inner-city areas gives way to dispersal to the suburbs and eventual assimilation into the host society. Enclaves of Dutch, French or Swedish workers and businesses may be a temporary staging point on the way, but according to this view 'social relations are ... inevitably correlated with spatial relations'[6] and the more dispersed an immigrant-origin community the more assimilated it was. The long-term persistence of clusters of descendants of immigrants indicated a social problem. In particular, the stark social disadvantage of the Black population, most of whom lived in areas where there were very few White residents, made residential segregation an emblem for inequality: end segregation and equal rights would have been achieved. A more politically conservative approach comes to the same conclusion that ethnic composition of neighbourhoods should be the target of policy, because 'conflict occurs when racial groups come into contact with each other' and 'too much ethnic heterogeneity will be disruptive of social relations'.[7] Complete mixing or assimilation of ethnic differences, so the theory goes, is the only way to gain peace, if complete separation is not an option. Thus, the idea that segregation is at least an indicator if not a cause of conflict gained widespread support.

However, it is also reasonable to distinguish 'good' segregation, which is on the whole voluntary, and 'bad' segregation, which is forced by the negative attitudes, behaviour and laws of the majority. Segregation should not then be seen as a problem in itself. Thomas Pettigrew suggested that 'the long term democratic goal is the transformation of these ghettos from today's racial prisons to tomorrow's ethnic areas of choice'.[8] Evidence from many countries supports the positive role of the solidarity of clusters of population both for minorities to achieve integration and for settled communities to maintain cultural practices whether mainstream or not.[9] Small preferences for sharing a neighbourhood with at least some of one's own ethnicity could account for significant degrees of ethnic clustering.[10]

So, residential segregation can mean different things to different people. A neighbourhood housing a mix of ethnic backgrounds that are not found in other neighbourhoods can be one person's damaging segregation and another person's cosmopolitan diversity. One will condemn the insularity of the minority for not moving fast enough away from its area of settlement, while the other will highlight the insularity of middle-class White rural neighbourhoods.

In Britain in the 1970s, residential mixing was encouraged by the dispersal of black tenants in Birmingham and the bussing of Asian pupils to achieve mixed schools in Bradford. Following the 1968 and 1976 Race Relations Acts, two decades of policy followed a more anti-racist ethos and those policies of dispersal were declared illegal, the institutional assumption being that immigrant families and their children's families were best left where they wished to be, while equal access to services and employment and housing markets could be tackled directly through legislation and training. Segregation received scant attention in government reports on housing strategy and neighbourhood policy through the 1990s up until 2001, as traced in Chapter Five whose arguments we summarise here. The same turning from segregation as a policy issue occurred in the US after the 1964 Civil Rights Act, only a little earlier than in Britain.[11]

Segregation became a policy issue again in Britain following disturbances in Bradford, Burnley and Oldham in 2001, in which mainly young Pakistani men battled with police. In each case the disturbances followed provocative actions by far-right political groups. One could say that the disturbances were a response to the failure of legislation either to curb racism or to reduce the racial disadvantage felt by the generation of young Asians born and educated in Britain with aspirations as British citizens but with far lower achievements in the labour and housing markets than their White peers.[12] Rather than identify the inequalities – including wealth inequalities – and injustices as a contributory factor both to the tensions and to settlement patterns, the reports to government, as we have seen at the start of this chapter and in previous chapters, highlighted ethnic differences and the settlement patterns themselves as reasons for fear, separation and ultimately the violent disturbances. The celebration of diversity under the multicultural banner almost immediately became suspect. Those worried about cultural differences sought 'a different kind of multiculturalism', culminating in 2007 in advice from the government's Commission on Integration and Cohesion to give no public funds for community facilities restricted by faith or culture.[13]

Greater ethnic diversity may have been created by immigration, but it is sustained in settled communities. These are now suspected not only of isolating themselves in ghettos, but of changing the nature of British city neighbourhoods too fast, causing 'indigenous' White families to flee to a more comfortable environment. There is thus a formidable array of academic and political thought that fears segregation and sees it not as a result of inequality and injustice but as the result of a lack of cohesion and the cause of disadvantage. As we shall see, the evidence supports neither isolation nor flight, but the evidence is a minor inconvenience to political will with the bit between its teeth to pursue community cohesion.[14] Before we can examine this evidence to assess the claims of increasing segregation and the development of ghettos, we need to define more closely what these terms refer to.

What is a ghetto?

Historically, ghettos were areas in which Jewish communities were walled and legally restricted, first in Venice, later in other parts of Europe[15] and infamously in cities controlled by the Nazis before deportation of ghetto residents to concentration camps. In the Jewish ghetto at the end of the 19th century in Whitechapel, East London, almost 100% of the population were Jews of East European origin. This settlement was very small and has had no parallel since then.[16]

A ghetto in more recent times refers to a considerable area of many streets in which one ethnic group forms 90-100% of the population. Ghettos have variously been identified on the basis of religion, such as the original Jewish ghettos, or the Protestant–Catholic segregation in Northern Ireland and Scotland,[17] and on the basis of race, such as the African American settlements in many US cities. The word ghetto is now also used figuratively, for urban areas of poverty, or for any place where a certain type of person is supposed to be found particularly often, as in 'student ghetto' or 'pensioner ghetto'. In this chapter we are talking of areas with an unusually high proportion of a particular ethnic group (more akin to racial than religious ghettos), and we include a wider discussion of the uneven spread of populations. If we were looking only for ghettos the chapter would be very short.

Geographers and sociologists have devised many measures of racial separation. The proportion of a minority ethnic group in an area needs to be high if it is to be identified as segregated. It is fair to ask, what degree of concentration constitutes a high proportion? If we draw a boundary around each house and call it an area, then clearly there are many 'ghettos' each with one family in them, while if we draw boundaries around whole cities none may be a ghetto. It makes sense to look at the local proportion of each group at a variety of spatial scales. The local proportion of a group, as experienced on average by its members, is the first of the measures used in this chapter, referred to as the 'Index of Isolation' because the higher its values the more likely are the group's members to meet only each other locally.

The research used by Trevor Phillips defined a ghetto as follows: an area or collection of areas within a city in which the White population is less than 30% and in which one minority is twice the size of the next largest, and in which live at least 30% of all that minority's residents in the city. The definition is part of a classification of areas that ranges from White citadels through minority enclaves before reaching ghettos. It has been devised by geographers Ron Johnston,

James Forrest and Mike Poulsen and we shall also examine its use to identify ghettos in Britain.[18]

Rather differently, if the spread of a group across a city or across a country is different from the rest of the population, then it may be considered that there is a degree of spatial segregation, labelled in the literature and here the 'Index of Dissimilarity'. We would expect every group to have some segregation when comparing the areas it lives in with the rest of the population.

For the third approach a very mixed area might sensibly be taken as one where groups are present in equal numbers. A mixed area may represent a vibrant metropolitan multicultured place, or alternatively might be seen as a place of competition and conflicts of interest, but could not be seen as a ghetto. The presence of multiple groups in an area is measured by the 'Index of Diversity'.

Fourth, if a minority ethnic group's residents were trapped in an area one would expect their migration away from it to be less than that of other groups. For example, one might expect White flight but net in-movement of the minority, reflecting retreat from each other. The measurement of migration adds a further dimension to the evidence in this chapter.

Finally, it is claimed that segregation leads to isolation, poverty and inequality. We will review the arguments and the evidence as to the direction of causality, for it could also be that poverty leads to residence in clusters of cheap housing.

Phillips was careful to talk of areas that are 'on their way' to becoming a ghetto. We need to look for evidence of *increasing* segregation, in addition to establishing whether ghettos already exist. To judge the claims of segregation and ghettos we need to measure both the degree of separation between different groups in Britain and how it is changing. We need to look at the process as well as the pattern.

Does Britain have ghettos?

Much of the evidence about segregation in Britain comes from the national census, because it records the ethnic group composition of each locality, and some details of migration. At the time of writing, the last census – taken in 2001 – is already somewhat out of date. Nonetheless it provides an invaluable picture of how Britain is changing. To the extent that the picture is repeated in many different areas, and can be explained by processes which continue and are likely to continue for many decades, we can make a diagnosis about current trends. This section is divided into several parts to help clarify the four aspects of segregation and ghettos identified in the previous section – isolation, spread, mixing and migration. We begin with an overview of the issues and measures by focusing on Bradford, the archetypal ghetto British city in the minds of many commentators.

An example: Bradford

Although frequently associated with problems of integration, Bradford turns out to be typical of most British cities in its dynamic population and lack of a ghetto. Bradford is home to half a million residents, 75,000 of whom recorded themselves as having a Muslim religion in the last census. In total, 101,000 people recorded an ethnic group other than White.

Bradford was the scene of a public burning of Salman Rushdie's book *The Satanic Verses* in 1989.[19] It faced disturbances in 1995 and 2001. The 2001 disturbance occurred in a context of inequalities and some argued that it was provoked by the authorities' lack of opposition to far-right groups, for example by cancelling a city festival after the National Front threatened to rally on the same day.[20] The disturbances involved young Asian residents in destructive sprees in their own neighbourhood of Manningham, inner Bradford. Bradford had been among the first cities to adopt *halal* meat dinners and a *salwar kameez* uniform as school options. Inner-city school head, Ray Honeyford, was dismissed after publicly insisting that Muslim children were held back in education by their own cultural affiliation. It is a city that might be expected to contain one of Trevor Phillips' ghettos of separate development, and to be full of 'fear and trepidation'.

Much of Bradford's Black and Asian population is certainly clustered in particular parts of the district. The White population is more than three quarters of the whole, but three of Bradford's 30 wards have a minority White population: Bradford Moor, University and Toller. Bradford Moor and University wards are the main areas in which pioneer migrants arrived from Pakistan in the 1960s and 1970s in answer to the call for workers to extend textile production into a nightshift, to improve productivity and compete with foreign industrial competition. Chain migration of family and friends changed the composition of these previously White wards. Shops and mosques added a colourful and noticeably Asian flavour to Bradford. However, the nightshifts and other initiatives were not successful in stemming industrial decline; most of the textile jobs had disappeared by 1985.[21] With such a history, these two areas might be chosen as prime candidates for being 'on their way to becoming fully fledged ghettos'.

However, the third ward with minority White population – Toller – is rather different. Many Asian families have moved to its better housing, up the hill and away from the inner settlement areas. It is an indication of dynamism within Bradford's Asian-origin population, which suggests something other than isolated ghettos.

The statistics show this dynamism in three ways: through more mixing and diversity, through natural growth of the Asian population in Bradford and through dispersal away from the inner settlement areas. The number of mixed areas, with significant populations of both White and other groups grew during the 1990s, whichever threshold one uses to define 'mixed'. Fifteen of the 30 wards had more than 10% of their residents from groups recorded as other than 'White', three more wards than 10 years previously. Even in the most Asian areas more than one in four residents were White. In University and Toller wards, the largest group – Pakistani – made up only just over half the population, and less so in Bradford Moor. These were mixed, diverse areas rather than ghettos of single origin. The person who told a government panel that theirs was the only White face seen in a week cannot have got out much. Since 2001, with the arrival of Eastern European and African immigrants, the areas are ever more diverse.

The growth of the minority population in these two wards is now not so much from new immigration as from natural growth – the census shows that the number of minority births each year is greater than the number of minority immigrants.[22] Finally, from lack of vacant housing or from preference, there is considerable movement *out* of the University ward by minority residents to other parts of the UK. The 2001 Census shows that 1,066 minority residents left the ward for other parts of the UK in the previous year while 622 arrived from elsewhere in the UK: 444 more left than arrived. In contrast, there were 185 more White residents who came to the ward from other parts of the UK than left it in the previous year. Not White flight but White arrival.

Thus, for Bradford the evidence stacks up to paint a picture of large clusters of mixed areas, a picture in which people of different ethnic groups are not retreating from each other. Indeed, there is not so much White flight as White movement into the largest minority ethnic cluster and minority movement out. Later in this chapter we will look at the figures for other cities in Britain to show how common this picture of growth and dispersal is, after examining other evidence for Britain as a whole.

Isolation

Geographers who have studied population patterns in Britain have not been quick to give support to Trevor Phillips' claims of ghettos. Ceri Peach of Oxford University has answered the question 'Are there ghettos in Britain?' with a clear 'no'.[23] However, most neighbourhoods have a growing minority population. Therefore one might ask whether minority populations are becoming isolated in the neighbourhoods in which they live.

White people are by far the most isolated group in Britain. They are more likely to live near to each other than any other group. This is a straightforward result of their making up six out of every seven residents. The average White person lives in an electoral ward that has more than 90% White people in it (the figures are for 2001). No other ethnic group reaches even 20% on this Index of Isolation used frequently by social scientists: Pakistanis in Britain live in wards that have on average 17% Pakistani residents. Even when measured for small neighbourhoods of a few streets of about 200 residents,[24] this Index of Isolation rises only to 26% for Pakistani residents, while it is 94% for White residents. The Index has gone up by a few percentage points as each group's population has grown.[25] But it hardly gives evidence of any group living in ghettos.

Diversity or mixing

Diversity, how close an area is to equal numbers of people from all ethnic backgrounds, has increased over time, according to a detailed analysis by the Greater London Authority (GLA).[26] Using standard indicators it found not only that diversity has increased in the obvious sense that the composition of England and Wales has changed as a whole, but that diversity of London's localities has also increased:

- All the 22 electoral wards with minority White populations were not dominated by one minority group but were among the most diverse wards of England and Wales.
- In the vast majority of wards ethnic diversity increased between 1991 and 2001; there were no wards where diversity decreased significantly, although 10 had a slight reduction, in every case due to an increase in the already dominant White population.

- Two wards – Southall Broadway and Spitalfields & Banglatown – with very high proportions of minority ethnic communities in 1991 saw a decline in the proportions of these communities by 2001.
- The ethnic diversity of London's children aged under 16 is greater than that of the adult population in the vast majority of wards.

Thus, the increasing population of minorities is making Britain more diverse both nationally and locally. There are no very high concentrations of particular ethnic groups, other than White, because the areas with fewest White residents are diverse and becoming more so.

The GLA report was published three months after Trevor Phillips' 'sleepwalking to segregation' speech, and was critical of the

> recent, and sometimes near hysterical, debate about 'ghettos' ... [which] has been based upon a type of analysis that suggests that too many Black people or too many Asians living together is a problem, while the same dominance by White people is acceptable. We find this suggestion offensive to the population of London, where the most diverse population in the country lives together and where there is no sign of classic ghettos.[27]

Spread or evenness

If there are no ghettos yet, perhaps overall the *movement* of people is nonetheless one of retreat into areas where they are already most concentrated, indicating ghettos of the future? There are two ways of looking at this. Is the spread of the minority ethnic population in Britain decreasing? More directly, are minority residents moving into their most concentrated areas (which we investigate below)? A standard measure of the spread of a population through localities is the Index of Dissimilarity. Both government and academic studies have shown that the Index of Dissimilarity in Britain as a whole and within each individual city indicates considerable clustering but a small reduction over time in that clustering. For any group, this Index takes values between 0 (no clustering at all, a spread the same as the rest of the population) to 100 (complete clustering: the group is found only in areas where there is no other population). The Index is around 60 for the minority ethnic population as a whole in England and Wales. It is by definition the same for the White population. It is highest for the Pakistani, Bangladeshi and African groups, and least for the Chinese group, although even for the Chinese group the degree of clustering is around 40. For every group the Index decreased in the 1990s (see Table 6.1).

Every group is more spread out and less clustered than it has been before. The decrease is apparent at each geographical scale – local authority districts, electoral wards and the street-level census areas. Finally, the decrease has been even greater within individual local authority districts.[28] The government report *State of the English cities* found only two districts in which segregation had significantly grown in the 1990s, and the authors have since admitted that even these two were computed using faulty data: consistent data shows no increase at all.[29] The spreading out within cities, to a greater extent than when measured for the country as a whole, suggests that there is movement out from inner wards to others within the same districts.

Migration

A more direct way of assessing the reality of claims of retreat is to count the number of migrants who move away from or into existing concentrations of minority ethnic populations. If there were 'black holes into which no-one goes without fear and trepidation, and from which no-one ever escapes undamaged', 'marooned communities … playing by their own rules', one would expect that people who moved to those areas would stay there. There would be retreat, a net movement of minority residents into areas that already had few White residents. The census shows that this is not the case.[30] In 2001 there were 118 electoral wards in Britain with a non-White majority (about one in each hundred of the 10,079 wards). In these minority White wards there were in total one million minority ethnic residents of Britain's total of 4.6 million, and 600,000 White residents. 78,964

Table 6.1: Index of Dissimilarity: degree of clustering between wards of England and Wales

	1991	2001
All minorities	61.4	58.8
Caribbean	68.9	67.0
African	71.1	70.6
Indian	65.3	62.1
Pakistani	75.1	71.7
Bangladeshi	74.2	71.6
Chinese	42.2	41.3

Source: Simpson (2007a)

minority ethnic residents moved from them to other parts of the UK in the year before the census, while 64,248 moved to them. That is a good deal of movement and a net movement out to other parts of the UK of 14,716 minority ethnic residents. Not retreat, but dispersal. White people moved out too, but interestingly the net movement out was less, at 9,747. As a proportion of each population, the movement was very similar. This same dispersal from the most concentrated clusters of minority ethnic population has been found at different spatial scales – for whole districts as well as for wards and for smaller street-level neighbourhoods. It is repeated in 1991 as well as 2001, and it is repeated for each minority ethnic group.[31]

In fact, Indians are leaving Leicester, Caribbeans are leaving Lambeth, Bangladeshis are leaving Tower Hamlets and Pakistanis are leaving Bradford, and within each of these areas the settlement areas are acting not as magnets but as generators of both population and migrants.

For the Indian group there is net out-migration from the highest Indian concentrations. In one year they lost 0.4% of their population to other parts of the UK. There is net in-migration of Indian residents to the lowest concentrations, equivalent to 1% of their existing population.[32] The same pattern of movement is evident for the minority ethnic groups taken as a whole (a loss of 1.0% from highest concentrations and a gain of 0.7% in the least concentrations), for the Pakistani/Bangladeshi group (a loss of 0.3% from highest concentrations and a gain of 0.7% in the least concentrations), for the Black group (including Caribbean, African and Other Black groups: a loss of 1.6% from highest concentrations and a gain of 1.8% in the least concentrations) and those of Mixed origins (a loss of 1.4%, and a gain of 1.7%).

What of White migration? Generally there is a net outward movement of White residents from the concentrations of each minority. If there is any retreat, it is of White residents to the most concentrated White areas (a gain in one year equivalent to 0.2% of their population, compared to a loss of 0.5% from the least White areas). However, it makes more sense to interpret the movement of all groups as 'aspirational movement' to areas of better housing. This is part of the general suburbanisation and counterurbanisation that has been such a feature of European urban change in the past 50 years.[33] The only exception to the pattern is that White residents moved, on balance, towards areas of highest Black concentration, including Lambeth.

Claims of White flight evaporate when confronted with the evidence that White and minority groups are moving in the same direction at the same rate. If there is flight, it is of those who can afford to move from depressed ex-industrial cities to jobs or to better housing. Affluent flight, perhaps. But the evidence shows no more evidence of White flight than Black flight or Brown flight.

Movement of the White population from cities of immigration is often presented as evidence of White flight, with the assumption that the White population has been displaced by immigrants. If this were true, one would expect immigration to have occurred before White out-movement. Both immigration to cities and migration out of cities have been occurring for many decades and so the sequence is not easy to pin down. However, as Table 6.2 shows for Leicester, city out-migration was strong before the major immigration of the 1960s and 1970s, and has lessened over time. In the year before the 1961 Census, Leicester lost the equivalent of 2.3% of its population through migration to other parts of Britain, while immigration was not yet substantial (the Ugandan regime of Idi Amin expelled many thousands of Asian residents in the late 1960s, many of whom arrived in Leicester). By the time of the 2001 Census, Leicester did not lose population through internal migration but was still gaining through immigration. Rather than displacement, the process may be one of replacement, as immigrants fill housing and jobs that are left *after* industrial restructuring has encouraged substantial numbers of White workers to move away from inner-city housing.

Claims of segregation that started this chapter referred to the declining White population in areas of growing minority populations. This is a further breathtaking flirtation with evidence, worthy

Table 6.2: Immigration and internal migration: the case of Leicester: Migration during one year (% of census population)

	Movement into Leicester from abroad[1]	Net movement out of Leicester to rest of Britain[2]
1960-61	0.4	2.3
1970-71	1.2	1.7
1980-81	0.5	0.6
1990-91	0.5	0.8
2000-01	1.0	−0.1

Notes: The administrative boundary of Leicester has not changed significantly since 1960.

[1] 1960–61: outside British Isles; 2000–01: outside UK; other years: outside Britain.

[2] 1960–61: England and Wales; 2000–01: UK; other years: Britain.

Source: Census reports, 1961 to 2001

only of those who are concerned more with their message than its truthfulness. We have already seen that internal migration away from cities is common to White and minority groups, and that it began before immigration. The shift in urban populations towards diversity is caused not only by migration but to a very significant degree by the different age structures of each group – such that minorities currently experience very few deaths compared to births. Chapter Seven returns to these dynamics of population change in more detail for particular cities.

Where are the ghettos?

The case study of Bradford has already shown evident natural growth of the minority ethnic population, its dispersal to other areas and the existence of many mixed areas. The discussion of national statistics has supported this picture of growth and dispersal of minority ethnic populations. These two processes and the resulting degree of residential clustering should be viewed as normal rather than through the prism of difference and danger. But are there particular cities where these benign processes are not at work, which may be candidate ghettos that the national picture has glossed over? Table 6.3 shows figures for all the 35 districts in Britain that have at least one ward where White residents are a minority. It is sorted so that the wards with highest proportion of minority ethnic residents are at the top. Wards are the electoral subdivision of districts that correspond to a large neighbourhood – in these districts they have an average population of about 10,000. The table is a large one but repays study, which the following paragraphs summarise.

A search for ghettos has to face the ethnic diversity of the 35 districts in Britain. Only six districts contain any ward with more than a three quarters minority population. In even the least White ward (Southall Broadway in Ealing), 12% of residents are White. Perhaps the most mixed district is Tower Hamlets where all of its wards have at least one quarter White population and one quarter minority ethnic population. In Newham, Birmingham, Redbridge, Croydon, Sandwell, Coventry, Lambeth, Trafford, Waltham Forest, Haringey, Manchester and Merton, the ward with the largest minority ethnic population is so diverse that no one minority group has a majority even among the minority ethnic population.

Table 6.3: Local authority districts with one or more wards of 50% minority ethnic population

	No. of wards in district	Wards with more than 3/4 White	Wards with more than 3/4 minority ethnic	Ward in the district with most minority ethnic residents	Minority ethnic residents (number)	Minority ethnic residents (%)	Largest minority ethnic group in ward	No. of residents in the largest minority group	No. of minority births	No. of minority immigrants	Net migration with UK, White residents	Net migration with UK, minority ethnic residents
Ealing	23	5	3	Southall Broadway	11,500	88	Indian	7,050	431	401	–99	–1,438
Newham	20	0	3	Green Street East	11,150	84	Indian	3,950	588	436	–160	–931
Leicester	22	13	2	Latimer	9,550	83	Indian	8,600	486	508	+35	–816
Birmingham	39	26	3	Handsworth	21,100	82	Pakistani	6,550	1,411	718	–786	–1,320
Blackburn and Darwen	23	16	2	Bastwell	6,000	81	Pakistani	3,100	284	112	–148	–193
Brent	21	0	1	Wembley Central	8,650	79	Indian	4,350	119	146	–128	–348
Bradford	30	21	0	University	16,650	74	Pakistani	12,450	403	302	+185	–444
Redbridge	21	10	0	Clementswood	8,050	71	Indian	2,900	159	103	–210	–155
Pendle	20	16	0	Whitefield	2,950	70	Pakistani	2,800	70	33	–23	–120
Tower Hamlets	17	0	0	Spitalfields and Banglatown	5,850	70	Bangladeshi	4,850	116	49	–50	–240
Southwark	21	3	0	Peckham	7,700	68	African	4,050	165	67	–13	–384
Luton	19	13	0	Dallow	8,800	67	Pakistani	4,450	214	172	–150	–89
Burnley	15	14	0	Daneshouse and Stoneyholme	4,050	66	Pakistani	2,550	115	78	–30	–159
Hounslow	20	11	0	Heston East	6,950	65	Indian	4,500	106	132	–139	–114
Croydon	24	13	0	West Thornton	10,500	64	Indian	3,250	193	215	–184	–27
Harrow	21	2	0	Kenton East	6,350	64	Indian	4,500	81	87	–181	+17
Sandwell	24	18	0	St. Pauls	7,300	64	Indian	3,550	137	67	–78	–84
Slough	14	5	0	Central	6,350	63	Pakistani	2,900	107	126	–89	–141
Wolverhampton	20	14	0	Blakenhall	6,900	61	Indian	5,150	100	66	+3	–139
Oldham	20	15	0	Werneth	6,800	58	Pakistani	4,600	190	99	–170	–50

Table 6.3: Local authority districts with one or more wards of 50% minority ethnic population *continued*

	No. of wards in district	Wards with more than 3/4 White	Wards with more than 3/4 minority ethnic	Wards in the district with most minority ethnic residents	Minority ethnic residents (number)	Minority ethnic residents (%)	Largest minority ethnic group in ward	No. of residents in the largest minority group	No. of minority births	No. of minority immigrants	Net migration with UK, White residents	Net migration with UK, minority ethnic residents
Coventry	18	16	0	Foleshill	10,150	57	Indian	4,400	208	183	–17	–346
Lambeth	21	1	0	Coldharbour	8,050	56	Caribbean	3,050	171	82	+145	–233
Lewisham	18	4	0	Evelyn	7,950	55	African	3,650	203	91	–204	–405
Peterborough	24	23	0	Central	4,800	55	Pakistani	4,050	124	54	–58	–111
Trafford	21	20	0	Clifford	5,500	55	Pakistani	1,650	98	80	+103	+23
Waltham Forest	20	6	0	Leyton	6,750	54	Caribbean	1,600	156	65	–130	+57
Wycombe	28	25	0	Oakridge and Castlefield	4,650	54	Pakistani	3,350	105	97	+114	–66
Bolton	20	17	0	Derby	7,000	53	Indian	4,950	145	88	–95	–103
Haringey	19	6	0	Northumberland Park	6,600	53	Caribbean	2,250	166	115	–55	–25
Manchester	33	23	0	Longsight	8,450	53	Pakistani	3,950	202	231	+32	–106
Merton	20	13	0	Graveney	4,950	53	Caribbean	1,150	64	79	+4	–180
Hackney	19	0	0	King's Park	5,700	52	African	1,900	121	42	+91	+91
Hyndburn	16	15	0	Central	2,500	52	Pakistani	2,300	67	19	–141	–33
Preston	22	16	0	Deepdale	3,000	52	Indian	2,300	70	31	+99	+4
Derby	17	15	0	Arboretum	6,900	50	Pakistani	4,700	157	104	–71	–201

Note: All figures are given directly in the census except the number of births, which is estimated as one fifth of the number of children aged under five. The final four columns refer to one year before the census, 2000-2001.

Source: 2001 Census, tables ST101, KS06 and KS24.

This diversity is dented on the one hand by the thousands of wards dominated by their White population, and by the eight wards in Britain that have a majority of one of the minority ethnic groups identified in the census. These eight wards are in Leicester, Bradford, Pendle, Ealing and Tower Hamlets. The highest proportion for a single minority group is 74%, the proportion of Indians in the population of Latimer ward in Leicester. This is far from domination and is why no ghettos have been found in Britain by academic studies. This is also different from the situation in the US where, for example, in Chicago over half of the Black population of Cook County lives in neighbourhoods that are more than 90% Black.[34]

There is considerable immigration to the most diverse areas but more often than not it is outnumbered by births, so that the growth of the minority ethnic population is rapid and mainly internally generated. For example there were an estimated 431 minority ethnic births in Southall Broadway and 401 non-White immigrants during the year before the census. This balance in favour of births is not the case for every district. If there is a pattern, it tends to be for the Indian group for whom immigration makes a greater contribution to population growth than births.

Dispersal away from minority concentrations is clear for 30 of the 35 districts, where the balance of minority ethnic migration from other parts of the UK was negative. In other words, migration was away from the minority concentrations. Of the five where movement of minority ethnic residents was inward, White residents also moved into the concentrations within Trafford, Hackney and Preston. These were regeneration areas in the 1990s. This leaves only Harrow and Waltham Forest as scenes of separation where the White population is leaving the concentrations of the minority population but minorities are going to them. Are Harrow and Waltham Forest the mystery ghettos? We do not think so. These two districts are on the northern edge of London; they are places to which migrants from inner London go, and many later move onwards to areas further away.[35] Once again, the picture is one of dynamism rather than a restricted ghetto.

There are other difficulties for those who might claim retreat into culture-bound enclaves. White residents on balance went *into* the minority concentrations of Leicester, Bradford, Lambeth, Wolverhampton, Wycombe, Manchester and Merton, at the same time as minority ethnic residents left. This is hardly a picture of White flight, especially when one adds the 16 further districts shown in the table where both White and minority ethnic residents were moving out, but minorities in greater numbers.

The evidence of diversity, growth and dispersal, and lack of evidence for ghettos and retreat and increasing segregation, comes not only from the 2001 Census and for electoral wards, although that source is by far the richest available to research. The consistency across Britain, for different spatial scales, and from the 1991 Census, is repeated in the government's updated estimates of ethnic composition for English districts, where the growth of the population in groups other than White is fastest outside the main city concentrations.[36] Evidence from focus groups since 2001, discussed in the previous chapter, makes it abundantly clear that growth and dispersal have continued in the 21st century.

Really, where are the ghettos? What is the fuss about?

So we have found, first, that Bradford, archetypal segregated city according to the national media, has White people moving to its most segregated neighbourhoods and Asian people leaving them. Second, that areas with highest concentrations of minority ethnic residents are usually losing population, both White and minorities. Third, that such areas are growth areas due to immigration and even more so due to natural growth of young populations. And that these areas are not mono-ethnic areas but are diverse. They are becoming more diverse as immigration from European and other new origins replaces migration linked to Britain's colonial past.

So is there no evidence for ghettos in Britain? Trevor Phillips has apologised for 'mangling' the work of academic Mike Poulsen in his 2005 speech, but both he and Poulsen agreed that he had got the conclusions correct, and that 'segregation was a growing issue amid a failure by policymakers and the media to properly understand how society was changing'.[37] Now we have segregation not growing but nonetheless a growing issue! Ceri Peach, who has studied segregation in Britain over five decades, finds that in the classification promoted by Poulsen, 'use of the "Ghetto" in its terminology has been mischievous and misleading, that the thresholds suggested do not so much reveal the existence of ghettos but manufacture them such that one can create ghettos if the thresholds are reduced sufficiently'.[38] In Leicester, three electoral wards have a little more than a 70% minority population, within that majority the Indian group makes up 64% (more than double the next group), and 39% of Indians in Leicester live in those three wards. These neighbourhoods do not approach the segregation of Chicago Cook County, larger than Leicester, where over half the Black population lives in areas that are more than 90% Black. On

Poulsen's classification, one could have 30% White population, 25% Indian and 10% each of four other groups, and label this a ghetto. So tempting is the identification of a 'ghetto' to the media, and so strong have been the criticisms from other investigators, that Poulsen has withdrawn the label ghetto in his most recent articles.[39]

If there are no ghettos, and if there is no White flight except that matched by ordinary movement to better homes by minority families as well as White families, is there anything about the changing ethnic composition of areas that should be worrying the government? There is nothing left to be worried about unless one is concerned simply about a falling proportion of White people in an area and finds diversity difficult. And of course some people do find diversity a challenge, feeling it is too much too fast. Chapter Seven returns to this theme in the context of population forecasts.

Poverty and segregation, which leads?

We are left with the claim that the clustering by ethnicity, however benign its sources, causes increased poverty and inequality. In 2006 Trevor Phillips claimed that '[s]eparateness in and of itself tends to encourage inequality of treatment ... living separately means that different groups of people have their life experiences defined by their ethnicity rather than their ambitions, [and] ... polarisation feeds a growing and dangerous tribalisation of our communities'.[40] The claim that separateness causes inequality is dealt with here.

There is a genuine concern that the lack of successful role models among family and neighbours, and the lack of information and encouragement that come with role models, may hold everyone back in a neighbourhood. The desperation of the insecure and unemployed may lower aspirations of those around them. But it could be the other way around – that lack of income prevents escape and indeed poor people are attracted to areas with cheap housing. This is a perennial debate in urban development with important policy consequences. If pervasive poverty holds an area back, then giving such areas housing that is attractive to middle-income families could be a reasonable policy target as a means of also improving the fortunes of the poorest. On the other hand, if the uplifting effect of rubbing shoulders with the successful in socially mixed areas is small or non-existent then the policy target should be to directly raise the chances of those with least success.[41] Where they live is immaterial.

When referring to race and ethnicity, the question becomes whether there are neighbourhoods with culturally separate lives in which experience is limited by separation from the mainstream, which therefore limits their residents' aspirations and success in work and education. This is the view reflected not only by Trevor Phillips but also in the UK government's focus on 'community cohesion'. Lower indices of segregation and greater ethnic mixing and dispersal would then be legitimate targets of policy, in which programmes focus specifically on an ethnic group's geographical and social integration. However, we have seen already in this chapter that persistent geographical segregation will continue irrespective of policy, due to the natural and benign dynamics of population growth.

Many commentators point to evidence of lower employment, lower earnings, lower participation in education and higher levels of deprivation in areas where most minority ethnic residents live. Table 6.4, for example, shows that unemployment when measured for all people in England and Wales is 10% in diverse areas with less than 50% White population, twice the national average. However, this does not solve the conundrum: does separateness cause inequality, or do inequalities guide us to live separately? Few studies follow individuals longitudinally to answer this question. One such study in Amsterdam showed that there was no greater likelihood of ending welfare claimant status in areas with few such claimants. Neighbourhood social mix was not the problem causing persistent poverty.[42] In Britain, a government report showed unemployment inequality to be as great outside the inner–city areas with minority White populations as inside them.[43] Table 6.4 is taken from that report. It shows that in areas where White residents are in a majority even greater than the national average (labelled 'unmixed' in the table), unemployment among Pakistani, Caribbean, African and Bangladeshi men is twice

Table 6.4: Male unemployment rate at age 25 and older (%)

	England and Wales	Diverse areas: less than 50% White	Mixed areas: between 50% and 87% White	Unmixed areas: more than 87% White
All people	5	10	6	4
White Briton	5	8	5	4
Chinese	5	8	5	4
Indian	5	7	5	3
Pakistani	12	14	12	9
Caribbean	13	16	13	8
African	14	16	14	8
Bangladeshi	16	21	13	7

Source: Simpson et al (2006, figure 6.18)

that of White Britons. This is the same as it is in the 'diverse' areas where White people are in the minority, which might be labelled 'segregated' by those still concerned with such labels.

The claim that culturally distinct areas trap people in poverty is a core part of the 'culture of difference', which assumes that those areas heighten inequalities. But this does not seem to be the case. We saw earlier that many people do move out of concentrations of minority ethnic populations; now it is clear that severe inequality continues outside those areas.

Conclusion

This chapter has reviewed the evidence and found neither ghettos nor increasing segregation. We find that the degree of separation between ethnic groups in Britain is not high, in the sense that those areas with relatively few White people are diverse and metropolitan in nature rather than exclusive. We find that residential segregation has a variety of causes, many of which are either benign or helpful to integration rather than unhelpful. The clustering of groups together is mainly a result of immigration and family-building. It is a fact that rather than retreating into their own areas, Britain's minority ethnic residents tend to move out from existing settlement areas to neighbouring areas or to the suburbs. In almost every city with a sizeable inner area that has been the focus of immigration in the past 60 years, children of immigrants have on balance moved away from those areas, not to them or between them.

Britain's so-called ghettos are diverse areas both ethnically and socially. Because of natural population growth and the addition of new migrants from a variety of origins, their minority ethnic population will increase even as many move away. There is little evidence with which to decide whether the composition of an area has any effect on holding back its residents, but no trail of evidence leads from the colour of an area to deepening poverty for its residents. Social inequality is evident irrespective of ethnic composition.

Policy should not aim to 'dilute' concentrations of minority ethnic residents, because the targeted areas are already among the most diverse in Britain, because their changing composition is not amenable to policy influence and because it is not the ethnic composition of areas that is holding people in vulnerable positions. A focus on ethnic composition will not have much impact on integration. It is more likely to have a perverse effect of stigmatising areas in which Black and Asian people live, leading to less likelihood of residential mixing.

It is the suburbs to which children of immigrants aspire to move that should be the focus of attention. A spotlight on fair treatment, choice in housing, positive social behaviour, job availability and neighbourliness in areas that are changing their composition are more relevant to the goal of an integrated society. Britain's changing ethnic composition, both nationally and locally, is evident and important, but it does not of itself constitute a problem.

Notes

[1] Phillips (2005).

[2] The quotes are taken from Herman Ouseley's (2001) report to the City of Bradford, written before the riots and echoed by post-riot government reports by Cantle (2001) and Denham (2001).

[3] Johnson (2006).

[4] MigrationWatchUK (2005, paras 2-4)

[5] Community Cohesion Panel (2004, p 16).

[6] Park (1952, p 177).

[7] These quotes are from the influential Irish geographer Frederick Boal (1976, p 54; 1999, p 45).

[8] Pettigrew (1969, p 63).

[9] Ceri Peach in Britain has long insisted on distinguishing good from bad segregation (1996a). Also Dunn (1998), Peleman (2002) and Rex (1981, p 25), who warned that 'Desegregation and dispersal might well be the principal threat to immigrant minority communities'.

[10] Schelling (1971) and Fossett (2006) use models of population dynamics to show this large impact of small preferences for cultural proximity.

[11] The history of attention to ethnic clustering in policy, its decline after equal rights legislation and the subsequent shift of focus back to cultural differences since 2001 have been charted by Phillips, D. (2006) and Kalra and Kapoor (2008).

[12] The 'ethnic penalty' continuing in the second generation is documented, for example, by Simpson et al (2006) and Heath and Li (2007).

[13] Commission on Integration and Cohesion (2007).

[14] Some would argue further, that multiculturalism is a threat to government because government relies on a commonly accepted culture to support its legitimacy. Eagleton (2007) takes this view but nonetheless argues for a new common culture drawn from the engagement of different traditions with common human values.

[15] Wirth (1928).

[16] Leech (1994).

[17] See Dorling and Thomas (2004).

[18] Johnston et al (2002).

[19] *The Satanic Verses* was alleged by some Muslims to be blasphemous, causing international controversy and debates about freedom of speech. The leader of Iran, Ayatollah Ruhollah Khomeini, called for Rushdie's death, causing an international diplomatic crisis.

[20] Kundnani (2001).

[21] Bradford Council (1985); Lewis (1994).

[22] The number of births to each ethnic group is estimated from the census by the number of infants aged under five, and divided by five to give an estimate of births in one year.

[23] Peach (1996b) and Peach (2008).

[24] The Census Output Area.

[25] Simpson (2007a) provides a definition of each index discussed in this chapter, with values for England and Wales at a variety of spatial scales.

[26] GLA (2005). The Office for National Statistics (ONS, 2006a) examined ethnic and religious diversity and came to similar conclusions as the GLA.

[27] GLA (2005, foreword).

[28] Simpson (2007a).

[29] Parkinson et al (2006); the correction takes into account ward boundary reviews as detailed in Simpson (2007a).

[30] The census measures migration as a change of usual residence since one year prior to census day.

[31] Simpson and Finney (2008).

[32] These statistics were derived by sorting local authority districts into quintiles of different group concentration, each of which contains one fifth of the group's population; the comparison is then between the most concentrated quintile of districts and the least concentrated quintile. Further detail and analysis is given in Simpson and Finney (2008).

[33] Champion (1989).

[34] Peach (2008).

[35] These interpretations of the experience of Harrow and Waltham Forest have been confirmed through conversations with local government research staff in these local authorities.

[36] ONS (2006b).

[37] Phillips' retraction and restatement are reported at http://news.bbc.co.uk/1/hi/uk/5297760.stm

[38] Peach (2008).

[39] Compare Poulsen and Johnston (2006) with Poulsen et al (2001).

[40] Phillips, T. (2006).

[41] See Andersson et al (2007) for a discussion of these issues and examination of the Swedish case.
[42] Musterd (2003).
[43] Simpson et al (2006).

7

Challenging the myth of 'Minority White Cities'

Whites will soon become a minority in Birmingham and other major British cities, posing a critical challenge to social stability, Britain's race relations watchdog has warned. *The Sunday Times newspaper*[1]

Introduction

Concerns about the consequences of immigration and residential segregation converge in a spectre of 'Minority White Cities', where White residents make up less than half of the population. There is a fascination with the year in which particular cities will lose their White majority both from those whose work encourages ethnic diversity and those who fear lack of integration. Thus, publicity from a global forum on Cities in Transition was headlined by the wholly unsubstantiated claim that 'Birmingham is set to join Toronto and Los Angeles as a "majority-minority city" by 2011' in order to raise questions for planning: 'What will it mean for public services and race relations when more than half the population is non-White?'[2] Similarly, the Commission for Racial Equality's factual profiles based on the 2001 Census and prepared in 2006 claim that 'Leicester is widely predicted, within the next five years, to become the first city in Europe with a majority non-white population. Nowhere else in Britain has proportionally fewer White British residents'.[3] Here 'widely predicted' needs to be interpreted as 'predicted wide of the mark' as no such predictions have been made. The coolly stated 'fact' of Leicester's extremely low proportion of White British residents is also false.[4] In 2007 a contributor to Wikipedia, a widely used free online encyclopaedia edited by its readers, used six such apparently authoritative reports to claim that 'The indigenous population is due to be a minority in Leicester, London and in Birmingham by the time of the 2011 Census'.[5]

Two claims about Minority White Cities are addressed in this chapter. First, that the phenomenon of a Minority White City has some democratic meaning or significance for city management. Second, that population change will be such that several British cities will have fewer than half their residents of White ethnicities by 2011.

The chapter examines the predictions and puts the evidence beside them, which demonstrates severe exaggeration. First, we argue that the notion of cities becoming plural in the near future (where no one racial or ethnic group has a majority) is simply a convenient hook on which to hang discussion of the challenges and opportunities of future multicultural cities. The supposed nearness of the event justifies urgency for policy recommendations. The next section follows the trail of unsubstantiated claims copied from one news item to another to demonstrate the perpetuation of the myth. Then we demonstrate the population dynamics that are changing the composition of cities, and examine more closely the population forecasts that have been completed for cities of Britain, painting the future based on evidence.

Minority White Cities and community cohesion

Concern about Minority White Cities is the crude expression of a fear for the ungovernability of diverse cities. It is an expression of the fear that increasing diversity will bring less social and community cohesion, resulting in people of different ethnic groups leading 'parallel lives'. The emergence of the community cohesion agenda as a successor to multiculturalism was discussed in Chapters Two, Five and Six.[6] Much like the image that ghettos are not conducive to social cohesion, the image of Minority White Cities warns of negative implications of diversity.

It is not the simple colour composition of a place's population that is a seen as the problem. Those expressing worries would not have the same concern for Black cities in the Caribbean. If the White majority in a British city were immigrants from Eastern Europe, the same fear would be expressed. The concern is about newcomers, both new immigrants and children of former immigrants (ethnic minorities), in particular those who may have different values and experiences to the prevailing values and experiences in Britain and who may therefore upset the applecart of the accepted way(s) of life.

There is, as we discussed in Chapter One in relation to integration, no easy consensus definition of the prevailing values and experiences and the accepted way(s) of life. Thus, discussions of the challenges of plural cities are as difficult to conclude as debates on 'Britishness' and core values. The Smith Institute[7] and the Commission for Racial Equality held a public discussion in March 2006, 'The age of plural cities: when we are all minorities'.[8] With contributors from four continents, terminology was one of the issues discussed. Trevor Phillips of the Commission for Racial Equality felt that 'it is hard to describe a situation which is about division by race and ethnicity without people feeling anxious, threatened and upset'. The response from Holland, Brazil and Tower Hamlets was to identify and to talk about concrete problems, including honour killings and homosexual discrimination, White power in government, racial and economic discrimination, and political leadership across communities.

Specific concerns about integration are poorly represented by any of the three defining elements of Minority White Cities. Why a minority, rather than 30% or 90%? Less than 50% White does not signify anything special, but is simply a metaphor for 'a lot of others'. Why White? Whiteness is hardly a good indicator of fitness to govern or consensus on values. Why cities? Brent and Newham are not cities but boroughs within London, and they already have a minority of White residents and have equal governance status to city local authorities outside London. Similarly, the city area of Bradford is far smaller than the local authority area whose statistics are debated. In many ways, the search for Minority White Cities is nonsensical, because the answer is entirely dependent on geographical scale.

These three elements – Minority, White and Cities – do not combine into a concept that has substantive meaning or significance unless an association is made between whiteness and cohesion, or whiteness and governability, and by implication a disassociation of diversity and cohesion. Such an association reflects a way of thinking, acting and structuring society that assumes and enforces White supremacy. The concept is a racist one because through this assumption it reasserts White power and maintains White privilege and also because it makes of White something more than an ethnic or racial category.

Critiquing the concept of whiteness in the 'Minority White Cities' claim is not to deny that whiteness or White identities or White ethnic group(s) are unimportant. On the contrary, whiteness is important culturally and politically, as an experience and as a form of power.[9] Considering whiteness as an (ethnic) identity is essential for understanding and challenging new forms of racism.[10]

Like any ethnic grouping, as we saw in Chapter Two, there is also a great deal of diversity within the White category. Of children who live in Britain but were born elsewhere, the largest number were born in Germany.[11] The variety of European origins within the changing White population matches the variety of language, religion and regional origin within Britain's Pakistani, Indian and Caribbean populations. It can be argued that 'Whiteness is a relevant but not an adequate category through which to engage a world where nationality and nationalism ... and religious and political values are starkly to the fore'.[12] Whiteness as an ethnic identity is about much more than colour; White identities are being claimed by people who would traditionally be seen as non-White.[13] To suggest that the White population is synonymous with a socially cohesive population is very misleading.

There are some who believe that the category of White, or more specifically White British, should have greater entitlements in Britain. However, few apart from the fascist British National Party (BNP) openly make the association of ethnicity with democratic rights. The BNP's careful and clear (if fanciful) calculations are chilling. They reduce the White population by deducting from census counts an allowance for those who 'do not belong to an ethnic group indigenous to the British Isles', to yield counts of areas that will have a minority of 'Native Londoners' and therefore be no longer British in the author's eyes.[14] This focus on the indigenous White population is not limited to the BNP. It is emphasised by the census's own distinction between White British and Other White categories and by the academic David Coleman's population forecasts as we shall see later in this chapter.

In fact, for many who use the term, Minority White City is not an indicator of any change in status, but simply a metaphor for the concerns that ring through claims discussed in this book, of segregation and integration. However, as with segregation, use of the term Minority White Cities to highlight problems is not impartial because it associates integration and stability with whiteness. 'Minority White City' associates a White majority with a superior value and a society that is more governable and cohesive than a diverse one. In doing this the concept and debate is a distraction from the particular problems of integration and stability that should be spoken about and addressed. The concept and term Minority White City has come to have such negative associations, which we will show to be unfounded, that it is better avoided or used with caution.

However, it is unfair to suggest that all those promoting the Minority White City debate do so through fear of diversity. The term has also been used to highlight not problems but the positive outcomes and opportunities of ethnic diversity. Thus, some of the claims of early plural cities have been made to underline the current importance of policies to establish diverse workplaces and inclusive employment policies. A plural Birmingham by 2010 is claimed in the city's argument for diverse business services,[15] and was a proud motif of the city's bid for European Capital of Culture. Again it is not that reaching 50% transforms a city's social relations; an approaching numerical plurality simply emphasises the already existing mix of ethnicities.

This lack of coincidence between reaching a minority White population in a city and any particular consequences of a diverse population whether seen as problematic or as positive, perhaps explains why commentators are prepared to be so glib with their claim of Minority White Cities. If it is simply a metaphor for a discussion they want to promote, why not bring the oncoming plurality as close as possible? However, the repetition of unsubstantiated claims by authoritative local and central government bodies cannot be so easily excused. It is to specific unsubstantiated claims that we now turn to illustrate how commonplace they have become.

Origins of the myth: a trail of unsubstantiated claims

The Sunday Times on 19 March 2006 under the headline 'Segregation warning as whites face being minority in cities' continued the story that heads this chapter as follows:

> Trevor Phillips, chairman of the Commission for Racial Equality (CRE), says tough decisions will have to be made as Leicester then Birmingham, Oldham and Bradford become plural cities where no one race holds a demographic majority.
>
> The warning comes as government statistics show that white and ethnic minority communities are becoming increasingly segregated by growing population movement and immigration.
>
> Phillips will highlight the issue this week at a conference in Leicester, which the CRE predicts will become a plural city by 2011, with the others crossing the threshold by 2016.[16]

The news report was a preview for the Smith Institute and Commission for Racial Equality conference mentioned earlier, but focuses entirely on patterns of residence as a 'critical challenge to social stability'. Its authority is emphasised by reference to government statistics. As it happens, government reports conclude the opposite of increasing segregation, as has been discussed in Chapter Six, but the focus in this chapter is on the report's claims of Minority White Cities, which also turn out to be untrue. Leicester is said to have been predicted by the Commission for Racial Equality to become a plural city by 2011, with Birmingham, Oldham and Bradford 'crossing the threshold' by 2016. At the time the news item was published, Oldham and Bradford local councils had produced forecasts that could have been referred to, showing majority White populations continuing beyond 2031. Birmingham and Leicester local authorities have only published population forecasts since 2006, but employ researchers who from simple calculations could have shown that the White majority would remain until after 2016. The current estimates are summarised in Table 7.1, and are discussed later in this chapter.

Table 7.1: Local authority population forecasts

Birmingham	Birmingham is likely to become minority White in 2024. The White population will remain twice the size of any other group.
Bradford	Bradford's White population is likely to be 65% of the total in 2021, and it is unlikely to be minority White before 2031.
Oldham	Oldham will not become minority White in the foreseeable future. In the furthest forecast, for 2028, the White population remains 70% of the total.
Leicester	Leicester's child population taken as a whole, the best indicator of the city's future composition, is majority White. The Office for National Statistics estimates that Leicester's Indian population has reduced since 2001, while it has grown in neighbouring Leicestershire districts. Research at Manchester University suggests a plural population by 2019.

Notes: The dates in this table are presented as 'expected' years for the cities to have a White population of under 50% based on current trends, but are not certain. If and when this population change happens will depend on future numbers of births, deaths and migration for each ethnic group. If there is more White immigration to Birmingham, for example, the date will be later. The dates given are the best estimates, but the change is only slightly more likely to happen in the years given as compared to similar years.

Sources: Simpson (2007b) for Birmingham; Bradford Council (2000) for Bradford; Simpson and Gavalas (2005) for Oldham; Danielis (2007) for Leicester.

Thus, all the claims that *The Sunday Times* attributes to the Commission for Racial Equality were false, and at the time of the article were verifiably false by consultation with appropriate government bodies. So, where did they arise from?

The Sunday Times claims no sources except the Commission for Racial Equality.[17] The Commission for Racial Equality Press Office and its Senior Policy Officer claimed that they had given only the information for Leicester to the press, but that Birmingham and Leicester Councils' chief executives had claimed a Minority White City in the near future. Between them, they gave a series of nine references to support the claim that Leicester would become minority White by 2011.[18]

Three of the references given by the Commission for Racial Equality give no claim about Minority White Cities in Britain.[19] Four – from the *Mirror* and *Daily Telegraph* newspapers, from the Leicester Partnership and from the Benefit Fraud Inspectorate – make a claim of Leicester becoming minority White in 2011 or 2012 but give no source.[20] A government-sponsored doctoral student's report claims that Leicester 'is to become the first "minority-majority" city in the UK' but sources a newspaper article that refers not to population but to school rolls.[21] Finally, the ninth source is an academic article that refers to unsourced claims about Leicester's future plural status, but concludes that 'Data for the 2001 Census indicate that the anticipated demographic changes are taking place at a lower rate than some of the more alarmist projections would appear to suggest'.[22]

Thus, no research had been undertaken or used to support any of the claims made for Birmingham, Bradford, Oldham and Leicester. It is as if the very making and repetition of the claim makes it true. Indeed, the Commission for Racial Equality's claim of Leicester's imminent White minority – which is repeated on the Commission for Racial Equality website within its factual profiles – is defended by it as 'information in the public domain' because it has been 'documented by various agencies', those same unsubstantiated claims passed from news item to public report and back again.[23]

The Sunday Times report was itself picked up by the local press in the cities concerned. For example, the *Bradford Telegraph & Argus* repeated the story verbatim with added comment from Marsha Singh MP, who said that non-White majority areas already existed within parts of Britain without terrible outcomes.[24] Later in the year, the Audit Commission's local authority report on Birmingham excluded the claim of plural status by 2016 after protest from the council, but it was picked up again for the Global Forum on 'Cities in Transition', this time assisted by two further newspaper reports claiming a plural Birmingham by 2010.[25]

The press are therefore partly responsible for perpetuating the myth of Minority White Cities by presenting inaccurate evidence, and deeming the idea to be newsworthy simply because another outlet has used it. In an industry where 'agreed news' has taken prominence over investigative journalism, 'there often isn't the time to get out and find things out: you rely on second-hand information'.[26] Over the last few decades, ownership and control in the British media industry has become more concentrated, reducing the audiences' access to a diversity of information and opinion.[27] Furthermore, the tendency of some of the media to uncritically reflect and promote the political arguments of the day has resulted in an 'absence of alternative information and comment in public debate'.[28] Nevertheless, one would expect some capacity to verify news, particularly its accuracy, within the better-resourced media.

Government bodies should perhaps have more access to research advisors. The Commission for Racial Equality's lack of research support is exemplified by its suggestion that an increase of Leicester's minority ethnic population from 28% in 1991 to 36% in 2001 results in a 'prediction' for 2011 of 'approximately a 50% ethnic minority population, making it Britain's first plural city'.[29] Adding the 8%

change between 1991 and 2001 gives a prediction of 44% in 2011, which perhaps the Commission for Racial Equality should not take as a majority.[30] The origins of the claim of early plurality for Leicester, and perhaps for Birmingham, may be in local authority monitoring of its schools' composition. Leicester City Council has shown a White minority among primary children, but this is not support for the claims about the near future for the population as a whole. The widespread use of unsubstantiated claims by important actors in integration policy provides a good example of how myths are perpetuated, spreading fear of diversity.

What makes Britain's cities diverse?

Britain's growing ethnic diversity is undisputable. Whether the whole of Britain or its city districts are considered, there are a greater number of ethnicities with more global origins represented than in the past. This is an interesting and important social change that need not be interpreted in a negative way. If we are to monitor this change, and make predictions, we need an accurate understanding of what is the cause of the increasing diversity of Britain. Chapter Six has already shown that immigration is only one source of change. The major and most predictable generator of population growth is the youth of immigrant-origin populations, even those whose main entry into Britain took place 40 years ago. Most immigrants are aged in their twenties when they arrive and have families soon after settling in Britain. For two generations and until the number of elderly adults matches the number of young adults, there are more children being born than people dying. For the Caribbean, Indian, Bangladeshi and Pakistani populations, natural growth has been greater than immigration as a cause of population change since the 1990s.[31]

Although natural growth of minority populations, the excess of births over deaths, is a source of diversity in Britain, its role in minority population growth is slowing down as differences in birth rates between ethnic groups become smaller and the pioneer immigrants reach an age where significant numbers of deaths balance the numbers of births. Without continued immigration, the size of the minority ethnic populations of Britain would stabilise and continued diversity would be a result of only residential movement and partnerships between people of different ethnicities. But those stable populations will be some decades in the future: the youthfulness of the minority populations will ensure growth of local populations such that several cities outside London are likely to become plural in the next decades. This is perhaps most easily seen by using the current composition of children as a crude indicator of the future composition of a city, in comparison with its current composition.

In each of the four local authority areas claimed by *The Sunday Times* to be set for plural city status by 2016, the minority ethnic group population is a greater proportion of children than it is of the population as a whole (see Table 7.2). This is an indication of the minority population's relative youth and the likelihood that it will grow in size, irrespective of policy on immigration or the housing market. Several London boroughs would rank above Leicester and Birmingham in Table 7.2 with Newham at the top of the list. One borough to the West of London – Slough – also has a higher minority ethnic population among both children and all people than either Leicester or Birmingham, but receives less press attention. Slough boasted Britain's first Black female Mayor, Lydia Simmons, in 1984, and has approximately equal numbers of Indian and Pakistani heritage residents, and no doubt its civic leaders are happy with its lack of media attention on racial grounds.

This discussion of the momentum for growth among young populations suggests that there is evidence to predict the future composition of local populations, as in the next section. However, before leaving this discussion of the growing diversity within Britain, it is relevant that within cities there are some areas that are already plural. There are no official statistics for areas smaller than local authority districts, except from the 10-yearly censuses. The census of 2001 shows already 105 plural areas where no ethnic group is a majority, among the 10,079 electoral wards of Britain. These tend to be diverse areas: in all of them the White population is at least 10% of the population, and in 58 there are at least three ethnic groups with 10% or more of the local population, including White.

Table 7.2: Minority ethnic population as a percentage, children and all people, 2004

	Percentage other than White among children	Rank	Percentage other than White among all people	Rank
Leicester	44%	14	37%	10
Birmingham	44%	16	32%	17
Bradford	35%	22	24%	28
Oldham	26%	36	15%	43

Note: Children aged 0-15 and all residents. Rank among 354 Districts of England. All ethnic groups other than White categories.

Source: ONS (2006b)

There is an undoubted association of particular areas with particular overseas origins. Northern towns can be distinguished not only by their centuries-old English accents but also from the predominance of a particular Caribbean island (Dominica in Bradford, Grenada in Huddersfield) or a particular region of the Indian subcontinent (Gujarati Jains in Leicester, Punjabi Valmiki in Coventry, Mirpuri Muslims in Bradford).[32] These affiliations arise from chain migration of friends and family to particular places, reinforced by culinary, cultural and religious support that a small but critical number of familiar residents can provide. But this is a far cry from single cultural heritage dominating the cities' demography, which remains firmly diverse. In Brent and Newham, the two London boroughs with minority White populations (but where the White British population remains the largest group), there are more than 15,000 residents from each of five other ethnic groups.

When will cities become plural, and how do we know?

On the one hand the claims of imminent plural cities in Britain are not based on evidence. On the other hand it is clear that diversity is growing and may well result eventually in plural cities. What *can* be said with some confidence about the timing of diversity's development? This section describes the art of population projections and reviews today's picture of the future.

Forecasts of the future composition of local areas can be justified without a focus on plural cities. Assessment of future needs is an essential element to help each local authority plan its services and use its resources effectively. The changing ethnic composition of an area is a guide to changing needs in as much as it indicates different preferences for housing size, for types of school meals, for care of older people, for cultural and entertainment facilities, for funeral services or for other aspects of local services. Consequently, local government research has led the way in Britain by developing methods of population forecasting with an ethnicity dimension.[33]

In the previous section the relatively high proportion of young children of minority ethnic groups was used to indicate a momentum that would lead to growth in the adult population. But how much growth? The change between two past censuses might be used to indicate each group's future growth. However, a forecast of a local ethnic group population is not as simple as extrapolating from current numbers of children, or from past growth, for at least five reasons:

- *Immigration to Britain* will add to the population, adding most to the number of young adults, and subsequently to new children (for White and other ethnic groups). The extent of future immigration is the major uncertainty for any forecast; it depends on future immigration policy, marriage practice and economics in both Britain and the origin countries. Emigration – international migration out of Britain – will also have an effect, although to date forecasts have focused less on this than on immigration.

- *Migration within Britain* shapes local population composition. All ethnic groups are moving from inner urban areas (see Chapter Six) but the minority ethnic populations are likely to move from inner areas to suburbs while the White population is more likely to move from and beyond suburbs and over city boundaries, speeding up the diversity of the remaining suburban population.

- *Fertility* tends to be high after immigration but then decreases, as it has among all minority ethnic groups in Britain identified by the censuses. For example, the British Pakistani and Bangladeshi populations' fertility rate has halved since the 1980s.

- *Momentum* of a relatively young age structure is by definition not a permanent feature. Table 7.2 earlier in this chapter showed that the proportion of minorities among Leicester's children was closer to the proportion among the whole population than in other cities. Leicester's momentum for growth is therefore less than in other cities.

- *Perceptions of ethnicity* change for both individuals and for society. The principle of allowing individuals to choose their own identity as they do in the census (which is the starting point for any projection) cannot be taken into account in projections because we do not know what ethnic identifications will be meaningful in the future. For example, the proportion of children of mixed parentage who will retain either parental identity or opt for a Mixed identity is unknown.

Population projections with an ethnic group dimension are not only technically difficult but also require a strong consensus about the labels used. The ethnic group categories of importance in 20 years' time, if any, are very unlikely to be those of today.[34] For this reason the methods of population projections with an ethnic group dimension are not only in their infancy but will have a difficult childhood, in spite of the expectations for them from the press and politicians.

In Britain, two long-term *national* projections of population have been published by David Coleman, the Oxford professor whose briefings are used extensively by MigrationWatchUK.[35] He uses the term indigenous to refer to those with family origins in the British Isles, measuring their current number by those who identify in the census as White British or White Irish. The inclusion of Irish among the British indigenous is a peculiarity in common with the British National Party.[36] Coleman projects the children of the 'foreign' White population (not British or Irish) to remain part of the foreign population whether or not in partnerships with indigenous people. Using a number of assumptions that are not at all extreme, the 'foreign population' of England and Wales rises from 11% in 2001 to 36% by 2050. In a projection for the UK, the non-White population becomes a majority in Britain by 2086. The proportion of the total population that has Mixed origin rises particularly rapidly, from 1% in 2001 to 8% in 2050, and becomes the most numerous minority group well before 2100. For Coleman, the Mixed group is included in the total 'foreign-origin population' rather than the remaining 'indigenous' population. Foreign-origin, foreign and foreign-background are used as interchangeable terms in his work.

There is a major difficulty with these concepts of indigenous origin and foreign origin. The current indigenous population includes many who by the same criteria are most definitely of foreign origin. Indeed, one would imagine that the majority of the population of Britain is already of foreign origin if one goes back as many generations as these projections attempt to go forward. The current Jewish population of Britain, for example, identifies as White British by a large majority[37] although almost all have at least one recent ancestor born outside Britain. The separation of individuals with foreign family origins from those who are indigenous is extremely distasteful to democrats because it is made in the context of British debates in which 'indigenous' means holders of greater rights than others.

The Joseph Rowntree Foundation commissioned a similar set of projections but with a less ambitious time horizon, to 2020. Produced from Leeds University by Professor Phil Rees,[38] the projections suggest that the highest rate of population growth will be among the residual 'Other' ethnic groups, highlighting the diversity of new immigration to the UK. These projections expect the White population to reduce from 88% to 82% among children aged under 16.

The Rees and Coleman projections for the UK differ significantly in their estimates of fertility (Black, Asian and White being higher in the Coleman projection, while Mixed is lower), as well as in migration, and in the projected populations at 2020. In comparing his own with Coleman's projections, Rees also found that:

we can recognise some strong commonalities: the White population will experience very little growth. The ethnic minority groups will see continuing strong growth to 2020 compared with 2001 ranging between 51 and 93% (current projections) and 79 to 156% (Coleman & Scherbov [2005]). This means that the ethnic composition of the population will continue to evolve. Coleman and Scherbov's projections see the pace of change over the [period] 1981–1991 continuing to 2020, whereas the current projection sees the pace drop, as a result of lower fertility and passing through of the demographic momentum effect.

Thus the 'strongest commonalities' include for example the Mixed population growing either at 93% or at 156% over 20 years, and the pace of change either continuing or dropping, and one can take these projections as further evidence of the difficulty of making reliable projections of ethnic composition for the future.

Leeds University has also provided forecasts for local authority areas in Yorkshire and Humberside. Like their national versions they carry warnings about their crude nature. They add to the forecasts made for every London borough by the Greater London Authority, by Bradford Council for its own area, and by Manchester University for Birmingham, Oldham, Rochdale, Stoke and Leicester, which also extend to forecasts of housing and employment needs.[39]

Each of these subnational forecasts is made with similar data and methods, using a *cohort component projection* method that estimates the impacts of internal and international migration, fertility, and the momentum of the current age structure – the main issues listed above. They each project up to 25 years into the future, no more than is needed for local planning, and can be thought of as state of the art forecasts, although that art is in its infancy. Figure 7.1 uses these local forecasts to show the expected year in which local authority areas in Britain will become plural. On the left axis is the total percentage of minority ethnic groups expected in the year 2026.

Thus, the two London Boroughs of Brent and Newham that were already plural in 2001 will be joined by Harrow in 2008, Tower Hamlets in 2011, and Redbridge, Hounslow, Croydon and Ealing before 2026. The only local authorities outside London that are expected to become plural by 2026 are Leicester in 2019 and Birmingham in 2024. All these local authority areas will gain a diverse population, in which the White population will remain between 25% and 50% during all of the forecast period. The suburbanisation of

Figure 7.1: Timeline of plural local authorities in Britain: year of achieving plural status and % minority ethnic population in 2026

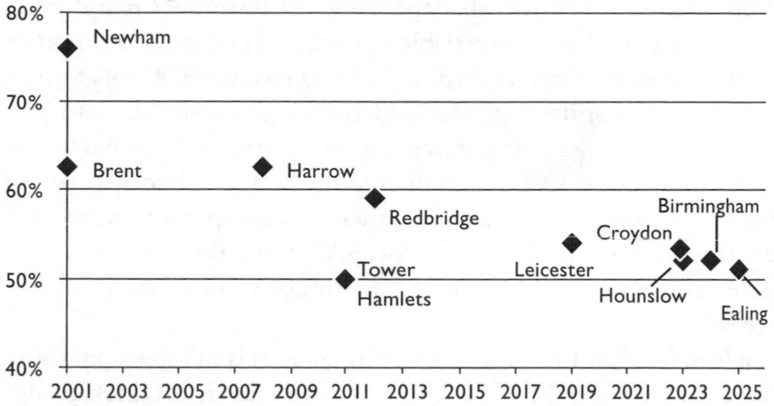

Sources: Danielis (2007), Greater London Authority (2007), Simpson (2007b)

the minority population is mainly to outer London, and the greater movement of the White population is to less urban areas as we have seen in Chapter Six. As has already been seen in city areas outside London, White and other groups' movement is in the same direction but the suburbs will see most growth in diversity and most reduction in the White population. The Greater London Authority emphasises that while there will be more diversity, the growth of the non-White minority populations is time-limited, lasting until they establish a stable age structure.

In summary, the changing population geography of Britain is to some extent predictable. Its separate determinants of migration, mortality and fertility can be measured and used in standard demographic projections to say something useful about the future of British cities in the next decade or two. Those who have made such projections for local authority areas agree that the future is of greater diversity. This is expected as a result of population dynamics and there is no reason to relate it to negative causes or consequences. Leicester is forecast to be the first plural local authority outside London in about 2019, followed by Birmingham in about 2024.

Conclusion

Plural cities, where ethnicity does not distinguish a majority and minorities, are a sign of 20th- and 21st-century global mobility.

People's mobility across the world has increased. Our children grow up in cities where diversity is the norm.

This chapter has shown that the myths of imminent plural cities in Britain are not based on reliable evidence. The repeated claims of Minority White Cities by 2010 are exaggerations. The collation of evidence to show that Leicester and Birmingham are likely to join London boroughs in plural status, but not before 2019, is helpful in dispelling the myths. But a challenge to the factual correctness of a myth is of secondary importance to a challenge to why, even if true, the myth would be problematic. Why would it be inherently problematic for White people to be a minority in a city, even if it were so?[40]

Understandably, the existence of plural cities is of interest to those who either welcome the increasing diversity or fear it. It is perhaps also understandable that there should be interest in when particular cities may become plural. But this marker of plural status has no relevance whatever to the development of diversity or for urban policy from any perspective. Diversity exists in any city, by income and by cultural practice whether or not there is any ethnic diversity. And where there is a mix of ethnic groups as there is in every British city, the advantages and challenges of such a mix are a fact whether the White population makes up 95% or 5%. The move from 51% White to 49% White involves no appreciable change, except to those whose politics involve judgement of rights based on colour and family origins.

The focus on plural status is an unhelpful one because it is used to suggest a loss of rights by the White population. When used more generally by sensationalist media and politicians it appeals to fears that skin colour and diversity are threats to social cohesion; in short it amounts to what is known in Britain as 'playing the race card'.

Thus, the Leicester Multicultural Advisory Group promoted by local newspaper editor Nick Carter since 2003 was 'a response to hysteria whipped up by speculation that the city would have a minority white population by 2011'. The group discussed all issues but was particularly concerned with an active approach to marginalising racist politics.[41] As some of the contributors at the Commission for Racial Equality forum on plural cities suggested, the need is to focus on issues of specific behaviour, policy and investment in cities, and not be distracted by racial stereotyping, or, one might add, by the statistics of racial stereotyping.

Notes
[1] Leppard (2006).

[2] *The Guardian*, 13 December 2006. The report itself exaggerated the forum organisers' own publicity of 8 December 2006, which claimed only a plural city 'in the next decade' (www.inta-aivn.org/index. php?option=com_content&task=view&id=201&Itemid=112). In fact, neither the report of the forum itself (www.bctrust.org.uk/reports/Cities-Transition-Forum-Report.pdf) nor its supporting research document on Birmingham (www.bctrust.org.uk/reports/Mapping-Birmingham-Report.pdf) make any claim that Birmingham will become a plural city. The forum was organised by prestigious charities, the Cadbury Trust and the Young Foundation.

[3] http://83.137.212.42/sitearchive/cre/diversity/map/eastmidlands/leicester.html

[4] Several London boroughs have proportions of White British under 50% recorded in the 2001 Census, much smaller than Leicester's 60.5%. Outside London, Slough also has a lower proportion than Leicester, at 58.3%.

[5] http://en.wikipedia.org/wiki/Ethnic_groups_of_the_United_Kingdom. The claim has since been removed.

[6] The Institute of Community Cohesion also provides an overview of the development of community cohesion, at www.coventry.ac.uk/researchnet/icoco/a/2471

[7] The Smith Institute reports on the 'relationship between social enterprise and economic imperatives', and more recently 'on the policy implications arising from the interactions of equality, enterprise and equity'.

[8] Published in *New Statesman*, 1 May 2006, www.newstatesman.com/200605010050

[9] White Studies has emerged since the 1990s as an interdisciplinary field. It has asserted the need to examine the meanings of White identities (and how they relate to gender and class identities) to understand their role in negotiations of social power structures, including in race relations. The field of study has emerged from critical race studies and its anti-racist motivations. See Bonnett (2008) and Widdance Twine and Gallagher (2008) for overviews of the discipline of White Studies; and Frankenberg (1993) and Anderson (2003) for overviews of whiteness.

[10] Volume 31, Issue 1 of *Ethnic and Racial Studies* is a special issue on whiteness and includes several articles on the formation, meaning and implications of White identities.

[11] Dorling and Thomas (2004).

[12] Bonnett (2008, p 189).

[13] The study of how White identities are formed among minority ethnic groups is identified by Widdance Twine and Gallagher (2008) as a focus of the 'third wave' of whiteness studies.

[14] www.bnp.org.uk/landandpeople/cwlonminor.htm. The article 'estimates the true extent of the relentless colonisation of London'. It deducts an arbitrary 5% from the count of White British to account for 'White British Londoners [who] do not belong to an ethnic group indigenous to the British Isles (i.e. are not English, Scottish, Welsh or Irish)', and who are 'more often than not in the form of White "asylum-seekers" from Eastern Europe, North Africa, the Middle East and South America'.

[15] Divercity, www.birminghamdivercity.co.uk/businesscase.html (which has removed the claim since 2007)

[16] Leppard (2006).

[17] David Leppard, personal communication, March 2006.

[18] Nick Johnson, personal communication, 5 April 2006.

[19] Two are Leicester City Council documents. Although City politicians may have claimed imminent plural city status, Council staff have not undertaken projections of the population.

[20] The four references from Nick Johnson that gave no source for their predictions are: (a) *The Daily Telegraph*, 8 December 2000: Minority White cities by 2010 'One forecast earlier this year....' and 'According to one demographer....' (no name or source given), www.telegraph.co.uk/news/main.jhtml?xml=/news/2000/12/08/npop08.xml; (b) *Daily Mirror*, 16 April 2005: Paul Routledge says 'According to the experts....' (no names given), www.mirror.co.uk/news/allnews/tm_objectid=1540 8342&method=full&siteid=50143&headline=05-05-05--the-election---routledge-on-the-road--the-city-saved-by-immigrants-name_page. html; (c) The Benefit Fraud Inspectorate in 2004: Leicester 'is predicted to become the first minority city by 2011' (no source given), www. bfi.gov.uk/reports/2004/bfi/leicester/summary/; (d) The Leicester Partnership, 11 May 2005: Leicester ' by 2012....' (no source given), www.leicesterpartnership.org.uk/Meetings/Meet110505/Paper%20D %20Appendix%202%20Introductory%20text.pdf

[21] Clayton (2004, p 5) sources the claim to *The Guardian*, Esther Addley, 1 January 2001, which itself sources the City Council's school rolls, but not a population projection.

[22] Singh (2003, p 52).

[23] Nick Johnson, personal communication, 5 April 2006.

[24] *Bradford Telegraph & Argus*, 23 March 2006, p 15.

[25] *Birmingham Post*, 2 November 2006, in articles by Mohammed Nazir of the West Midlands Minority Ethnic Business Forum and Professor

Richard Scase, it is stated that 'one of the UK's most authoritative business forecasters' refers to 'the robust statistics offered in terms of Birmingham's changing demography' but without revealing who offered the particular claim of 'a black and ethnic majority in the make-up of its population by 2010'.

[26] Jeremy Paxman in the 2007 James MacTaggart Memorial Lecture blamed loss of purpose and loss of resources for the victory of 'agreed news' over investigation.

[27] See McCombs (1994) and O'Sullivan et al (1994) for discussions about media ownership and the management of the news.

[28] Philo (1999, p xi).

[29] CRE (2006).

[30] Four similar cases of misquoting and ignoring government and other statistics were the subject of a complaint to the Statistics Commission in 2007, discussed in Chapter Eight.

[31] Finney and Simpson (2008).

[32] Discussed in Ballard (1994).

[33] Simpson (2002) and Storkey (2002) note the lone contribution of local authority forecasts with an ethnic group dimension in the 1980s and 1990s, particularly in Bradford, Oldham and London. Earlier government national projections were discontinued in the 1970s. Academic work has flourished only since 2000.

[34] Ellis (2001) claims that it is impossible to usefully interpret projections of racial composition further than a few years from the present.

[35] Coleman and Scherbov (2005); Coleman (2006).

[36] See note 14 above. The other national and sub-national forecasts discussed in this chapter amalgamate all the White sub-groups, mainly to take advantage of the time series of demographic rates for 1991 and 2001 that this allows.

[37] Of 286,000 people who identified themselves as of Jewish religion in the 2001 Census, 218,000 also identified as White British.

[38] Rees (2008a). See also Rees (2008b, p 8) for a comparison of his projections with those of Coleman and Scherbov.

[39] GLA (2007); Bradford Council (2000); Stillwell et al (2006); University of Manchester (2007).

[40] This dual approach to myth-busting, tackling both statistics and ideology, is at the heart of many educational projects, for example the Bradford Anti-Racist Projects schoolkits (www.barp.yorks.com/).

[41] *Connections*, CRE magazine, Winter, 2003/04, http://83.137.212.42/sitearchive/cre/publs/connections/03wi_unitedfront.html

8

Conclusion

The myths and the litany

Myths about migration and race have been discussed separately in the chapters of this book. But the separate myths are often joined together as a larger cohesive story that describes the dangers of too much immigration, of segregation and of strongly independent ethnic communities. This larger story can be described as a litany, because of the way the dangers are repeated as a guide to policy, without reference to current and lived reality. The litany goes like this: 'Immigrants are a burden, taking jobs and resources, living piled together in segregated areas; segregation prevents integration, clashes with British culture, heightens tension and breeds violence'.

The litany is also made in reverse: 'Cultural tension makes people afraid, leading to White flight, self-segregation and ghetto-like parallel communities; instead of integrating, isolated minorities find devious ways of bringing new immigrants for marriage and work'. The litany equates immigration, diversity and segregation, labels all as problems and opposes them to integration, an equation that we have challenged in this book by investigating the evidence behind separate claims and showing them to be myths.

Looking at the claims as one bigger story in this concluding chapter allows us to find their consistencies and expose the views of the world that the claims represent. This in turn helps to understand why a range of politicians, commentators and the media find it convenient to recount the litany in spite of its mythical status.

The evidence

The reality shown by research gives very little support to the litany. We have shown that the history of immigration is one of concentration in available and cheaper housing followed by slow dispersal as integration proceeds. There are many reasons why separation might be expected to remain or to increase over time – racist or xenophobic hostility to newcomers, new immigration of family members, strong loyalty to family and to the place of one's upbringing, minority disadvantage in the housing and labour markets, the natural growth of immigrant populations through births, and the litany itself, which suggests to people who do not live in them that minority concentrations are particularly dangerous places. Yet despite all this, the evidence shows very clearly that minorities and the White population are more evenly spread than in the past. Migration of minorities away from settlement areas and increased mixing are occurring despite all those reasons for separation.

The litany ignores a great deal of other evidence, which is worth summarising here before we discuss *why* it is ignored. Segregation is greatly exaggerated. The average proportion of any of the ethnic groups across all the areas they live in did not exceed 30% in the last census, even when measured for the smallest areas of 150 households each. Britain's non-White areas are diverse, very rarely mono-ethnic. The only way in which segregation is increasing is when it is measured by the size of the minority populations, which is indeed increasing, but from births more than from immigration. The Pakistani, Bangladeshi and Black African groups are the most separated in Britain, in the sense of most unevenly spread. The White group is the most separated in Britain, in the sense of living in areas with only themselves.

The best indicator of integration is the size of the Mixed ethnic population, which is the fastest-growing minority. Minority ethnic groups are as likely to enter a family union outside their own group as White people are with minorities. The same goes for Muslims, who are as likely to enter a family union with non-Muslims as are Christians with non-Christians. Individual differences and choice in key areas of life – work, education, family, household – are the basis of liberal notions of creativity and development; differences abound in Britain and are defined as much by class, age and location as by one's ethnicity or religion. For example, when parents choose to send children to state schools that are not their closest, this sorts children more by income than by ethnicity.

Immigration to Britain is not exceptional in the world: Britain's proportion of immigrants is slightly less than the world average, and has grown between 1960 and 2005 at the same rate as world international migration. White flight is a myth except as an observation of White moves out of urban minority concentrations; the rate of movement out is the same for minorities. White movement out of cities preceded immigration, which can therefore be seen as replacing the out-migrating population rather than displacing it. In some cases, White movement is inward to minority concentrations, including in Bradford, Leicester and South London.

Violence is not unique to any ethnic group and is best dealt with through courts and with intelligence about criminal activities rather than through accusing whole communities of being soft on criminality. Muslims are no more likely to have been charged with terrorism if they live in concentrations of Muslim population than other areas of Britain. Similarly, race inequality is not best reduced by blaming its victims. Inequality in employment, for example, is as great outside minority concentrations as within them.

The myth-makers

Many claims about race and migration that are held up as received wisdom have been shown in the chapters of this book to be untrue or misleading interpretations of the evidence. Trevor Phillips has featured frequently, his importance deriving from his appointment by the government as a senior champion of equality, first as chair of the Commission for Racial Equality and now as chair of the Equality and Human Rights Commission. Together with his director of policy, Nick Johnson, at the Commission for Racial Equality, Phillips was the subject of a complaint that their behaviour

> brought official statistics, the use of statistics and statistical work by official and public bodies into disrepute; has increased misunderstanding of key social trends in Britain and on this basis could easily contribute to a rise in fear and racial hatred; [and] has set a bad example of how it is possible to argue your case by misquoting statistical evidence, deliberately misleading the public and policy makers on statistics as a result.[1]

The complaint, to the Commission for Racial Equality and the Statistics Commission, cited the lack of response to *The Sunday Times*, which had quoted Phillips' false claims on population forecasts discussed in Chapter Seven, Phillips and Johnson's misquoted statistics on residential and school segregation, Phillips' misleading interpretation of an unreliable survey on friendship groups discussed in Chapter Five and an argument from Johnson wrongly claiming increasing birth rates in China and India.

The Statistics Commission was constitutionally able to respond only to comments on official statistics. Having identified a number of inconsistencies in the Commission for Racial Equality website statistics, the Statistics Commission chair, Professor David Rhind, continued 'We do recognise that the CRE [Commission for Racial Equality] may wish to express and gather together opinions and predictions. We think though that any statements that suggest a basis in official statistics should be confirmed with the Office for National Statistics'.[2] As a public note from the chair of one government commission to another it was as about as forthright as possible, but it has not halted Trevor Phillips' misleading claims. His comment in January 2008 that 'We know that white flight is accelerating' was reported for a week as a news story from the government's head of its equalities body. When we requested the evidence behind this claim, Trevor Phillips sent a polite reply to say that he did not have time to discuss footnotes.[3] As we describe in Chapter Six, the evidence shows not White flight but a general movement from inner cities of all ethnic origins. The government appointee of Britain's equality commission should not be able to continue with such a cavalier attitude to evidence, such that truth can be bent according to the needs of his and the government's political perspective.

Another frequent myth-maker appearing in the pages of this book has been MigrationWatchUK, whose bogus and alarmist interpretations of population change were discussed in Chapters Three and Four. Their arguments lay every ill in Britain at the door of net immigration to Britain, and in particular immigration from non-Western cultures. The same arguments could be used equally to blame every ill on the fertility of working people since this contributes more to population growth, but perhaps such arguments would not be very popular. We wonder why racist and nationalistic views get such favoured coverage in some newspapers, television and parliamentary committees.

The response of government to diversity has also played a role in perpetuating the litany. When government minister Jack Straw lamented in 2006 that his constituents' use of the *niqab* (veil) was unhelpful to his understanding of their concerns, he let leash a storm of prejudice that ran the breadth of the litany. Phil Woolas, the minister in charge of government community cohesion policy declared his support by blaming veil-wearers for inviting discrimination and racism: 'Most British-born Muslims who wear it do so as an assertion of their identity and religion. This can create fear and resentment among non-Muslims and lead to discrimination. Muslims then become even more determined to assert their identity, and so it becomes a vicious circle where the only beneficiaries are racists like the BNP [British National Party]'. And counter-terrorist agencies in Britain and Europe had apparently long been concerned about the readiness of male Islamist terrorists to wear female clothing to escape detection.[4]

A cultural marker of Islam was identified by an experienced politician as also a sign of separation and inconvenience. Wearing of the *niqab* was depicted as self-inflicted disadvantage that causes discrimination and racism; and a hiding place for terrorists who will use it to avoid immigration controls. This 'them and us', 'with us or against us' view of community relations and integration is not floated in an obscure, extreme blog, but is put forward by government ministers and agencies, and reported as a news item by *The Times*. The message is clear: the choice is yours, but if you display such a marker of difference or allow others of your community to do so, then you are to blame for the racism, discrimination, harassment and attention from police services that your whole community will receive. It seems that 'the claiming of minority rights or affiliations is policed by a 'zone of moderation' that is ultimately defined by New Labour'.[5]

Why does the litany thrive?

An environment for ignoring the evidence

If the evidence undermines the litany of dangerous segregation, and shows more mixing and less segregation, why does the litany get so much space and such a good reception in British politics? When thinking about why this set of myths is repeated, it is clear that although there is coherence to the litany, it is adopted with different emphases. There is a range of personal and political perspectives that are supported by the litany. Some focus on bad segregation, some on bad immigration, some on bad religion and others on bad ethnicity, each making their own set of connections between these various elements of the litany. But it is the general acceptance of the whole litany that allows its elements to be repeated with impunity.

The litany has many characteristics of a moral panic: a consensual concern about the threats of segregation, perceptions of the problem disproportionate to the evidence, and hostility towards the minorities who are seen to be its cause. Periods of moral panic are not unusual and not necessarily detrimental. However, the moral panic about immigration has been identified as unique in its extent and in the role of government and the media in fuelling it. The segregation moral panic can be seen as an extension of the immigration moral panic, which could have 'serious and long lasting repercussions and might produce such changes as those in legal and social policy or even in the way society conceives itself'.[6] The segregation moral panic is extreme, and dangerously extreme because it is founded on myths.

Myths are powerful because, as we saw in Chapter One, they provide a means to understand society. If they become pervasive they can become folklore: 'So ever-present in the background of people's lives that it becomes almost invisible, folklore nonetheless shapes people's behaviour and reactions to events ... folklore is more pervasive than any number of public service announcements or posters and has a greater weight of authority, combining as it does from the collective wisdom and transmitted as it is on a personal, individual level'.[7] The litany, which does not represent the evidence of reality, is a candidate for folklore because of the attractiveness of its simple storyline, within which there is room for various perspectives to find justification.

The moral panic and the litany are strong because the threat or blame is placed on people or groups of people who are both visible and structurally weak. The 'problem' communities can be easily stereotyped and constructed as different from the mainstream. It is at times of intense social concern that 'othering' is most active, producing a self-reinforcing cycle of identifying difference and associating it with danger.[8] Stereotyping makes difference manageable by simplifying and generalising the other. It simultaneously perpetuates fear by keeping the other distant and distorted.[9] For MigrationWatchUK, the British National Party and others who link immigration to segregation and danger, the unwanted are those with non-Western culture.

Identifying the 'baddies' gives a more secure and definite identity to the 'goodies'. For example, there is such great difficulty defining what it means to be British that it becomes easier to assert a sense of Britishness by emphasising what is not British. When the British reject the foreigner, the asylum seeker, the immigrant, the minority, they are constantly defining and redefining their national identity.[10] Othering, therefore, is very much to do with belonging; with defining who belongs and who doesn't. A fierce and reactionary nationalism is undoubtedly behind some of the fear of new communities, however British those communities now are by birth and sentiment.

Identifying the 'baddies' can also serve political purposes and maintain the status quo:

> The pariah and stigmatised 'other' are an easy target for scapegoating and hence a useful tool in the hands of political leaders who wish to divert the blame for a critical situation from themselves onto the outgroup ... it is also readily taken up by the native population, as it saves them finding a culprit among their own group and challenging their reassuring order to which they are accustomed.[11]

Racism is not necessarily overt in the promotion of the litany. However, its role in perpetuating the myths should not be overlooked. Ideologies of race and race prejudice are historically embedded into British society and culture. The historical development of racism is ingrained in thinking, culture, institutions, ways of conduct, communications and emotions and is constantly reinforced.[12] It is unlikely that the institutional racism that was at the height of political concern at the end of the 1990s has been eradicated despite its relegation down the political agenda.[13] Writers on race and politics have commented that 'despite New Labour's gestures towards cultural diversity and inclusion, its body politic beats to the rhythm of a white heart'.[14]

The environment in which the litany thrives is also one influenced by a colonial history. It has been argued that Britain is still coming to terms with the loss of empire and that 'postcolonial melancholia' characterises the current phase of uncertainty about national identity.[15] This melancholia 'dictates that immigration can only be experienced as invasive war'[16] and the story becomes that the British are the main victims of their own colonial history. Current struggles for power on the international stage, including war in Iraq and Afghanistan, sit easily with a desire to limit dissent within Britain.

The illusive goals of integration

The problem with stereotyping and generalising in a framework of nationalist and conservative politics is that, in ignoring the evidence and perpetuating the litany, specific problems of integration are not addressed. And when specific problems are not identified and addressed the environment that nurtures the myths thrives, thus reinforcing the litany. The avoidance of naming specific problems in favour of the generalities of segregation, immigration and parallel communities may be the political route of least resistance. But this route has resulted in the abuse of evidence that we have seen in this book.

As we discussed in Chapter One, integration is a complex and multidimensional concept. So, there is no surprise that devising strategies that result in a perfectly integrated society is a difficult if not impossible task. What is this ideal society that we aspire to? It is easy for the aspiration to fail and for panic to emerge when the initial goals are unrealisable.

The cohesion agenda of integration is developing in some ways that cause concern because they seem more concerned with the litany than improving people's lives. In particular, recent thinking has equated successful integration not only with equal life *chances* – educational outcomes, access to housing and jobs and so on – but also with equal life *choices* – where people work, go to school and live. This philosophy suggests that integration will only be achieved with the elimination of all difference including in individual preference. This is surely an impossible as well as morally questionable target.

Where we work and live, and which school our children go to are only partly our choice, and depend crucially on where we lived when we were young and on our economic means. For immigrants it can be advantageous to gain the support of those who speak the same language and understand concerns about settling in a foreign and sometimes unwelcoming land. For some Black children, schooling in a minority ethnic environment is a positive advantage so that there is no need to 'act White' to achieve, in the same way as some girls thrive in all-girls schooling.

There is also a strongly repressive element to the notion that government should discourage differences in choice by breaking down segregation in where people live.[17] The rapid churn in populations that would be required to achieve constant equal residential spread along ethnic lines would bring about what one renowned sociologist of race called the death of community, through the tearing apart of families and friendship groups built during childhood and loyal to their neighbourhood. To engineer such 'integration' would demand a turning away from identity and a suicidal level of cultural self-abuse.[18] The focus on different life choices rather than life chances is particularly unhelpful because no line can be drawn to say when a difference is so large that it is dangerous. It is very difficult, if not impossible, to define what signifies an unacceptably different choice.

What is the alternative to the litany?

Naming specific problems

The dilemmas of a generalised litany of the problems of segregation and generalised solutions to integration that call for sameness can be somewhat overcome by breaking down the issues into specific problems. Forced marriages, the lowest wages and poorest working conditions are all illegal practices that affect immigrants and minorities more than others, but are best tackled explicitly rather than by blaming all immigrants and minorities and by setting improvements as conditions of cohesion or integration of whole communities. It does not help to hide problems in blanket terms of isolationism or segregation or life choices, which every immigrant and minority can fear may or may not apply to them. It is a matter of identifying and targeting specific problems.

Equally, the lack of housing, neighbourhood violence and terrorism in Britain are all serious issues,[19] but none is solved by hitching them to the immigration and social cohesion policy as is done all too frequently by those quoted in this book. The practice of blaming fundamental problems on immigrants and minorities in order to gain short-term political advantage or media prominence is known in Britain as 'playing the race card'. Direct discriminatory remarks about minorities are rightly rounded on in political circles, no longer acceptable. But it remains possible to cast whole communities into moral shadow by claiming a wilful lack of integration that burdens the rest of society. This 'rest of society', unnamed but certainly voters, are presumed well integrated although it is not clear with whom. This version of playing the race card involves the labelling of inner-city diverse areas as ghettos, of asylum seekers and immigrants as freeloaders, of Muslims as isolationists. If ghettos, freeloading or isolationism are the problems, they should be the target of political debate, rather than diversity, asylum seekers, immigrants and Muslims.

Calls for integration that ascribe attitudes to whole groups can therefore have a perverse effect, as Brendan Barber, the General Secretary of the Trades Union Congress (TUC), warned in 2005: 'We have had too many cheap calls for Muslims to integrate, some of which have come close to asking people to give up crucial parts of their identity. Building a tolerant liberal society ... will be that much harder when some groups suffer from such extreme levels of deprivation and poverty'.[20]

Perhaps one-sided cheap portrayals of reality come easily to politicians, who need to make a public impact, and to the media, who need to encapsulate a whole story into a headline. But one frequent result appears to be the easy invention and acceptance of negative stereotypes of segregation and immigration.

A prime example is the concern that followed claims that young Asians have fewer friendships with white folk than their parents. We saw in Chapter Five that this is not the case and that nevertheless same-ethnicity friendships need have nothing to do with a wilful isolationism. In fact, given the young age structure of the Asian population, the likelihood that children will become friends with their neighbours, particularly those of similar experiences and language, and that they may seek shelter from racism, it might be cause for celebration that roughly half or more of the friends of most minority ethnic residents of Britain are of a different group. This goes for Pakistanis and Bangladeshis as much as for Indians and Africans in Britain. The integration of young Asian men and women in gaining greater qualifications is good news and makes the ethnicity of one's friends rather less of an issue. The point here is that for many young people the demand that they choose friends according to some ethnic or religious code is a humiliating one that is most likely to turn them against authority. There are other subjects that get stigmatised in a litany of suspicion and dismissal: Muslims, Gypsies, black youth, segregated communities and single mothers are all fair game in the British press, although their punch-bag status varies in intensity over time. Lone mothers, for example, are alternately painted as sinners and scroungers. Although the alternative picture of struggling saints is too one-sided, it has to be made to break through the stigma and stereotyping. Similarly, one can show that so-called segregated areas are, in fact, usually diverse and supportive, without claiming that all is rosy in the inner-city neighbourhoods where most minorities live. And there is plenty of evidence that young Muslims are usually well integrated with aspirations and concerns familiar to any other British young person, without claiming that they are all saints.

A real evidence base

The misinterpretation of a social trend as a race issue is a characteristic of many of the myths we have discussed. Statistical research often shows an association between two factors (such as the ethnic composition of an area in which someone lives and their employment). Interpretation is then needed to try to explain the association and identify which is the cause and which is the effect (for example, that unemployment restricts many people's residence to poorer housing, which is also where ethnic concentrations are most likely to be). When the policy world is awash with fears of race conflict, immigration and segregation, it is not surprising that these have been handy clothes to drape over studies of social trends. We have shown, however, that it is possible to investigate the extent to which reality is racially painted. Very often it is the interpretation that is racial rather than the reality.

We feel that the evidence is abundant and conclusive that the patterns of minority and majority settlement do not reflect increasing segregation but historic employment and housing conditions, and that there is a level of ethnic mixing unprecedented in British history. This mixing involves social and residential mobility that is largely non-racial in magnitude and direction, and is apparent not just in a few isolated places but in British cities generally. The evidence is not hidden but readily available from national statistics agencies. Government agencies and the media should use it more seriously.

Whether all our arguments are accepted or not, we have shown that there are ways of using evidence that help to resist dogmatic assertions that immigration and segregation in Britain are causes of problems: on the contrary, immigration and segregation are results of much deeper global, political and economic processes. Some of these processes are benign demographic growth and dispersal, which are making Britain and much of the rest of the world more diverse places, and suggest that concern over segregation is entirely misplaced. Other processes concern the regulation of employment, and they may be partly under the control of government. But these processes are certainly no more the responsibility of immigrants and minorities than other members of society. Yet immigrants and minorities are too frequently the subject of humiliating demands to change in order to solve other people's problems.

Statistics and research more generally have a clear role in describing the world as it is, and the aspirations of the people who live in it. Those aspirations tend to be common across social groups, in favour of better housing, environment, training, education and leisure, along with respect for others. The abuse of statistics in the litany can and should be tackled. Evidence-based policy is only valuable if the evidence is robust; policy will only be evidence based when it escapes the lens of the litany.

Towards a fresh perspective

So what might be an alternative lens? If issues of segregation and integration are not to be framed within the litany, what is an alternative philosophy for thinking about our diverse society? We cannot offer a comprehensive solution and indeed that has not been the primary aim of this book. Rather, we hope to have opened debate towards recognising that a new policy framework is needed and developing ideas of what that new framework might look like. However, having identified the myths, we advocate a number of directions for thought.

A diverse society should not be thought of as a threat. Sameness cannot be an ideal, not least because it is impossible. There is no reason to give attention to ethnic difference any more than differences by class or gender or other lines of social identification. Diversity can be taken as an advantage rather than a disadvantage.[21] Similarly, the increased movement of people across international borders is a social change to be embraced rather than feared. As then Prime Minister Tony Blair said in 2000: 'We have a chance in this century to achieve an open world, an open economy, and an open global society with unprecedented opportunities for people and business'.[22] Besides, 'states that restrict movement are fighting a rearguard action'.[23] They are also contributing to global inequalities: 'Our efforts to keep poor people out while the rich and the educated circulate freely are a form of global apartheid. And like apartheid, they look increasingly unsustainable'.[24]

Any pursuit of nationalist ideas to create cohesion, as in the citizenship and cohesion agendas with their focus on shared values, should recognise that identities are multiple and transnational.

The strategies for a strong society should focus on meeting human rights and basic needs. There is more reason to focus on equality and living standards than on whether people are friends with each other or who lives near to whom. Policy should recognise what it can and cannot change. It can change the housing conditions of deprived populations (irrespective of ethnicity) but it cannot stop the Pakistani population having children. Tensions in society result from inequalities and perceptions of inequalities. Ethnicity per se is not the cause, except where racism is a driving force.

Finally, we should recognise that successful integration may be very messy. It may not follow the schemes of policies and programmes; it may not lend itself to being systematically monitored. Instead, it may be a more organic development of interactions between peoples; it may be 'an unruly, untidy and convivial mode of interaction in which differences have to be actively negotiated'.[25] In many ways, ethnic differences are ordinary and banal.[26] It is the litany that makes them a threat.

Notes

[1] The complaint was made by Ludi Simpson and by Daniel Dorling, Professor of Social Geography at the University of Sheffield. It is reproduced together with the CRE response at http://www.ccsr.ac.uk/staff/Ludi/race.html#CREcomplaint2007

[2] The Statistics Commission response is at www.statscom.org.uk/C_1201.aspx

[3] *Daily Mail*, 15 January 2008, '"White flight" from city centres is getting worse, says equality chief Trevor Phillips'. Phillips to Simpson, personal communication, 22 January 2008.

[4] The information and quote are from *The Times*, 9 October 2006, 'Suspect in terror hunt used veil to evade arrest', www.timesonline.co.uk/tol/news/uk/crime/article666149.ece

[5] Back et al (2002, p 450).

[6] Cohen (1987, p 9). Stanley Cohen's seminal work (1972) introduced the theory of moral panic in a study of mods and rockers in the UK in the 1960s and this ushered in research that looked at delinquent youth subcultures as reactions to growing up in a class society. In an updated version of the book (Cohen, 2002), Cohen discusses how the characteristics of moral panics have changed and identifies the immigration and asylum moral panic as distinct from others.

[7] Whatley and Henken (2000, p 8).

[8] The concept of 'othering' was popularised in the 1980s by Edward Said (1987) in his work on Western views of the Orient.

[9] Sibley (1995) discusses the processes, themes and images of stereotyping.

[10] Cohen (1994). See also Anderson (1991).

[11] Joly (1998, p 5).

[12] Jackson and Penrose (1993) discuss the social construction of racism. Jones (1997) gives definitions of prejudice and racism. Joly (1998) discusses processes and meanings of racism across Europe.

[13] Kundnani (2007b).

[14] Back et al (2002, p 453).

[15] See Gilroy (2005).

[16] Gilroy (2005, p 437).

[17] The wish for a reduction in difference is also in contradiction with policies that are intended to increase choice in the public service sector.

[18] Rex (1981).

[19] Although not as great a national risk as traffic accidents or a flu pandemic according to the National Risk Register published by the Cabinet Office in August 2008, available at www.cabinetoffice.gov.uk/reports/national_risk_register.aspx

[20] Brendan Barber, TUC, www.tuc.org.uk/equality/tuc-10401-f0.cfm

[21] The Intercultural Cities project is one example of a perspective seeing diversity as advantageous. See Wood and Landry (2007). Tariq Modood

is prominent among writers defending the concept of multiculturalism as a framework for a positive diverse society. See Modood (2007).

[22] Tony Blair, Davos, January 2000, quoted in Glover et al (2001, p 1).

[23] Dowty (1987, p 256).

[24] Legrain (2007, p 324).

[25] Gilroy (2005, p 438) introduces the concept of convivial multiculture. Amin (2002) also discusses negotiation of difference as a localised and everyday experience.

[26] This is the conclusion of Gilroy (2005) and also of Robinson (2005) in his review of the community cohesion agenda.

Myths and counterarguments: a quick reference summary

Immigration

The evidence: The UK experience of international migration is not remarkable when set in a global context

The myth: Britain has an unfair share of immigrants

- The number of immigrants in Britain (foreign-born) increased from 2.6 million in 1961 to 5.4 million in 2005. This rise of 110% is the same as the worldwide increase. These UN calculations take into account the changes in boundaries in Europe and the Soviet Union (pp 55–56).
- Increased international migration is a common experience for developed, economically strong nations. Immigration is expected for countries with strong economies as international moves are shaped by patterns of supply and demand of jobs and labour (pp 59, 84–85).
- Not only has the UK's immigration grown in line with world migration, but the UK has a smaller proportion of immigrants and lower rates of net immigration than the US, Canada, Australia and several large European countries (pp 55–56, 59–60, Table 3.2).
  - Less than 3% of the world's migrants live in the UK compared with 5% in Germany and 20% in the US (pp 59–60).
  - Migrants (those born outside the country) make up 9% of the population in the UK compared with 12% in Germany and 13% in the US. 9% is the average for Europe (p 60, Table 3.2).
  - The UK's net in-migration rate is 2 per 1,000 population compared with 3 in Germany and 4 in the US (p 60, Table 3.2).

For more on Britain's immigration experience in global context, see Chapter Three.

The evidence: Measurement of international migration requires care, and recognition of the diversity of migrants

The myth: We all know how much immigration there is (too much)

- The challenges of measuring international migration do not justify an assumption that levels of immigration are problematically large (pp 54–56).

- Ethnicity and immigration should not be confused: half of all minority residents were born in the UK and two thirds of immigrants are White (p 57).
- Undocumented migration is by its nature not measurable (and can only be estimated), except after an amnesty (p 57).

For more on measuring immigration, see Chapter Three.

The evidence: Immigrants are diverse and increasingly short-term stayers

The myth: Britain's flooded with problem immigrants

- Immigration to Britain in the year prior to the last census was equivalent to less than 1% of the population. In total, around 6% of residents in Britain are foreign nationals (residents who do not have British citizenship) (p 57).
- The myth of too many immigrants only has weight because it focuses on so-called 'problem' immigrants and in doing so draws on negative stereotypes (pp 56-57).
- Only 6% of recent immigrants to Britain were asylum seekers (p 56).
- Of the 205,000 migrants from European Union (EU) Accession countries in 2005, almost two thirds intended to stay for less than three months and would therefore not be classed as immigrants. The significance of short-term international migration is increasing (p 56).

For more on the diversity of immigration to Britain, see Chapter Three.

The evidence: Immigrants are a select group: young, motivated and skilled

The myth: Immigrants are lazy, good-for-nothing scroungers

- Immigrants are entrepreneurial, fill labour market gaps and improve productivity (p 62).
- Immigrants tend to be professionals and managers and this has been the case for three decades. Even refugees, often thought of as a burden, are more highly skilled than the population of Britain on average: 23% of refugees have a skilled trade compared with 12% of the rest of the UK population, and 22% of refugees are managers or

senior officials compared with 15% of the rest of the UK population (p 62).

- Immigrants are more likely than people born in the UK to be graduates (p 83, Table 4.4).
- Immigrants tend to be young – 91% were of working age in 2004. This redresses the balance of an ageing population, reducing the dependency of the economically inactive on the economically active (p 63).

For more on the selectivity of immigrants, see Chapter Three.

The evidence: Neither immigrants nor minorities take up most space in Britain

The myth: Not enough space and not enough housing because of immigration

- Myth-makers blame problems of population growth on immigrants. But they identify problem populations by ethnicity. Undoubtedly immigration and ethnicity are related but they must not be conflated. Half of all people in minority ethnic groups have been born in the UK and two thirds of immigrants are White (p 57).
- The apparent pressure on space and housing is much more a result of a trend for smaller household sizes and larger houses than it is the result of population growth through immigration (pp 79–80).
- Ethnic minorities are less responsible for this space and housing pressure than the White population. For example:
  - On average, White Britons live in households of 2.3 people whereas Bangladeshis live in households of 4.2 people (p 80, Table 4.1).
  - 30% of White Britons live in one-person households compared with 9% of Bangladeshis (p 80, Table 4.2).
  - White Britons take up three times the land area that Bangladeshis take up (p 80, Table 4.3).
- If the whole population lived in flats, with an average household size of four, without using up any more land than is currently used for housing, 201 million people could be accommodated in Britain (p 80).
- Immigration is not the reason for greenfield development. Residential movement out of cities has been occurring for at least half a century and is not unique to the UK. This counterurbanisation is as much to do with lifestyle choice as it is to do with population pressure.

People are not being pushed to the suburbs and rural areas because of immigrants. There is a stronger case that immigration is a consequence of counterurbanisation as immigrants take on the low-wage jobs and cheap housing that are left in urban centres (pp 81-82).

- MigrationWatchUK claims that England is overcrowded at 390 people per square kilometre but this is very sparse compared with London's 4,700 people per square kilometre. The population density of the UK (250/sq km) is similar to that of Germany (p 81).

For more on who is really putting pressure on space and housing in Britain, see Chapter Four.

The evidence: Economic bonus of immigration

The myth: Immigrants are an economic burden

- There is consensus – among government, the House of Lords, researchers and even anti–immigration organisations such as MigrationWatchUK – that immigration has an overall positive economic effect in Britain (p 61).
- On average, wage growth is encouraged by immigration. Immigrants are more likely than others to experience employment conditions that do not meet minimum standards (p 61).
- The UK is a net gainer of remittances. That is, more money is sent to the UK from people living abroad than is sent abroad from people living in the UK (pp 61-62).

For more on economic benefits of immigration, see Chapter Three.

The evidence: Immigrants use fewer public services than they pay for

The myth: Immigrants are a burden on the state

- Migrants are self-selective – they are more likely to be young, in good health, well qualified and of high socioeconomic status than people who do not migrate to Britain (p 82).
- Immigrants are more likely to be managers or professionals, and more likely to be graduates, than people born in the UK (p 83, Table 4.4).
- Immigrants contribute more in taxes than they use in benefits and public services (p 84).

- 6% of non-British nationals in Manchester are claiming out-of-work benefit compared with 20% of the total working-age population of the district. The figure for England and Wales as a whole is 8% (p 85).
- Asylum seekers do not have the right to work. They are eligible to apply for accommodation and subsistence support from the National Asylum Support Service but not for other benefits. Since 1993, levels of destitution among asylum seekers have markedly increased (p 85).

For more on why immigrants aren't a burden, see Chapter Four.

The evidence: Services that respect ethnic diversity are no more costly than other equality services

The myth: The burden of ethnic diversity is too great for service providers

- Responding to diversity of needs is nothing new, and there is no reason for the costs associated with service provision for ethnic diversity to be any more seen as a burden than costs associated with service provision for gender, dietary or any other kind of diversity (p 86).
- If diversity is framed as competition, so that one person's demands are seen as a threat to others, then the minority easily becomes the scapegoat for more structural problems of scarcity of resources (p 86).

For more on why ethnic diversity isn't a burden, see Chapter Four.

The evidence: MigrationWatchUK selects its figures to make a political case

The myth: MigrationWatchUK is a reliable source for immigration information and comment

- MigrationWatchUK sustains the myth that there is too much immigration by presenting evidence that is far from balanced, using claims that are factually inaccurate. Its use of immigration figures out of context promotes fear of immigration and of immigrants. MigrationWatchUK does not make clear why it is only population growth through immigration that it considers a problem.

MigrationWatchUK holds political weight due to its acceptance by parts of the media and political elite, not because its logic and statistics hold water (pp 63-69).

- MigrationWatchUK claims that it is only concerned about the balance of migration but is clearly anti-immigration with prejudices against non-Western immigrants (p 66).
- MigrationWatchUK's claim that 83% of the UK's population growth is due to immigration is a nonsense calculation – it might as well have said that immigration accounts for 211% of the UK's growth. MigrationWatchUK chooses the figure that gives it the best headline (pp 65-66).
- MigrationWatchUK's arguments are founded on the concept that population growth (through immigration) is costly for Britain. But the evidence shows that immigrants are not more costly than others in terms of use of space, housing requirements or benefits claims. And immigrants overall have a positive impact on Britain's economy (pp 66-69, 78-82).
- MigrationWatchUK argues that the cost of children of immigrants should be taken into account when calculating the economic effect of immigration. But in this logic, at what point – after how many generations – does one stop being an immigrant (p 68)?

For more on MigrationWatchUK's fanciful footwork with figures, see Chapter Three.

Integration

The evidence: More mixed-ethnicity friendship groups
The myth: More segregated friendship groups

- For most ethnic minority young people, roughly half or more than half of their friends are White (p 96).
- Minorities born in Britain are less likely to have exclusively minority friends than those born outside Britain. This is despite there being twice as many minority young adults (in their twenties) as minority old adults (in their fifties), which could lead to an expectation that young minorities have more friends among minorities than their parents (p 97, Table 5.1).
- Less than 20% of minorities born in Britain have friends only from their own group (p 97).

- White people are the most isolated in their friendships – more than half have only White friends (pp 97–98).
- Neighbourhoods with fewest White people are where people have most ethnically diverse friends – probably because these neighbourhoods have most ethnic diversity among residents (p 97).
- Most people of Mixed ethnic groups have parents of different ethnicities. The growth of the Mixed group is therefore an indicator of the most intimate form of inter-ethnic friendship. There are 650,000 people of Mixed ethnic group in England alone, making it the third largest minority after the Indian and Pakistani groups. It is one of the fastest-growing ethnic groups (p 99).
- Asian Muslims, Sikhs and Hindus all marry out of their own groups just as often as White Christians (p 99).
- When the Chair of the Commission for Racial Equality claimed in 2005 that 'alarmingly, we showed that young people from ethnic minorities were twice as likely to have a circle of pals exclusively from their own community as were older ethnic minority folk', he was using a judicious compound of alarmist language and false claim to scientific rigour to create a striking message about friendship groups, unsupported by the evidence, of dangerous inward-looking communities, harbingers of a bleak future for the UK (p 99).

For more on mixed ethnicity friendships, see Chapter Five.

The evidence: Greater tolerance in social attitudes

The myth: A population 'gripped by fear' of racial unrest

- British Social Attitudes surveys going back to the 1980s reveal that the White population in Britain is now much more accepting than in the past of having a minority ethnic boss and of a close relative marrying someone from a minority ethnic group (pp 102–103).
- The growth in tolerance is the result of general changes in social attitudes and also due to younger generations being more tolerant than the older generations whom they are replacing (pp 102–103).
- International opinion surveys reveal that Britain is more tolerant towards ethnic difference than many other European countries (p 103).
- Local studies have demonstrated that these tolerant attitudes are evident across the country including in Oldham and Bradford, which were affected by ethnic conflict in 2001 (p 104).

- In Oldham, 82% of those aged under 25 were optimistic that people from different ethnic backgrounds could get on well together, compared with 52% of those aged 75 and older (p 104).

For more on ethnicity and social attitudes, see Chapter Five.

The evidence: Desire for mixed schools not being met

The myth: Minorities choose segregated schools

- School ethnic composition is a little more polarised than residential polarisation but the difference is not more than one would expect from social selection by income, and is not growing over time (pp 106–107).
- Headline claims that schools are becoming more segregated than the areas they sit in are not based on evidence (pp 105–106).
- School selection is less associated with ethnicity than with income. It may be that the two types of selection are confounded, that is, selection of schools by the better off results in ethnic selection as a by-product because minorities are generally economically disadvantaged in comparison with White people (pp 106–107).
- School choice does not operate evenly or equally across social groups. Some people are more likely to be allocated the school of their choice than others. Some people's choices are more restricted, for example by financial means to travel to schools further away or pay for private education (pp 107–108).
- There is a desire for ethnically mixed schools among White and minority families but the operation of the system of school choice is preventing this. School segregation, to the extent that it can be shown to exist, is not a result of desire for self-segregation but a result of a mismatch between choice and outcome. This poses a challenge for schools, which must meet their responsibilities to promote good race relations (pp 107–108).

For more on school choice and mixing, see Chapter Five.

Segregation

The evidence: Minorities want to live in mixed neighbourhoods
The myth: Minorities want to live in segregated neighbourhoods

- Housing aspirations of young people from White and minority ethnic groups are very similar: they all desire safe neighbourhoods with good environments, no anti-social behaviour and to be near to family and friends (p 100).
- Minority youngsters look to live in areas that are ethnically mixed and are not in search of ethnic isolation (pp 100-101).
- Barriers to minorities achieving their preferred housing include racism, lack of affordable housing and housing market structures that may steer people of different ethnicities to live in particular areas (pp 101-102).

For more on the housing aspirations of minority ethnic people, see Chapter Five.

The evidence: Bradford is ethnically mixed with no sign of ghettos, just like the rest of Britain
The myth: Bradford's experience illustrates how Britain is sleepwalking to segregation

- There are no ghettos in Britain and no change towards ghettos. The case study of Bradford clearly shows that this district, like all others, can by no means be considered to contain a ghetto (pp 122-124).
- Only 3 of the 30 wards in the district of Bradford have 50% or more of their population from ethnic groups other than White (Bradford Moor, University, Toller) and each of these has more than 25% White population. These are mixed areas rather than ghettos of single origin (pp 122-123).
- The number of mixed wards (which are conceptually opposite to ghettos) in Bradford increased from 12 in 1991 to 15 in 2001 (p 123).
- The minority populations in Bradford are growing primarily as a result of more people being born than dying, which is expected from populations with young age structures (such as Pakistani and Bangladeshi populations). In-migration is not the main driver of minority population growth (p 123).

- There is considerable movement of people from minority ethnic groups out of the minority ethnic areas of Bradford, such as University ward, to elsewhere in the UK. In 2000-01, 1,066 minority ethnic residents left the ward for other parts of the UK, while 622 arrived from elsewhere in the UK: 444 more minority residents left than arrived (p 123).
- There is a movement of White populations on balance into the diverse areas of Bradford. In 2000-01, 185 more White residents moved to University ward from other parts of the UK than left it (p 123).

For more on ethnic mixing in Bradford, see Chapter Six.

The evidence: Greater ethnic mixing in neighbourhoods across Britain

The myth: Britain is becoming a country of ghettos

- British population dynamics are not those of ethnic division and separation. The picture of growth, dispersal and mixing seen in Bradford is common across Britain (pp 129-133).
- The White population is by far the most isolated ethnic group. The only concentrations which are anything like ghettos are of White people. At the scale of a few streets, the average White person lives in an area that has more than 94% White people in it. Pakistanis in Britain live in street-level areas that on average have 26% Pakistani residents (p 124).
- There are no very high concentrations of particular ethnic groups, other than White, because the areas with fewest White residents are diverse and becoming more so (pp 124-125).
- The spread of the population of each minority ethnic group has become more even and less clustered over time. This is true at each geographical scale: local authority districts, electoral wards and street-level census areas. This is indicated by the Index of Dissimilarity, which for the minority ethnic population taken as a whole has decreased from 61.4 in 1991 to 58.8 in 2001 (p 126, Table 6.1).
- Academic and government reports (*State of the English Cities*) agree that residential ethnic clustering has not increased for any city in Britain (pp 125-126).
- Only six districts (out of 408) in Britain contain any ward with more than three quarters minority ethnic residents. Even in the least White ward in Britain – Southall Broadway in the London Borough of Ealing – 12% of the population is White (p 129, Table 6.3).

- Tower Hamlets is the most ethnically mixed district in Britain. All of its wards have at least one quarter White population and one quarter minority ethnic population (p 129, Table 6.3).
- Thousands of wards have a majority White population. Eight wards have a majority of a single minority ethnic group. These wards are in Leicester, Bradford, Pendle, Ealing and Tower Hamlets (p 132, Table 6.3).
- The highest proportion for a single minority group is 74%, the proportion of Indians in the population of the Latimer ward of Leicester. This is far from a ghetto, and cannot be compared with Chicago, where over half the Black population live in neighbourhoods that are more than 90% Black (p 132, Table 6.3).

For more evidence against claims of ghettos, see Chapter Six.

The evidence: Ethnic clustering can and does result from positive causes and has positive consequences

The myth: Residential segregation is a cause and consequence of social breakdown

- Clustering – be it along the lines of ethnicity or class or occupation or any other social indicator – can be a matter of choice as a result of positive affiliations. Negative causes or consequences of clustering cannot be assumed. A distinction should be made between 'good segregation' and involuntary segregation that is the result of inequalities and discrimination (p 118).
- Ethnic inequalities are not caused by areas with high proportions of minorities. For example, minority unemployment is double that of White unemployment in areas with mainly White population as well as in areas with less than 50% White population. Social inequality is evident irrespective of ethnic composition, and this inequality should be the focus of concerns (p 135, Table 6.4).

For more about the meaning of residential clustering, see Chapter Six.

The evidence: For terrorists, there's nothing special about 'segregated' areas

The myth: Segregation breeds terrorism

- Muslims are not more likely to be charged with terrorism if they live in areas of Muslim concentration rather than in any other area of Britain (pp 109-110).
- A Muslim from Bradford is no more likely to be a terrorist than a Muslim from Bexley. There is no reason to link particular levels of Muslim concentration with terrorism (p 110).

For more on the association between terrorism and ethnic composition, see Chapter Five.

Population change

The evidence: Larger minority neighbourhoods result from natural growth (less from immigration and not at all from retreat)

The myth: Growth of minority clusters is caused by retreat

- Residential clustering is the result of neither White flight nor minority retreat, but much more benign demographic change, mostly non-racial in character (Chapters Six and Seven).
- Natural change (births minus deaths) adds more to Indian, Pakistani and Bangladeshi populations in Britain than does immigration (p 149).
- Population growth in areas with large minority ethnic populations is predominantly a result of natural change, that is, more people being born than dying (p 132).
- In the districts with highest minority ethnic population, births add more to the minority population than does immigration or migration from elsewhere in the UK. For example, for minorities during one year (pp 130-131, Table 6.2):
  - in Ealing's minority concentration there were 431 births and 401 immigrants;
  - in Birmingham's minority concentration there were 1,411 births and 718 immigrants;
  - in Bradford's minority concentration there were 403 births and 302 immigrants.
- Family-building is an expected demographic process for population groups that have a young age structure, which is more the case for

Britain's minority ethnic groups than for the White population (p 151).

For more on demographics of population change, see Chapters Six and Seven.

The evidence: Shared migration experiences which result in more mixed neighbourhoods

The myth: White flight and minority retreat

- There is movement out of minority clusters by each minority ethnic group and the White group at similar rates. Dispersal of this kind is evident for each minority ethnic group, for the 1990s and the 2000s, and for districts, wards and street-level neighbourhoods (p 127).
- Indians are leaving Leicester, Caribbeans are leaving Lambeth, Bangladeshis are leaving Tower Hamlets and Pakistanis are leaving Bradford (p 127).
- Minorities are moving away from their concentrations and into areas where they are least concentrated (p 127):
  - The highest Indian concentrations annually lost 0.4% of their Indian population to other parts of the UK.
  - The highest Black concentrations annually lost 1.6% of their Black population to other parts of the UK.
  - The highest Pakistani/Bangladeshi concentrations annually lost 0.3% of their Pakistani/Bangladeshi population to other parts of the UK.
- The highest White concentrations gained the equivalent of 0.2% of their existing White population. The areas with fewest White residents lost 0.5% of their White population (p 127).
- There is White movement into minority concentrations in Leicester, Bradford, Lambeth, Wolverhampton, Wycombe, Manchester and Merton (p 132, Table 6.3).
- In 23 of the 35 minority concentrations in Britain more minorities than the White group moved out to elsewhere in the UK (Table 6.3).
- These patterns have non-racial explanations. They represent aspirational movements reflecting the well-established trends of movement from cities to suburban and more rural areas (counterurbanisation) (pp 127-128).

- Immigration replaces the White population, rather than displaces it. Significant migration out of Leicester began before significant immigration to it (p 128, Table 6.2).
- Comments such as 'We know that White flight is accelerating' have no basis in evidence. White and minority groups are moving in the same direction and at the same rate (pp 128-129).

For more on migration patterns, see Chapter Six.

The evidence: Leicester is likely to be the first Minority White City, around 2019

The myth: Leicester will be minority White by 2011, followed by Bradford, Oldham and Birmingham by 2016

- It is possible to project ethnic group populations. Ethnic group population methodology, especially for small areas, is in its infancy and faces many technical and conceptual difficulties. Forecasts can act as a guide to changing needs and can thereby inform policy development (pp 151-155).
- To the extent that it can be predicted, Birmingham's population will be less than 50% White around 2024, Bradford's after 2031 and Leicester's around 2019 (p 147, Table 7.1 and Figure 7.1).
- All the local authorities that have been forecast to have less than 50% White population sometime in the next few decades will remain ethnically mixed with between 25% and 50% White population (p 155).
- Claims from the government equalities body of Leicester's future population were not based on evidence but on uncritical repetition of unfounded claims made by others (pp 146-149).

For more on minority ethnic population projections, see Chapter Seven.

The evidence: We're already diverse, and so what?

The myth: Imminent threat of Minority White Cities

- The three elements of the 'Minority White Cities' myth do not combine into a concept that has substantive meaning or significance. There is no reason to focus on 50%, on whiteness or on cities as markers of critical change in ethnic diversity (p 144).

- 'Minority White City' associates a White majority with a superior value and a society that is more governable than a diverse one. The concept is racist (pp 144–146).
- The 'Minority White Cities' myth has been created by a trail of unsubstantiated claims made by the media and the (former) Commission for Racial Equality (pp 146–149).
- The focus on 'Minority White Cities' is a distraction from particular material problems of integration (pp 143–144).
- At sub-city scales there are already areas where White people make up less than half the population, and these are predominantly diverse areas where no one ethnic group dominates (pp 150–151 and Chapter Six).

For more on the claims of 'Minority White Cities', see Chapter Seven.

References

Abbas, T. (2007) 'Muslim minorities in Britain: integration, multiculturalism and radicalism in the post-7/7 period', *Journal of Intercultural Studies*, 28(3): 287–300.

Alam, Y. (2007) *Made in Bradford*, Pontefract: Route.

Alba, R. and Nee, V. (1997) 'Rethinking assimilation theory for a new era of immigration', *International Migration Review*, 31(4): 826–74.

Alba, R. and Nee, V. (2005) *Remaking the American Mainstream: Assimilation and Contemporary Immigration*, Harvard: Harvard University Press.

Alba, R.D., Logan, J.R., Stults, B.J., Marzan, G. and Zhang, W. (1999) 'Immigrant groups in the suburbs: a reexamination of suburbanization and spatial assimilation', *American Sociological Review*, 64(3): 446–60.

Alba, R.D., Logan, J.R. and Stults, B.J. (2003) 'Enclaves and entrepreneurs: assessing the payoff for immigrants and minorities', *International Migration Review*, 37(2): 344–88.

Amin, A. (2002) 'Ethnicity and the multicultural city: living with diversity', *Environment and Planning A*, 34: 959–80.

Amin, A. (2005) 'Local community on trial', *Economy & Society*, 34(4): 612–33.

Anderson, B. (1991) *Imagined Communities: Reflections on the Origin and Spread of Nationalism*, London: Verso.

Anderson, M.L. (2003) 'Whitewashing race: a critical perspective on whiteness', in A. Doane and E. Bonilla-Silv (eds) *White Out: The Continuing Significance of Racism* (pp 21–34), New York: Routledge.

Andersson, R., Musterd, S., Galster, G. and Kauppinen, T.M. (2007) '"What mix matters?": Exploring the relationship between individuals' incomes and different measures of their neighbourhood context', *Housing Studies*, 22(5): 637–60.

Aspinall, P. (2000) 'The challenges of measuring the ethno-cultural diversity of Britain in the new millennium', *Policy & Politics*, 28(1): 109–18.

Aspinall, P. (2001) 'Operationalising the collection of ethnicity data in studies of sociology of health and illness', *Sociology of Health and Illness*, 23(6): 829–62.

Athwal, H. (2001) 'The racism that kills', *Race & Class*, 43(2): 111–23.

Back, L., Keith, M., Khan, A., Shukra, K. and Solomos, J. (2002) 'New Labour's white heart: politics, multiculturalism and the return of assimilation', *The Political Quarterly*, 73(4): 445–54.

Bailey, N. and Livingstone, M. (2005) *Determinants of Individual Migration: An analysis of SARs Data*, SCRSJ Working Paper No 3, Glasgow: Scottish Centre for Research on Social Justice, University of Glasgow.

Bailey, N. and Livingstone, M. (2006) *Population Turnover and Area Deprivation: Final Report*, Glasgow: Scottish Centre for Research on Social Justice, University of Glasgow.

Ballard, R. (ed) (1994) *Desh Pardesh: The South Asian Presence in Britain*, London: Hurst & Co.

Barrett, G.A., Jones, T.P. and McEvoy, D. (2001) 'Socio-economic and policy dimensions of the mixed embeddedness of ethnic minority business in Britain', *Journal of Ethnic and Migration Studies*, 27(2): 241-58.

Berthoud, R. (1998) 'Defining ethnic groups: origin or identity', *Patterns of Prejudice*, 32(2): 53-63.

Berthoud, R. (2000) 'Ethnic employment penalties in Britain', *Journal of Ethnic and Migration Studies*, 26(3): 389-416.

Beynon (2006) 'Race and immigration: is it the end of the affair?', available at www.jcwi.org.uk/policy/uklaw/raceandimmigration_ spring06.html

Blackaby, D.H., Leslie, G.G., Murphy, P.D. and O'Leary, N.C. (2002) 'White/ethnic minority earnings and employment differentials in Britain: evidence from the LFS', *Oxford Economic Papers*, 54: 270-97.

Blair, T. (2006) *Our Nation's Future, Multiculturalism and Integration*, London: HM Government.

Blum, A., Guérin-Pace, F. and Le Bras, H. (2007) 'La statistique, piège ethnique', *Le Monde*, 10 November, www.lemonde.fr/web/ article/0,1-0@2-3232,36-976492,0.html

BMJ (British Medical Journal) (1996) 'Ethnicity, race and culture: guidelines for research, audit, and publication', *BMJ*, 312: 1094.

Boag, J. (2001) 'Taking the politics out of the census?', *Radical Statistics*, 78: 40-7.

Boal, F.W. (1976) *Social Areas in Cities*, Vol 1 (eds: Herbert, D.T. and Johnston, R.J.), London: Wiley, pp 41-79.

Boal, F.W. (1999) 'From undivided cities to undivided cities: assimilation to ethnic cleansing', *Housing Studies*, 14(5): 585-600.

Bonnett, A. (2008) 'White studies revisited', *Ethnic and Racial Studies*, 31(1): 185-96.

Booth, H. (1988) 'Identifying ethnic origin: the past, present and future of official data production', in A. Bhat, R. Carr-Hill and S. Ohri (eds; The Radical Statistics Race Group) *Britain's Black Population*, Gower: Aldershot.

Bourne, J. (2001) 'The life and times of institutional racism', *Race & Class*, 43(20): 7–22.

Bradford Council (1985) *District Trends 1984*, Bradford: City of Bradford Metropolitan District Council.

Bradford Council (2000) *Population Forecasts for Bradford 1999-2021: Age, Sex and Ethnic Group*, Bradford: City of Bradford Metropolitan District Council, Policy and Research Unit.

Brimblecombe, N., Dorling, D. and Shaw, M. (1999) 'Mortality and migration in Britain: first results from the British Household Panel Survey', *Social Science and Medicine*, 49: 981–8.

Brimblecombe, N., Dorling, D. and Shaw, M. (2000) 'Migration and geographical inequalities in health in Britain', *Social Science and Medicine*, 50: 861–78.

Bromley, M. and Sonnenberg, U. (eds) (1998) *Reporting Ethnic Minorities and Ethnic Conflict: Beyond Good or Evil*, Maastricht: European Journalism Centre.

Bross, I. (1960) 'Statistical criticism', *Cancer*, 13: 394-400, Reprinted in E.R. Tufte (ed) (1970) *Quantitative Analysis of Social Problems* (pp 97–108), London: Addison–Wesley.

Brown, C. and Gay, P. (1985) *Racial Discrimination: 17 years after the Act*, London: Policy Studies Institute.

Browne, A. (2000) 'The last days of a white world', *The Observer*, 3 September.

Browne, A. (2002) *Do We Need Mass Immigration? The Economic, Demographic, Environmental, Social and Developmental Arguments against Large-Scale Net Immigration to Britain*, London: Civitas: the Institute for the Study of Civil Society.

BSSRS (British Society for Social Responsibility in Science) (1981) *Race: The Case Against Including any Question on Race or Ethnic Origin in the 1981 Census*, London: BSSRS.

Burrows, R. (1999) 'Residential mobility and residualisation in social housing in England', *Journal of Social Policy*, 28(1): 27-52.

Cabinet Office (2000) *Minority Ethnic Issues in Social Exclusion and Neighbourhood Renewal*, Report from the Social Exclusion Unit, London: Cabinet Office.

Cantle, T. (2001) *Community Cohesion: A Report of the Independent Review Team*, London: Home Office.

Carter, B., Harris, C. and Joshi, S. (1987) *The 1951-1955 Conservative Government and the Racialisation of Black Immigration*, Policy Papers in Ethnic Relations No 11, Warwick: Centre for Research in Ethnic Relations, University of Warwick.

Champion, T. (ed) (1989) *Counterurbanisation: The Changing Pace and Nature of Population Deconcentration*, London: Edward Arnold.

Champion, T. and Fielding, T. (eds) (1992) *Migration Processes and Patterns, Volume 1: Research Progress and Prospects*, London: Belhaven.

Chiswick, B.R. (2005) *The Economics of Immigration*, London: Edward Elgar.

Chiswick, B.R. and Miller, P.W. (2007) *The Economics of Language: International Analyses*, London: Routledge.

Clayton, J. (2004) The everyday politics of the multicultural city, ESRC/ODPM Postgraduate Research Programme Working Paper 7, http://www.communities.gov.uk/documents/corporate/pdf/146832.pdf

Cohen, R. (1994) *Frontiers of Identity: The British and the Others*, London: Longman.

Cohen, S. (1987) *Folk Devils and Moral Panics* (2nd edition), Oxford: Blackwell

Cohen, S. (1972) *Folk Devils and Moral Panics*, London: MacGibbon and Kee.

Cohen, S. (2002) *Folk Devils and Moral Panics* (3rd edition), London: Routledge.

Coleman, D. (2006) 'Immigration and ethnic change in low-fertility countries: a third demographic transition', *Population and Development Review*, 32(3): 401–46.

Coleman, D. and Salt, J. (eds) (1996) *Ethnicity in the 1991 Census: Volume 1: Demographic Characteristics*, London: OPCS.

Coleman, D. and Scherbov, S. (2005) 'Immigration and ethnic change in low-fertility countries – towards a new demographic transition?', Paper presented at the Population Association of America annual conference, Philadelphia, USA.

Commission on Integration and Cohesion (2007) *Our Shared Future*, London: Department for Communities and Local Government, www.integrationandcohesion.org.uk

Community Cohesion Panel (2004) *The End of Parallel Lives? The Report of the Community Cohesion Panel*, London: Home Office.

CRE (Commission for Racial Equality) (1996) *We Regret to Inform You ...*, London: CRE.

CRE (2002) Ethnic monitoring categories for England and Wales, http://83.137.212.42/sitearchive/cre/gdpract/em_cat_ew.html

CRE (2006) *Scoring goals for integration in Leicester*. Press release, 21 March.

CRE (2007) *A Lot Done, A Lot To Do: Our Vision for an Integrated Britain*, London: CRE.

Daniel, W. (1968) *Racial Discrimination in England*, Harmondsworth: Penguin.

Danielis, J. (2007) 'Ethnic population forecasts for Leicester using POPGROUP, Dissertation in support of Social Research Methods and Statistics Masters degree, University of Manchester.

DCSF (Department for Children, Schools and Families) (2008) *The Composition of Schools in England*, London: DCSF, www.dfes.gov. uk/rsgateway/DB/SBU/b000796/index.shtml

Denham, J. (2001) *Building Cohesive Communities: A Report of the Ministerial Group on Public Order and Community Cohesion*, London: Home Office.

DIUS (Department for Innovation, Universities and Skills) (2008) *Promoting Good Campus Relations, Fostering Shared Values and Preventing Violent Extremism in Universities and Higher Education Colleges*, London: DIUS.

Dobson, J., Koser, K., McLaughlin, G. and Salt, J. (2001) *International Migration and the United Kingdom: Recent Patterns and Trends*, London: Research Development and Statistics Directorate, Home Office.

Dodd, V. (2008) 'New strategy to stem flow of terror recruits', *The Guardian*, 28 February, p 1, www.guardian.co.uk/uk/2008/feb/28/ uksecurity.islam

Dorling, D. and Rees, P. (2003) 'A nation still dividing: the British census and social polarisation 1971–2001', *Environment and Planning A*, 35(7): 1287–313.

Dorling, D. and Thomas, B. (2004) *People and Places: A 2001 Census Atlas of the UK*, Bristol: The Policy Press.

Dowty, A. (1987) *Closed Borders: The Contemporary Assault on Freedom of Movement*, London and New Haven, CT: Yale University Press.

Dunn, K. (1998) 'Rethinking ethnic concentration: the case of Cabramatta, Sydney', *Urban Studies*, 35(3): 503–27.

Dustmann, C., Fabbi, F., Preston, I. and Wadsworth, J. (2003a) *Labour Market Performance of Immigrants in the UK Labour Market*, Home Office Online Report 05/03, London: Home Office, http://www. homeoffice.gov.uk/rds/pdfs2/rdsolr0503.pdf

Dustmann, C. Fabbi, F., Preston, I. and Wadsworth, J. (2003b) *The Local Labour Market Effects of Immigrations in the UK*, Home Office Online Report 06/03, London: Home Office, http://www.homeoffice.gov. uk/rds/pdfs2/rdsolr0603.pdf

Dustmann, C., Frattini, T. and Preston, I. (2007) *A Study of Migrant Workers and the National Minimum Wage and Enforcement Issues that Arise*, London: Low Pay Commission.

Eagleton, T. (2007) 'Those in power are right to see multiculturalism as a threat', *The Guardian*, 21 February.

Ellis, M. (2001) 'What future for whites? Population projections and racialised imaginaries in the U.S.', *International Journal of Population Geography*, 7: 213-29.

Esmail, A. and Everington, S. (1993) 'Racial-discrimination against doctors from ethnic minorities', *British Medical Journal*, 306: 691-2.

EUMC (European Monitoring Centre on Racism and Xenophobia) (2002) *Racism and Cultural Diversity in the Mass Media*, Vienna: EUMC.

Fieldhouse, E. and Cutts, D. (2008) 'Mobilisation or marginalisation? Neighbourhood effects on Muslim electoral registration in 2001', *Political Studies*, 56(6): 333-54.

Finney, N. (2003) *The Challenge of Reporting Refugees and Asylum Seekers*, Bristol: ICAR/Presswise.

Finney, N. and Robinson, V. (2008) 'Local press negotiation and contestation of national discourses on asylum seeker dispersal', *Social and Cultural Geography*, 9(4): 397-414.

Finney, N. and Simpson, L. (2008) 'Internal migration and ethnic groups: evidence for Britain from the 2001 census', *Population, Space and Place*, 14(2): 63-83.

Fisher, R.A. (1917) 'Positive eugenics', *Eugenics Review*, 9: 206-12.

Flint, J. and Robinson, D. (eds) (2008) *Community Cohesion in Crisis? New Dimensions of Diversity and Difference*, Bristol: The Policy Press.

Ford, R. (2008a) 'British attitudes towards immigrant ethnic minorities 1964-2005: Reactions to diversity and their political effects', Unpublished DPhil thesis, University of Oxford.

Ford, R. (2008b) 'Is racial prejudice declining in Britain?', *British Journal of Sociology* 59(4): 609-36.

Fossett, M. (2006) 'Ethnic preferences, social distance dynamics, and residential segregation: theoretical explorations using simulation analysis', *Journal of Mathematical Sociology*, 30(3): 185-274.

Frankenberg, R (1993) *White Women, Race Matters: The Social Construction of Whiteness*, Minneapolis, MN: University of Minnesota Press.

Frost, L. (2006) *National Insurance Number Allocations to Overseas Nationals*, Manchester: Policy Unit, Manchester City Council.

Galton, F. (1869) *Hereditary Genius: An Inquiry into its Laws and Consequences* (2nd edition 1892), London: Macmillan.

Galton, F. (1892) *Hereditary Genius: An Inquiry into its Laws and Consequences* (2nd edition), London: Macmillan.

Gans, H.J. (1997) 'Toward a reconciliation of "assimilation" and "pluralism": the interplay of acculturation and ethnic retention', *International Migration Review*, 31(4): 875-92.

Gilroy, P. (2005) 'Multiculture, double consciousness and the "war on terror"', *Patterns of Prejudice*, 39(4): 431-43.

GLA (Greater London Authority) (2005) *London's Changing Population, Diversity of a World City in the 21st Century*, Greater London Authority Data Management and Analysis Group Briefing 2005/39, London: GLA.

GLA (2007) *GLA 2006 Round Ethnic Group Population Projections* (Baljit Bains and Ed Klodawski), Greater London Authority Data Management and Analysis Group Briefing 2007/14, London: GLA.

Glazer, N. and Moynihan, D.P. (1963) *Beyond the Melting Pot: The Negroes, Puerto Ricans, Jews, Italians, and Irish of New York City*, Cambridge, MA: MIT Press.

Glover, S., Gott, C., Loizillon, A., Portes, J., Price, R., Spencer, S., Srinivasan, V. and Willis, C. (2001) *Migration: An Economic and Social Analysis*, RDS Occasional Paper No 67, London: Home Office.

Gordon, M.M. (1964) *Assimilation in American Life: The Role of Race, Religion and National Origins*, Oxford: Oxford University Press.

Gott, C. and Johnston, K. (2002) *The Migrant Population in the UK: Fiscal Effects*, RDS Occasional Paper No 77, London: Home Office.

Gould, S. (1996) *Mismeasure of Man*, New York: Norton.

Halfacree, K., Flowerdew, R. and Johnson, J. (1992) 'The characteristics of British migrants in the 1990s: evidence from a new survey', *The Geographical Journal*, 158(2): 157-69.

Hall, R., Ogden, J. and Hill, C. (1997) 'The pattern and structure of one-person households in England and Wales and France', *International Journal of Population Geography*, 3(2): 161-81.

Hall, S. (1987) 'Urban unrest in Britain', in J. Benyon and J. Solomos (eds) *The roots of urban unrest*, Oxford: Pergamon Press.

Hamnett, C. (1991) 'The relationship between residential migration and housing tenure in London, 1971-1981: a longitudinal analysis', *Environment and Planning A*, 23(8): 1147-62.

Hargreaves, A.G. (1996) *Immigration, Race and Ethnicity in Contemporary France*, London: Routledge.

Harris, N. and Coleman, D. (2003) 'Does Britain need more immigrants?', *World Economics*, 4(2): 57-102.

Harris, R. and Johnston, R. (2008) 'Primary schools, markets and choice: studying polarization and the core catchment areas of schools', *Applied Spatial Analysis*, 1: 59-84.

Harrison, M., Phillips, D., Chahal, K., Hunt, L. and Perry, J. (eds) (2005) *Housing, 'Race' and Community Cohesion*, Coventry: Chartered Institute of Housing.

Haskey, J. (ed) (2002) *Population Projections by Ethnic Group: A Feasibility Study*, Studies in Medical and Population Subjects No 67, London: The Stationery Office.

Heath, A. and Li, Y. (2007) 'Measuring the size of the employer contribution to the ethnic minority employment gap', Unpublished paper prepared for the Business Commission of the National Employment Panel, available from the authors at Nuffield College, Oxford University, Oxford, OX1 1NF, UK.

Herrnstein, R. and Murray, C. (1994) *The Bell Curve: Intelligence and Class Structure in American Life*, New York: Free Press.

HM Government (1978) *1981 Census of Population*, Census White Paper, Cm 7146, London: The Stationery Office.

Home Office (2001) *Race Equality in Public Services*, London: Home Office.

Home Office (2002) *Secure Borders, Safe Haven*, White Paper, Cm 5387, London: The Stationery Office.

Home Office (2006) *Control of Immigration Statistics 2005, United Kingdom*, Cm 6904, London: Home Office.

Home Office (2008) *Accession Monitoring Report, May 2004 – March 2008*, London: Home Office UK Borders Agency, DWP, HM Revenue and Customs and DCLG, www.ukba.homeoffice.gov.uk/sitecontent/documents/aboutus/reports/accession_monitoring_report/

Hubbuck, I. and Carter, S. (1980) *Half a Chance: A Report on Job Discrimination amongst Young Blacks in Nottingham*, Nottingham: Nottingham CRE.

ICAR (Information Centre about Asylum and Refugees) (2004) *Media Image, Community Impact: Assessing the Impact of Media and Political Images of Refugees and Asylum Seekers on Community Relations in London*, London: ICAR.

ICAR (2006) *Reflecting Asylum in London's Communities*, London: ICAR.

Independent Asylum Commission (2008) *Fit for Purpose Yet? The Independent Asylum Commission's Interim Findings*, London: Independent Asylum Commission, http://www.independentasylumcommission.org.uk/

Institute of Community Cohesion (2007) *Estimating the Scale and Impacts of Migration at the Local Level*, London: Local Government Association, www.lga.gov.uk/lga/publications/publication-display.do?id=22422

Jackson, P. and Penrose, J. (eds) (1993) *Constructions of Race, Place and Nation*, London: UCL Press.

Jenkins, R. (1967) *Essays and Speeches*, London: Collins.

Johnson, N. (2006) 'We must choose equality', *The Guardian*, 1 March.

Johnston, R., Burgess, S., Harris, R. and Wilson, D. (2006) *Sleep-Walking Towards Segregation? The Changing Ethnic Composition of English Schools, 1997-2003 – an Entry Cohort Analysis*, Working Paper Series No 06/155, Bristol: Centre for Market and Public Organisation, Bristol University.

Johnston, R., Forrest, J. and Poulsen, M. (2002) 'Are there ethnic enclaves/ghettos in English cities?', *Urban Studies*, 39(4): 591-698.

Joly, D. (ed) (1998) *Scapegoats and Social Actors: The Exclusion and Integration of Minorities in Western and Eastern Europe*, Basingstoke: Macmillan.

Jones, J.M. (1997) *Prejudice and Racism* (2nd edition), London: McGraw-Hill.

Joshua, H., Wallace, T. and Booth, H. (1983) *To Ride the Storm: The 1980 Bristol 'Riot' and the State*, Bristol: Heinemann.

Kalra, V. and Kapoor, N. (2008) 'Interrogating segregation, integration and the community cohesion agenda', *CCSR Working Paper 2008-16,* Manchester: University of Manchester, http://www.ccsr.ac.uk/publications/working/2008-16.pdf

Kaye, R. (1998) 'Redefining the refugee: the UK media portrayal of asylum seekers', in K. Koser and H. Lutz (eds) *The New Migration in Europe: Social Construction and Social Realities* (pp 163-82), London: Macmillan.

Kaye, R. (1999) 'The politics of exclusion: the withdrawal of social welfare benefits from asylum seekers in the UK', *Contemporary Politics*, 5(1): 25-45.

Kirk, R. (2004) *Skills Audit of Refugees*, London: Home Office.

Kitchen, S., Michaelson, J. and Wood, N. (2006) *2005 Citizenship Survey: Community Cohesion Topic Report*, London: Department for Communities and Local Government.

Kitzinger, J. (1999) 'A sociology of media power: key issues in audience reception research', in G. Philo *Message Received* (pp 3-20), Harlow: Longman.

Koser, K. and Lutz, H. (eds) (1998) *The New Migration in Europe: Social Constructions and Social Realities*, Basingstoke: Macmillan.

Kundnani, A. (2001) 'From Oldham to Bradford: the violence of the violated', *Race and Class*, 43(2): 105-10.

Kundnani, A. (2002) 'The death of multiculturism', Commentary from *Race & Class*, April, 43(4): 67–72.

Kundnani, A. (2007a) 'Integrationism: the politics of anti–Muslim racism', *Race and Class*, 48(40): 24–44.

Kundnani, A. (2007b) *The End of Tolerance: Racism in Twenty-First Century Britain*, London: Pluto Press.

Law, I. (1997) *Privilege and Silence: 'Race' in the British News During the Election Campaign 1997*, Research report for the CRE, Leeds: Leeds University Press.

Law, I., Hylton, C., Karmani, A. and Deacon, A. (1994) *Racial Equality and Social Security Service Delivery: A Study of the Perceptions and Experiences of Black and Minority Ethnic People Eligible for Benefit in Leeds*, Leeds: University of Leeds.

Layton-Henry, Z. (1992) *The Politics of Immigration: Immigration, 'Race' and 'Race' Relations in Post-War Britain*, Oxford: Blackwell.

Lee, P. and Murie, A. (1999) 'Spatial and social divisions within British cities: beyond residualisation', *Housing Studies*, 14(5): 625–40.

Leech, K. (1989) *A Question in Dispute: The Debate about an 'Ethnic' Question in the Census*, London: Runnymede Trust.

Leech, K. (1994) *Brick Lane 1978: The Events and their Significance*, London: Stepney Books Publications.

Legrain, P. (2007) *Immigrants: Your Country Needs Them*, London: Little, Brown.

Leslie, D., Lindley, J. and Thomas, L. (2001) 'Decline and fall: unemployment among Britain's non–white ethnic communities 1960–1999', *Journal of the Royal Statistical Society*, Series A, 164(2): 371–87.

Leppard, D. (2006) *The Sunday Times*, 19 March, www.timesonline. co.uk/tol/news/uk/article742756.ece

Lewis, P. (1994) *Islamic Britain: Religion, Politics and Identity among British Muslims*, London: I.B. Tauris.

Lomborg, B. (2001) *The Skeptical Environmentalist: Measuring the Real State of the World*, Cambridge: Cambridge University Press.

MacKenzie, D. (1999) 'Eugenics and the rise of mathematical statistics in Britain', in D. Dorling and S. Simpson (eds) *Statistics in Society: The Arithmetic of Politics*, London: Arnold.

Malik, K. (2007) 'Thinking outside the box', *Catalyst, Magazine of the Commission for Racial Equality, UK*, January–February. http://83.137.212.42/siteArchive/catalystmagazine/Default.aspx. LocID-0hgnew0ov.RefLocID-0hg01b00100k.Lang-EN.htm

Malthus, T. (1798) *An Essay on the Principles of Population*, London: J. Johnson.

Marschall, M.J. and Stolle, D. (2004) 'Race and the city: neighbourhood context and the development of generalized trust', *Political Behaviour*, 26(2): 125-53.

Massey, D.S. and Denton, N.A. (1993) *American Apartheid: Segregation and the Making of the Underclass*, Harvard, MA: Harvard University Press.

Massey, D.S. and Mullan, B.P. (1984) 'Processes of Hispanic and black spatial assimilation', *American Journal of Sociology*, 89(4): 836-73.

Massey, D.S., Arango, J., Hugo, G., Kouaouci, A., Pellegrino, A. and Taylor, J. (1993) 'Theories of international migration: a review and appraisal', *Population and Development Review*, 19(3): 431-66.

McCombs, M. (1994) 'News influence on our pictures of the world', in J. Bryant and D. Zillmann (eds) *Media Effects: Advances in Theory and Research* (pp 1-15), Hove: Lawrence Erlbaum Associates, Inc.

MigrationWatchUK (2005) 'The impact of chain migration on English cities', Briefing Paper 9.13, http://www.migrationwatchuk.com/Briefingpapers/migration_trends/impact_of_chain_migration_on_english_cities.asp

MigrationWatchUK (2006) *The Effect of Immigration on the Integration of Communities in Britain*, Briefing Paper 9.19, http://migrationwatch.co.uk/briefingpapers/migration_trends/effect_of_immigration_onthe_integration_communities_britain.asp?search=segregation

MigrationWatchUK (2007a) 'Submission to the House of Lords Select Committee on Economic Affairs on The Economic Impact of Immigration', Briefing Paper 1.18, 23 September, available at www.migrationwatchuk.com/Briefingpapers/economic/1_18_submission_to_the_hol.asp

MigrationWatchUK (2007b) 'The impact of immigration on housing in England', Briefing paper 7.9, available at www.migrationwatchuk.com/Briefingpapers/housing/7_9_impact_of_immigration_on_housing_in_england.asp

MigrationWatchUK (2008) 'House of Lords Select Committee: Supplementary evidence from MigrationWatch', Economic Briefing Paper 1.20, 14 January, www.migrationwatchuk.com/Briefingpapers/economic/1_20_hol_economic_affairs_committee.asp

Modood, T. (1992) *Not Easy Being British: Colour, Culture and Citizenship*, Stoke-on-Trent: Trentham Books.

Modood, T. (2003) 'Muslims and the politics of difference', *The Political Quarterly*, 41(1): 100-15.

Modood, T. (2005) 'Remaking multiculturalism after 7/7', London: openDemocracy, www.opendemocracy.net/conflict-terrorism/multiculturalism_2879.jsp

---

Modood, T. (2007) *Multiculturalism: A Civic Idea*, Cambridge: Polity Press.

Morning, A. (2008) 'Ethnic classification in global perspective: a cross-national survey of the 2000 census round', *Population Research and Policy Review*, 27(2): 239-72.

Musterd, S. (2003) 'Segregation and integration: a contested relationship', *Journal of Ethnic and Migration Studies*, 29(4): 623-41.

O'Sullivan, T., Dutton, B. and Rayner, P. (eds) (1994) *Studying the Media*, London: Arnold.

ONS (Office for National Statistics) (2003) *International Migration: Migrants Entering or Leaving the United Kingdom and England and Wales, 2001*, Series MN No 28, London: ONS.

ONS (2005a) *Focus on People and Migration*, London: ONS, www.statistics.gov.uk/focuson/Migration/

ONS (2005b) *Consultation Document: Initial View on Content for England and Wales – Second Residences*, London: ONS, www.statistics.gov.uk/about/consultations/downloads/2011Census_consultation_second_residences.pdf

ONS (2006a) *Focus on Ethnicity and Religion*, London: Palgrave Macmillan.

ONS (2006b) *Population Estimates by Ethnic Group (Experimental)*, Titchfield: ONS, www.statistics.gov.uk/StatBase/Product.asp?vlnk=14238

ONS (2007) *Population Trends*, 130, Titchfield: ONS.

Ouseley, H. (2001) *Community Pride not Prejudice: Making Diversity Work in Bradford*, Bradford: Bradford Vision.

Owen, D. and Green, A. (1992) 'Migration patterns and trends', in A. Champion and A. Fielding (eds) *Migration Processes and Patterns, Volume 1: Research Progress and Prospects* (pp 17-40), London: Belhaven.

Parekh, B. (2000) *The Future of Multi-Ethnic Britain* (Report of the Commission on the Future of Multi-Ethnic Britain: Chair B. Parekh), London: Profile Books.

Park, R.E. (1950) *Race and Culture*, London: Free Press.

Park, R.E. (1952) *Human Communities: The City and Human Ecology*, Glencoe, IL: The Free Press.

Parkinson, M., Champion, T., Evans, R., Simmie, J., Turok, I., Crookston, M., Katz, B., Park, A., Berube, A., Coombes, M., Dorling, D., Glass, N., Hutchins, M., Kearns, A., Martin, R. and Wood, P. (2006) *State of the English Cities, 2 Volumes*, London: Office of the Deputy Prime Minister.

Pascoe-Watson, G. (2007) '5 million more here in 9 years', *The Sun*, 24 October, available at www.thesun.co.uk/sol/homepage/news/article380579.ece

Paul, K. (1997) *Whitewashing Britain: Race and Citizenship in the Post-War Era*, Ithaca, NY: Cornell University Press.

Peach, C. (1996a) 'Good segregation, bad segregation', *Planning Perspectives*, 11(4): 379-98.

Peach, C. (1996b) 'Does Britain have ghettos?', *Transactions, Institute of British Geographers*, 21(1): 216-35.

Peach, C. (2008) *Slippery Segregation*, Institute for Social Change Working Paper, Manchester: University of Manchester.

Peach, G. and Winchester, S. (1974) 'Birthplace, ethnicity and the undernumeration of West Indians, Indians and Pakistanis in the census of 1966 and 1971', *New Community*, 3(4): 386-93.

Peleman, K. (2002) 'The impact of residential segregation on participation in associations: the case of Moroccan women in Belgium', *Urban Studies*, 39(4): 727-47.

Pettigrew, T. (1969) 'Racially separate or together?', *Journal of Social Issues*, 25: 43-69.

Phillips, D. (1998) 'Black minority ethnic concentration, segregation and dispersal in Britain', *Urban Studies*, 35(10): 1681-702.

Phillips, D. (2006) 'Parallel lives? Challenging discourses of British Muslim self-segregation', *Environment and Planning D: Society and Space*, 24(1): 25-40.

Phillips, D., Simpson, L. and Ahmed, S. (2008) 'Shifting geographies of minority ethnic settlement: remaking communities in Oldham and Rochdale', in J. Flint and D. Robinson (eds) *Community Cohesion in Crisis? New Dimensions of Diversity and Difference*, Bristol: The Policy Press.

Phillips, T. (2005) 'After 7/7: sleepwalking to segregation', Speech to the Manchester Council for Community Relations, 22 September, www.equalityhumanrights.com

Phillips, T. (2006) Speech to the Royal Geographical Society Annual Conference, 30 August, Commission for Racial Equality, http://83.137.212.42/sitearchive/cre/Default.aspx.LocID-0hgnew0jl.RefLocID-0hg00900c002.Lang-EN.htm

Phillips, T. (2008) 'Not a river of blood, but a tide of hope: managed immigration, active integration', London: Equality and Human Rights Commission, www.equalityhumanrights.com/en/newsandcomment/speeches/Pages/powellspeech.aspx

Philo, G. (ed) (1999) *Message Received: Glasgow Media Group Research 1993–1998*, Harlow: Longman.

Philo, G. and Beattie, L. (1999) 'Race, migration and media', in G. Philo (ed) *Message Received* (pp 171-96), Harlow: Longman.

Pickering, S. (2001) 'Common sense and original deviancy: new discourse and asylum seekers in Australia', *Journal of Refugee Studies*, 14(2): 169-86.

Pinkerton, C., McLaughlan, G. and Salt, J. (2004) *Sizing the Illegally Resident Population in the UK*, Home Office Online Report 58/04, London: Home Office, www.homeoffice.gov.uk/rds/pdfs04/rdsolr5804.pdf

Platt, L. (2007) *Poverty and Ethnicity in the UK*, Bristol/York: The Policy Press/Joseph Rowntree Foundation, www.jrf.org.uk/bookshop/eBooks/2006-ethnicity-poverty-UK.pdf

Portes, A. (2008) 'Migration and social change: some conceptual reflections', Keynote address to the conference 'Theorizing Key Migration Debates', Oxford University, 1 July, available at www.imi.ox.ac.uk/news-store/theories-of-migration-and-social-change-conference-july-2008

Portes, A. and Zhou, M. (1993) 'The new second generation: segmented assimilation and its variants', *Annals of the American Academy of Political and Social Science*, 530: 74-96.

Poulsen, M. and Johnston, R. (2006) 'Ethnic residential segregation in England: getting the right message across', *Environment and Planning A*, 38: 2195-9.

Poulsen, M., Johnston, R. and Forrest, J. (2001) 'Intraurban ethnic enclaves: introducing a knowledge-based classification method', *Environment and Planning A*, 33: 2017-82.

Prewitt, K. (2005) 'Racial classification in America: where do we go from here?', *Daedalus*, 134(1): 5-17.

Putnam, R.D. (2007) 'E pluribus unum: diversity and community in the twenty-first century: the 2006 Johan Skytte Prize lecture', *Scandinavian Political Studies*, 30(2): 137-74.

Radical Statistics Education Group (1982) *Reading Between the Numbers: A Critical Guide to Educational Research*, London: BSSRS Publications.

Rees, P. (2008a) 'What happens when international migrants settle? Projections of ethnic groups in United Kingdom regions', in J. Raymer and F. Willekens (eds), *International Migration in Europe: Data, Models and Estimates* (pp 330-58 (ch 15)), London: John Wiley,.

Rees, P. (2008b) 'Chapter 15 Appendices' (to 'What happens when international migrants settle? Projections of ethnic groups in United Kingdom regions' in J. Raymer and F. Willekens (eds), *International Migration in Europe: Data, Models and Estimates*, London: John Wiley), http://www.wiley.com/legacy/wileychi/raymer/supp/Chapter15_Appendices.pdf

Rees, P. and Boden, P. (2006) *Estimating London's New Migrant Population: Stage 1 — Review of Methodology*, London: Greater London Authority.

Rex, J. (1981) 'Urban segregation and inner city policy in Great Britain', in C. Peach, V. Robinson and S. Smith (eds) *Ethnic Segregation in Cities* (pp 25-42), London: Croom Helm.

Robinson, D. (2005) 'The search for community cohesion: key themes and dominant concepts of the public policy agenda', *Urban Studies*, 42(8): 1411-27.

Robinson, V. (ed) (1993) *The International Refugee Crisis*, Basingstoke: Macmillan.

Robinson, V., Andersson, R. and Musterd, S. (2003) *Spreading the Burden: A Review of Policies to Disperse Asylum Seekers and Refugees*, Bristol: The Policy Press.

Rocheron, Y. (1997) 'Families on the front line: mixed marriage in France', in M. Cross and S. Perry (eds) *Population and Social Policy in France*, London: Inter.

Said, E. (1987) *Orientalism*, New York: Vintage Books.

Saleheen, J. and Shadforth, C. (2006) 'The economic characteristics of immigrants and their impact on supply', *Bank of England Quarterly Bulletin*, Winter, available at http://ssrn.com/abstract=950924

Salt, J. (2006) *International Migration and the United Kingdom*, Report of the UK SOPEMI Correspondent to the OECD, London: Migration Research Unit, UCL.

Schelling, T.S. (1971) 'Dynamic models of segregation', *Journal of Mathematical Sociology*, 1: 143-86.

Schumacher, E.F. (1973) *Small is Beautiful: Economics as if People Mattered*, New York: Harper and Row.

Select Committee on Economic Affairs (2008) *The Economic Impact of Immigration, 1st Report of Session 2007-08*, HL Paper 80-I, London: House of Lords.

Shaw, C. (2004) 'Interim 2003-based national population projections for the United Kingdom and constituent countries', *Population Trends*, 118: 6-16.

Sibley, D. (1995) *Geographies of Exclusion*, London: Routledge.

Simpson, L. (2002) 'Estimating methodologies and assumptions for projections: current practice for population projections by ethnic group', in J. Haskey (ed) *Population Projections by Ethnic Group: A Feasibility Study* (pp 53-72), London: The Stationery Office.

Simpson, L. (2007a) 'Ghettos of the mind: the empirical behaviour of indices of segregation and diversity', *Journal of the Royal Statistical Society: Series A (Statistics in Society)*, 170(2): 405-24.

Simpson, L. (2007b) *Population Forecasts for Birmingham, with an Ethnic Group Dimension*, Birmingham: Birmingham City Council, www.birmingham.gov.uk/Media?MEDIA_ID=191412

Simpson, L. and Akinwale, B. (2007) 'Quantifying stability and change in ethnic group', *Journal of Official Statistics*, 23(2): 185-208.

Simpson, L. and Brown, M. (2008) 'Census fieldwork in the UK: the bedrock for a decade of social analysis', *Environment and Planning A*, 40(9): 2132-48.

Simpson, L. and Finney, N. (forthcoming, 2009) 'Spatial patterns of internal migration: evidence for ethnic groups in Britain', *Population, Space and Place*, 15.

Simpson, L. and Gavalas, V. (2005) *Population Forecasts for Oldham Borough, with an Ethnic Group Dimension*, Manchester: University of Manchester, http://www.ccsr.ac.uk/research/documents/PopulationForecastsforOldhamCCSRReportMay05.pdf

Simpson, L., Purdam, K., Tajar, A., Fieldhouse, E., Gavalas, V., Tranmer, M., Pritchard, J. and Dorling, D. (2006) *Ethnic Minority Populations and the Labour Market: An Analysis of the 1991 and 2001 Census*, DWP Report No 333, London: Department for Work and Pensions, http://asp.ccsr.ac.uk/dwp/

Simpson, L., Ahmed, S. and Phillips, D. (2007) *Oldham and Rochdale: Race, Housing and Community Cohesion*, Manchester: CCSR, University of Manchester.

Simpson, S. (1997) 'Demography and ethnicity: case studies from Bradford', *New Community*, 23(1): 89-107.

Singh, G. (2003) 'Multiculturalism in contemporary Britain: reflections on the "Leicester Model"', *International Journal on Multicultural Societies*, 5(1), pp 40-54.

Singleton, A. (1999) 'Measuring international migration: the tools aren't up to the job', in D. Dorling and S. Simpson (eds) *Statistics in Society: The Arithmetic of Politics* (pp 148-58), London: Arnold.

Sivanandan, A. (1983) 'Challenging racism: strategies for the 80s', *Race & Class*, 25(2): 1-11.

Sivanandan, A. (1985) 'RAT and the degradation of black struggle', *Race & Class*, 25(4): 1-33.

Sivanandan, A. (1990) *Communities of Resistance: Writings on Black Struggles for Socialism*, London: Verso.

Southworth, J. (2001) 'Count me in?', *Radical Statistics*, 78: 32-9.

Spencer, I. (1997) *British Immigration Policy since 1939*, London: Routledge.

Sproston, K. and Nazroo, J. (eds) (2002) *Ethnic Minority Psychiatric Illness Rates in the Community (EMPIRIC)*, London: The Stationery Office.

Stein, R.M., Post, S.S. and Rinden, A.L. (2000) 'Reconciling context and contact effects on racial attitudes', *Political Research Quarterly*, 53(2): 285-303.

Stillwell, J., Rees, P. and Boden, P. (2006) *Yorkshire and the Humber, Population Projections: Age and Ethnicity*, Leeds: School of Geography, University of Leeds.

Storkey, M. (2002) 'A review of literature on ethnic group projections', in J. Haskey (ed) *Population Projections by Ethnic Group: A Feasibility Study*, Studies on Medical and Population Subjects No 67 (pp 1-16), London: The Stationery Office.

Stratham, P. (2002) 'United Kingdom', in European Monitoring Centre on Racism and Xenophobia (ed) *Racism and Cultural Diversity in the Mass Media* (pp 295-419), Vienna: EUMC.

Stratham, P. and Morrison, D.E. (1999) *Racist Sentiments, Movements and the Mass Media: A Mediated Xenophobia*, available at www. esrcsocietytoday.ac.uk/ESRCInfoCentre/ViewOutputPage. aspx?data=v9XrjLJ6xhFnOjui6buMVALQrrBfql0Q93FxKYbGhce 89VSaUfyNEZXa06uGUEh%2fkDn%2fG02yHhA%2bzTV935ZC jO4pVZ9QY0Qragslqf1Su0a0%2fCxi5HR6IA%3d%3d&xu=0&isA wardHolder=&isProfiled=&AwardHolderID=&Sector=

Tausch, A., Bischof, G., Muller, K. and Kastrun, T. (2006) *Why Europe has to Offer a Better Deal Towards its Muslim Communities: A Quantitative Analysis of Open International Data*, Malaga: Universidad Malaga.

Twomey, B. (2001) 'Labour market participation of ethnic groups', *Labour Market Trends*, January, 109: 29-41.

UN (United Nations) (2001) *Replacement Migration: Is It a Solution to Declining and Ageing Populations?*, New York: Department of Economic and Social Affairs, United Nations Population Division.

UN (2006) *Trends in Total Migration Stock: The 2005 Revision*, New York: Economic and Social Affairs, Population Division, UN.

University of Manchester (2007) *Ethnic Group Population Forecasting*, Manchester, University of Manchester, www.ccsr.ac.uk/research/egpf. htm

van Dijk, T.A. (1991) *Racism and The Press*, London: Routledge.

Vertovec, S. (2007) 'Super-diversity and its implications', *Ethnic and Migration Studies*, 29(6): 1024–54.

Voas, D. (2008) *The maintenance and transformation of ethnicity: Evidence on mixed partnerships in Britain*, Institute for Social Change Working Paper, Manchester: University of Manchester.

Wahlbeck, O. (2005) 'Turkish immigrants as entrepreneurs in Finland: local and transnational social capital', *Janus*, 13(1): 39–53.

Wallman, S. (1986) 'Ethnicity and the boundary process in context', in J. Rex and D. Mason (eds) *Theories of Race and Ethnic Relations*, Cambridge: Cambridge University Press.

Watt, N. (2007) 'Revealed: UK schools dividing on race lines', *The Observer*, 27 May, p 1.

Weekes-Bernard, D. (2007) *School Choice and Ethnic Segregation: Educational Decision Making among Black and Minority Ethnic Parents*, London: The Runnymede Trust.

Whatley, M. and Henken, E. (2000) *Did You Hear about the Girl Who…? Contemporary Folklore, Legends and Human Sexuality*, New York: New York University Press.

Whelpton, P.K. (1938) *Needed Population Research*, Lancaster, PA: Science Press Printing.

Widdance Twine, F. and Gallagher, C. (2008) 'Introduction: the future of whiteness: a map of the "third wave"', *Ethnic and Racial Studies*, 31(1): 4–24.

Wirth, L. (1928) *The Ghetto*, Chicago, IL: University of Chicago Press.

Wood, P. and Landry, C. (2007) *The Intercultural City: Planning for Diversity Advantage*, London: Earthscan.

Woodbridge, J. (2005) *Sizing the Unauthorized (Illegal) Migrant Population in the United Kingdom in 2001*, Home Office Online Report 29/05, London: Home Office, www.homeoffice.gov.uk/rds/pdfs05/rdsolr2905.pdf

Wright, L. (1994) 'One drop of blood', *The New Yorker*, July 25.

Wyly, E.K. and Holloway, S.R. (2002) '*Invisible cities: geography and the disappearance of "race" from mortgage-lending data in the USA'*, Social and Cultural Geography*, 3(3): 247–82.

Zelinsky, W. and Lee, B.A. (1998) 'Heterolocalism: an alternative model of the sociospatial behaviour of immigrant ethnic communities', *International Journal of Population Geography*, 4: 281–98.

Zuberi, T. (2001) *Thicker than Blood: How Racial Statistics Lie*, Minnesota, MN: University of Minnesota Press.

Index

Note: Page references for notes are followed by *n*.